FOUCAULT'S DISCIPLINE

FOUCAULT'S DISCIPLINE

The Politics of Subjectivity

John S. Ransom

DUKE UNIVERSITY PRESS *Durham and London*

© 1997 Duke University Press

Printed in the United States of America on acid-free paper ∞

Typeset in Minion by Tseng Information Systems, Inc.

Library of Congress Cataloging-in-Publication Data

appear on the last printed page of this book.

Dedicated to the memory of my mother, Julie Ransom

C O N T E N T S

PREFACE

The varying images that the name "Foucault" provokes have a great deal to do with the kind of reading he is given. Foucault, it appears, is a symbol that serves different functions in discrete narratives.[1] Indeed, much of the ink that fills the Great Lakes of Foucault scholarship (to which this effort contributes its modest pond) is dedicated first to defining Foucault the symbol; the actual reading of Foucault's texts merely confirms in increasingly predictable ways the original reception of the symbol. Thus, if Foucault the symbol represents the flighty, bombastic, overdrawn, incoherent, overexposed, and merely (and briefly) fashionable Continental intellectual, a certain reading follows: Foucault prefers people who are mad over Enlightenment reason; opposes hospitals; is capable of writing unreadable prose; thinks ripping people apart with horses is better than putting them in prison; first characterizes the whole West as a dystopic nightmare of inescapable power and then, without missing a beat, tells us to turn our lives into works of art.[2]

Among those writers who read Foucault more sympathetically, an effort is being made to find in him or extract from him a normative standpoint of some kind that will provide a grounding for the critical activity he appeared to endorse. Perhaps, some authors propose, Foucault can be thought of as promoting the value of an untamed force, Life with a capital *L*, over the rigid and restrictive forms it has taken in the present. Others suggest that Foucault, like Derrida, can be seen as a philosopher of *différance*, a theorist and champion of excluded voices and suppressed identities. These arguments about the principle with reference to which Foucault pursued his work lead, perhaps inevitably, to notions about the kind of political community a Foucauldian ethos would be willing and able to support. Such a move explicitly or implicitly concedes the force of the main objection his work has provoked, namely, that he offers no positive vision of the political world as it should be and no normative framework for his critical activity.

I reference and briefly discuss a number of these commentaries on Foucault in the chapters that follow. My own reading flows from an emphasis on Foucault's valorization of critique, independent of utopian projects for radical change. Secondary works that simply dismiss Foucault rarely include detailed, much less convincing, argumentation. These authors assume that if Foucault did not include a normative grounding for oppositional activity, it was due to some perverse and merely personal whim on his part. The truth is that the political world Foucault describes for us has developed a kind of immunity to oppositional moves based on normative ethics and that serious efforts must be made to rethink how opposition might function and justify itself. Authors who are tempted to reread Foucault and postmodernism generally as perhaps providing a normative grounding for critical activity make the same error from a more sympathetic perspective. Personally, I doubt we will be able to put the normative genie back in the oppositional lamp.

Foucault called himself a "specific intellectual." By this he meant that he worked in particular fields of concern to him and did not try to extract from them an overall theory of how the world did or should work.[3] His work is both better understood and more useful to practitioners when seen in the light of this desire for specificity. The fact that so many of Foucault's interpreters see no way to defend or employ him without reference to an "ought" is solid evidence of the difficulty involved in separating critique from dreams of a liberated existence. It is just this separation, however, that Foucault wished to effect.

My primary intellectual debt is to Raymond Geuss of Cambridge University, who repeatedly discussed the twists and turns of this book with me and aided me immensely by exploring and experimenting with Foucault's thought in long discussions both in and out of the classroom. James Schmidt of Boston University generously gave of his time to discuss a late version of the manuscript with me; I benefited greatly from his advice.

Special thanks are due my wife, Jane, and our son, Mark. Without them, this book would have been finished earlier, but the process wouldn't have been as much fun. My father's advice and proposed changes were invaluable. The encouragement I received from my brother James meant more than I can express. Thanks also to Patricia Bratnober for her support and faith in this project. Finally, my friendship with Robert and Kathy Devigne has sustained me throughout the long march that culminates in this book.

FOUCAULT'S DISCIPLINE

I N T R O D U C T I O N   Rethinking "Critique"

A fundamental distinction in social and political thought is between the "ought" and the "is." One of the tasks of political science, for example, is to explain how particular societies and institutions actually work. Political philosophy produces theories of how the world ought to be, though this task is by no means its exclusive domain. Frequently, these two branches of political thought — describing how things are as opposed to how they should be — stand in a critical relation to each other, with theorists of the world as it is and thinkers concerned with how it ought to be squaring off in a combative manner.[1]

This distinction is not an exclusive one. In a class on American government, for instance, students learn not only how Congress, the presidency, interest groups, and the like actually function but also about the normative grounds underlying the existence of representative institutions and other elements of modern democracies. The description of the world as it is can, in principle, coincide with arguments concerning how it ought to be organized. At this juncture political *science* and political *philosophy* meet.

More often, however, a tension exists between these two ways of thinking about the political world, with political philosophy playing the role of critic. This tradition goes back at least to Plato. In his *Republic* and in other works, Plato criticized the political arrangements of the Athenian polis and developed proposals for a revolutionary reconstitution of it.[2] We can see, then, that criticism is frequently a two-step intellectual process. First, there are the elements of the world as it is that the critic confronts, disapproves of, and wants to change. The critic can spend quite a bit of time elaborating on this step. Before his *Republic*, Plato wrote a number of dialogues that criticized Athenian society without sketching out his alternative vision of political life.

The second step is precisely the one that Plato took in the *Republic:* the critic moves beyond a denunciation of the world as it is and tells those listening or reading how it should be remade. In the modern era, this link between criticism and the specification of an ought has, if anything, become more marked. The French Revolution of 1789, which declared the Rights of Man, is a frequently cited model of the relationship between criticism and political change. During the Enlightenment, the intellectual movement that preceded the Revolution, a broad-ranging criticism of the French monarchy was initiated. This was followed by the Revolution, which transformed French society in terms of the "ought" which was implicit in those criticisms and which developed in the course of debate and struggle. In the nineteenth century, Karl Marx tightened the relationship between criticism and revolution by linking his "critique of political economy"—the subtitle of *Capital*—to a revolutionary transformation of European society. In the twentieth century, successful revolutions in Russia, China, Cuba, and elsewhere, mirrored by "cultural revolutions" in the West during the 1960s, seemed to point to the continuing efficacy of a project of criticism tied to countervisions of the social world.

Foucault was a critical thinker. One of the things he wanted to criticize, however, is the way critical thought has usually functioned in the modern era. In particular, he wanted to distance criticism from an association with revolution that, to be frank, weighed criticism down with increasingly difficult, ancillary justifications on behalf of its partner. In a 1978 talk titled "What Is Critique?" Foucault defines it as "the art of not being governed so much."[3] What we first notice is that Foucault separates critical thought from positive visions of social worlds that will replace today's reality. As we shall see in more detail later, Foucault wants to rearrange—in other words, destroy and reorient—the current conceptual grid in which "critique" functions.

Beginning in the eighteenth century, critical thought was progressively absorbed in the transformations of European economic and political life. More and more openly, what was criticized was contrasted with an account of how the world should be ordered. This "ought," in turn, was made plausible by the rapid expansion of human control over the environment and over humanity itself, understood in terms of population. Criticism was now able to draw on the emotional attachments to an increasingly secularized millennialism. Critique became associated with the desire for another world. This gave it the blush of life, a profane mask and costume in which it could walk around. Critique was represented as something real and concrete; it not only worked against this or that objectionable exercise of power but stood "for" something as well.

Revolution gave critique the gift of life, of positive existence. Instead of acting as one of life's shadows—always following it around but lacking its own substance—critique could stand in the world and speak to it of its future. There are obvious risks associated with this coupling. One is that as the fortunes of the revolution went, so went the fortunes of critique. As the possibility of revolution—and, in general, the possibility of the transformation of human existence—wanes as an acceptable or compelling project, it seems as though critique has fallen into ill repute. What has actually happened, however, is that the flesh and bones given it by revolution have begun to fall away, reducing it to a shadow once again.

As part of the operation separating criticism from revolution, Foucault wants to return this shadow to a sense of its own dignity, independent of dubious projects for fundamental social change. In "What Is Critique?" for instance, he refers to criticism as a kind of "virtue," that is, an endeavor worthwhile in its own right. Criticism needs to stop being thought of as purely a means and instead should take its place in the world as an end, as a purpose all its own.

The various ways in which Foucault resuscitates criticism are discussed in the present work. Foucault draws selectively on three traditions: Heidegger and the critique of the gesture, Nietzsche and genealogy, and Kant and the Enlightenment. Some of these, of course, overlap, but sufficient distinction exists between them to make a discussion of each worthwhile, beginning with two questions: What kind of opposition and critique are made possible by the traditions mentioned above? How does Foucault relate to them?

Heideggerian Critique

The critical power of this approach (as Foucault uses it) can be found in Heidegger's discussion of the deceptively neutral and natural practices we engage in as part of our everyday world. Our "being," Heidegger argues, can best be understood in terms of the practices and contexts into which we find ourselves "thrown."[4] But the "being" that is revealed here is not made natural by virtue of its thoughtless or thrown character. There is, in addition, an ambiguity in the claim that our world is best understood through these practices.

As an example, Heidegger discusses our relation to a hammer.[5] We pick up the hammer and use it to drive in a nail. As long as it does what we want, we do not think much about the hammer. Its "being" as a hammer—and our relation to it—comes to the fore only when it does not do what we want it to do. Perhaps the head is too big or too small for the job, or maybe the hammer as a whole is too heavy. A tool that is ready to use, one that fits seamlessly and without interruption into the uses we have assigned to it, is not noticed. Its status as a discrete, constructed object becomes apparent only when a "breakdown" occurs. Then we do stop, look at the hammer, and say, "This hammer is no good." At that point, too, we begin to reflect on what would be the right kind of hammer—what size or shape would be appropriate to the task at hand.

Which perspective is more "real" or more "accurate"—when we use the hammer effectively and unthinkingly, or when we stop using the hammer to think about it as a hammer and about its attributes? Heidegger's answer is that neither perspective is "preferable" or "more accurate" than the other. Both are equally real modes of our being-in-the-world. Heidegger does argue, however, that the first, unthinking mode of being is our primary mode of being, whereas the second, more reflective mode is derivative.[6]

For Foucault, however, it is the second perspective that has greater possibilities for critical thought. As he says in volume 1 of the *History of Sexuality,* power is tolerable only if it masks a substantial portion of itself.[7] In addition, as his histories on the prison and on the treatment of those who are insane and sick have shown, some of the most significant developments in the functioning of power have been in the areas of gestures and invisible practices. It is true, as Heidegger points out, that our use of the hammer and in general our relation to the world we are "thrown" into is, at the primary level, thoughtless. But that does not mean that no thought has gone into producing these phenomena. That is, Heidegger recognizes that the world we live in is not "natural" but made—however natural our experience of that (produced) world might be.

One mode of Foucault's critique, then, is Heideggerian in the sense that it works to denaturalize the phenomenal world and turn aspects of it into matters for reflection. This Heideggerian mode is well captured in Foucault's comment that "critique is not a matter of saying that things are not right as they are. It is a matter of pointing out on what kinds of assumptions, what kinds of familiar, unchallenged, unconsidered modes of thought the practices that we accept rest."[8]

Nietzsche

Foucault often referred to himself as a Nietzschean.[9] What kind of critique does the Nietzschean approach yield?

Nietzsche engaged in a historical investigation of institutions and practices that he called "genealogy." Earlier we saw Heidegger provide the analysis for a critical approach to the mundane, and there is something of the same impulse in Nietzsche. Like Heidegger, Nietzsche believed that certain consequential practices and beliefs have become routine, unquestioned, thoughtlessly accepted conventions that need to be scrutinized.[10] And, like Heidegger, Nietzsche argued that these customary modes of being have a historical origin. But Nietzsche put much more of his emphasis on, first, the conflictual elements of this history and, second, its psychological dimensions.

The practices, institutions, and so forth that make up the world we live in have their origin in conflict, in the opposition between contrasting wills to power. The battles between opposed wills to power that created such things as morality, conscience, Christianity, the philosophic will to truth, the aesthetic temperament, and so on are not the focus of historians, and so we are deceived into believing in a myth concerning the purity and self-identity of these origins. Genealogy works to uncover the battles that gave birth to the world we accept as natural, to make it questionable again, and to make it possible to fight over it once more.

In the context of these same histories, Nietzsche probes the deep psychological sources of practices and institutions that we have trouble questioning in the present. In *On the Genealogy of Morals*, Nietzsche presents the conflict between two "wills to power," those of the Roman noble and of the oppressed Jews. Out of this confrontation, a new morality developed. But Nietzsche does not show us just the clash of these opposed wills—he also traces their psychological roots and effects. A class of priests, for instance, developed out of and broke away from the "warrior" class to give a positive valuation to religious and contemplative activity. Speaking very loosely, this happens as follows: Take an individual warrior, whom we'll call Bjornson. Once respected as a warrior, he has unfortunately been injured and can no longer participate in the adventures and raids that had been his life up to that point. This new and restricted physical condition prompts Bjornson to rethink his position in the community. Or, in Nietzschean terms, we could say that he needs a new outlet for his "will to power." What Bjornson does is to shift the site of the battlefield on which he will act away from the kind more familiar to his still-active brethren back onto himself. He will turn his mental life into a series of contests between what is godly and what is evil and as a result will produce a new and different hierarchy of values. After a while he looks on the activities of his still-intact colleagues with a certain disdain. Instead of being jealous of them and their bloodfests, he begins to wonder if their pleasures are not coarse and superficial.

What has actually happened, according to Nietzsche, is not that the warrior-turned-priest has developed an absolutely superior outlook on the human condition but that his condition of existence and thus his valuations have changed. A new mode of being has produced a new set of oughts. Bjornson, however, is unwilling simply to reflect on this—he attempts to convince (Nietzsche would say "infect") his former colleagues with the new valuation concerning spirituality and its superiority over mere physicality. This new valuation does not, however, fit the conditions of existence of healthy young warriors. That is why Nietzsche says that morality at times can act like a poison that literally makes individuals sick.[11]

With accounts like the above, Nietzsche gives the "will to power" a primarily psychic expression.[12] The most significant level on which the will to power works, according to Nietzsche, is in terms of the penetration and reconstruction of psychic states. Nietzsche explicitly links the formation of subjective states to *political* success when he argues that "a concept denoting political superiority always resolves itself into a concept denoting superiority of *soul*."[13] The "empirically verifiable" expressions of will to power on the political stage are themselves a consequence of a more important psychic foundation, which in turn can be traced to changes in the physical or environmental condition of individuals and classes. The formation and mass production of psychic states is the essential first step for political action and thought. But this precondition for political analysis is quickly joined by another factor, which both complicates and enriches Nietzsche's account of the quality of human interaction. Like Freud, Nietzsche denies that an individual's psyche is a singular entity. Instead, it is a plurality, a combination and even a hierarchy among diverse psychic entities. Freud identifies three influential actors: the id, the ego, and the superego. The battle between these psychic monads, in Freud's account, is complex enough. Nietzsche, however, does not restrict himself to a simple threefold division, though he does at times identify primary actors.

From these two points (the centrality of psychic states and their concomitant plurality), a dual conclusion results for political analysis: the first question that must be asked about the disposition of a political battlefield is, Who controls the production and regulation of subjective states? The second is, What are the relevant valuations of those in control? A central consideration here is the location of dominant forces inside as opposed to outside the individual. Is the "governance" of the individual carried on primarily by external forces or by internal ones? As it is unlikely—perhaps impossible—for an individual to be wholly constituted by one or another will to power, whether external or internal, we must go on to ask what battle lines separate diverse valuations, what conduits connect them, and what hierarchy orders them. Only when these two questions are answered will we be able to orient ourselves politically.[14] Human nature is not a constant but something produced from a plurality of influences, both internal and external. Determining the specific character of the diverse wills to power in individuals, as well as the balance of power among them, is crucial for political analysis.

We can see, then, that genealogy as critique slips imperceptibly into a consideration of oppositional tactics. The unsuspected gaps separating forces that were thought to be unified—the ignoble causal mechanisms revealed by genealogy—double as revelations of weakness in the structure of power, a structure that is nowhere more influentially located than in the psychic dispositions of "subjects."

Kant and the Enlightenment

Kant's essay "What Is Enlightenment?" is a frequent theme of Foucault's reflections.[15] What he finds valuable there is twofold. First, Kant focuses on the meaning and significance of his own present. Although a participant in the Enlightenment, Kant still thought it necessary to distance himself from it by questioning its value for humanity. The focus of Kant's attention is, then, on the present and its importance. Foucault reads Kant as saying that the present is not valuable in terms of some future for which it will act as the doormat but as something with independent merit.[16] The first element of Kant's essay that appeals to Foucault, then, has to do with its presentation of a critical ethos that remains firmly rooted in the world and in the present. Kant's suggestion, as Foucault recasts it, is that we ask, "What is happening right now, and what are we, we who are perhaps nothing more than what is happening at the moment?"[17]

The second element of Kant's approach to enlightenment that attracted Foucault is that he "defines *Aufklärung* in an almost entirely negative way, as an *Ausgang*, an 'exit,' a 'way out.'"[18] What we need to exit from, according to Kant, is our own immaturity, which condemns us to obey the authority of others in a thoughtless and uncritical manner.[19] Each of these related themes— exiting a particular state, maturity, and the authority of others—speaks in its own way to the new style of criticism that Foucault wanted to inaugurate. If we exit from a determinate condition, it is not to achieve something positive or to gain access to a new order of reality but simply to escape; stated another way, what is positively achieved is the act of exiting itself. Maturity means taking responsibility not only for what we know but also for what we have become and the various forces that have shaped us. Finally, the authority of others has to do not only with those specific individuals who lay down the law of what can be done or thought but with the authority of traditions and the seemingly unassailable stability of the various constructs that make up our world.

For Foucault, both criticism and political analysis still need to be invented, not, of course, once and for all, but for the world as it is.[20] Heidegger's focus on the gesture, Nietzsche's genealogical historical method, Kant's focus on the present and Ausgang—these are the interlacing elements of a critique which has been stripped of metaphysical pretensions and which can properly be labeled "Foucauldian."

Oppositional thought must reorient itself in light of the two most important developments in recent decades, the first of which is the explosion, both in number and in kind, of ways of being "governed." These modes of governance do not rely solely, or even primarily, on rational discourse over ends and means. Nor can their efficacy be traced to a coercive use of power that can then be labeled illegitimate. Instead, they work "below" the level of either discourse or violence to focus on the body, producing gestures and dispositions. Quite simply, the usual critical tools do not apply to them. The second development is the fall of the socialist regimes in the East. This was not a mere regime change. A whole category of critical thought became effectively extinct in 1989 with the collapse of the Berlin Wall—though it had been gravely ill for a long time already.

The above two *empirical* developments, along with others, are the reasons Foucault is worth taking seriously. If we look around, he thinks we can see that the forms of power have multiplied and changed shape and that the usual critical methods have lost their efficacy. To reclaim the critical advantage, two changes in the way we think must take place, which mirror the above points:

we need a more accurate and up-to-date assessment of power formations, and we need to develop tactics that provide a more effective response to the world as it is.

Foucault supplies answers on both issues. First he provides a wide variety of pictures — sometimes sketches — of the new ways in which power functions. By looking at them we can gain an idea of what Foucault's views were on the shape and methods of power, views that can be assembled from a number of his books, with assistance from more occasional studies. He then discusses an equally wide range of oppositional responses, more frequently in his interviews and essays, and these can be used to produce a picture of what oppositional activity might look like.

What Foucault gives us is a different way of looking at and responding to the myriad ways of being governed that surround us — in short, a new depiction of the political world. In this book I will try to present that view. I begin in chapter 1 by briefly discussing Foucault's view of power and its relation to knowledge. The constitution of the individual by modern forms of power is then traced, first from the perspective of "disciplinary" methods and then from that of "reason of state" (chapters 2 and 3). In light of the political field that is described in chapters 2 and 3, oppositional responses developed by Foucault are reviewed in chapters 4 and 5. Finally, in chapter 6 I discuss Foucault's overall vision of politics.

I Confronting New Forms of Power

All political theory is concerned with the conundrum of *power*. Two questions can be asked with regard to power. First, how does it function? Borrowing an old definition, we can say that *power* is the ability of individual A to make individual B do something that B would not otherwise have done.[1] It turns out, on closer inspection, that this process is anything but straightforward and that there are all sorts of strange and unexpected ways in which individuals exercise power over others.[2] This first question — the "how" of power — is the one Foucault is most interested in.

The second question is asked most frequently in traditional treatments of political theory such as those provided by Locke, Hobbes, Rousseau, Rawls, Habermas, and others: What makes the functioning of power legitimate or acceptable? What (good) reasons convince us to accept this or that operation of power? Parents discipline children and see to it that they are educated. Good reasons can be adduced that legitimate such exercises of power — which is not to say that these good reasons cannot be called into question or their specific applications criticized.

Once justifications for the exercise of power are shown to exist, we see the simultaneous emergence of rational restrictions on power. If power is justified because it gets us on our way to widely desired goals, then power is *un*justified when it is exercised without regard to those goals. For instance, a range of co-ercive measures is available to parents so that they may redirect the behavior of children in ways that, it is argued, benefit them.[3] But punishment meted out not for the good it does but only to satisfy the parent's desire for raw and unrestricted exercises of power is not *justified*. It is "illegitimate" and can be rationally and justifiably opposed.

Consider now the same phenomenon first in relation to government and then in the context of what is often called civil society.[4] Both Hobbes and Locke imagine a "state of nature" where formal governmental powers do not yet exist.[5] They then ask what reasons individuals might have for exiting this state of nature. Both conclude that individuals in the state of nature will agree to establish governments to protect their interests in preserving their lives and property. The power thus conferred is legitimate for two reasons: it results from the common agreement of the members of society, and its purpose is to protect the interests of the members of society.[6]

In the traditional liberal model, power's origins and goals are publicly ac-knowledged and understood. The way in which exercises of power might be unacceptable are equally clear. Power that does not have its origins in the con-sent of the governed or that violates the purposes for which it was erected is illegitimate.[7]

Of course, many have found this classic liberal account of political power to be incomplete at best. John Stuart Mill is perhaps the best-known theo-rist—but by no means the only one—who worried about the kinds of power exercised informally by society over its members.[8] Mill believed it would be unfortunate if unpopular opinions were restricted by *law*, but even when the law respected minority and individual views, one had to be concerned about the harmful effect of public opinion on free thought. In democracies, majori-ties made up the ruling class. The potentially tyrannous effects of majority rule could, in fact, be more easily curbed by statutory or constitutional fiat than throughout society as a whole. Government action could be effectively restrained through a conscious effort to undermine its efficiency. This restraint is part of the purpose of constitutions and the American "division of powers" concept of governance. Something like the American Bill of Rights could also be used to restrict government's fields of action with regard to private indi-viduals and groups. But there is no way to legislate against popular disapproval of minority viewpoints and lifestyles and ostracism or discrimination as weapons against nonconformity. In this area of culture and lifestyle, then, there existed a kind of power that was not subject to legislative restrictions.

We need to notice the opposing assumptions and effects of the two kinds of power reviewed above—governmental and societal. In the social contract tradition, individuals are aware of themselves as individuals with rights and property to defend. They know why they are entering into a contract with others. The aims of the political association they agree to form are publicly acknowledged. If goals other than those agreed to are pursued by the newly created governmental power, the social contract is breached. We have, then, a group of individuals with clearly perceived interests who wish to enter into an association with one another for obvious reasons so as to achieve the equally obvious goals of security and peace. Power's origins and purposes are pellucidly clear.

But no one "agrees" to the functioning of nongovernmental social powers. Indeed, the interests and rights of the individual are not at all the standard by which this form of power regulates itself. The particular danger associated with this form of power is that it in part shapes the subjective states of the individuals it affects. One of democracy's insidious effects is its tendency to reduce large numbers of individuals to the same intellectual level. Under the "old regime" an elite class—such as the nobility or the monarch and his or her court—set the cultural standard for taste and intellectual and artistic achievement. In a democracy, the ruling class still sets the standard, but it is no longer a minority elite with high standards but a common majority class with moderate or low standards. It was this kind of power—one that can decisively influence the subjective self-assessment of the individuals it affects—that Mill (Tocqueville can also be mentioned here) wanted to make us conscious of and therefore capable of resisting.

In classic liberal theory, then, there is a consciousness of the kinds of power that escape the original formulations of power by Locke and Hobbes. What was lacking in Mill's argument, however, was a discussion of how these two forms of power—nonformal social control and state power—supported and interacted with each other. This deficiency was made up by members of the Frankfurt School, who argued that through both a kind of widespread bribery and an active suppression of oppositional ideological elements, potentially rebellious factors in Western societies were robbed of the capacity to resist what was in fact an oppressive system. The educational system, the economy, the press, and cultural outlets—all nongovernmental means of persuasion—shaped individuals' expectations and self-perceptions to such an extent that they no longer saw the need to reshape the world around them.[9] The problem now was not the potential for tyranny by the majority but the capacity of a cultural, political, and economic elite to create pliant majorities.[10]

The dilemma of the Frankfurt School and others is that they provided an analysis of power whose explanatory force was achieved at the cost of effective opposition to power. If our very subjective states are molded by forces that work in support of dominant social powers, where can opposition be anchored?

But before moving on to the Frankfurt School's answer to this last question, we should note the importance of its contribution to social theory as it concerns Foucault. Foucault agrees with the Frankfurt School on two points: (1) political power is far from the only or necessarily the most important kind of power for theorists to consider, and (2) not all exercises of power (in or out of the political arena) have the *form* of sovereignty. "What we need," Foucault says, "is a political philosophy that isn't erected around the problem of sovereignty, nor therefore around the problems of law and prohibition. We need to cut off the king's head: in political theory this has still to be done."[11] Clearly, the Frankfurt School goes at least part of the way toward achieving this goal. What it challenges is the dominant view in political theory as to the site of power. This is the view associated with Hobbes (mentioned frequently by Foucault) — that is, power resides in a centrally located sovereign. In principle, all the activities of power will be traceable to this source. It follows that this centrally located sovereign will be accountable for the effects of its operation. To regulate this power, traditional political theory has developed the notion of consent to describe the relationship of the subjects of power to its operations. There can be no consent to the workings of power if it is not visible and identifiable as to situs. It is in this context that rights and duties are defined. Coercion is consent's opposite and is just as identified with the existence of a sovereign as is consent. If rights are unjustly transgressed, if force is inappropriately applied, subjects will have both the right to rebel against a now illegitimate sovereignty and a knowledge of where to direct the rebellion: against the sovereign. In this version Foucault notes, "the conception of power as an original right that is given up in the establishment of sovereignty, and the contract, as matrix of political power, provides its point of articulation. A power so constituted risks becoming oppression whenever it over-extends itself, whenever — that is — it goes beyond the terms of the contract. Thus we have contract-power, with oppression as its limit, or rather as the transgression of this limit."[12] For both the Frankfurt School and Foucault, this is simply an inadequate picture of power.

Pointing to the ways in which individuals are conditioned by diverse operations of power such that consent is either manufactured by forces outside the
individual or never becomes an issue enables the critical tradition that Foucault and the Frankfurt School share to move beyond the poles of consent and
coercion and the limited critical range that they embrace.

We might think of Foucault's point this way: not all kinds of power can be
described by the terms "legitimate" or "illegitimate." These terms refer to a
previously agreed purpose for the exercise of power. If Janine is elected president of the Chess Club and proceeds to use club funds to organize backgammon tournaments, we can reasonably say that she is using her power illegitimately. If, however, Janine is put in charge of a group of bored and troubled
young teens at the local YWCA and teaches them how to play backgammon
as a way of keeping them off the streets and out of trouble, she has exercised
power, but the terms "legitimate" and "illegitimate" do not apply to it.[13]

To illustrate this idea of form of power that escapes the consent-coercion
duality of the social contract tradition, imagine a young man who agrees to
enter a monastery. Through long periods of training this individual is "subjugated" to the monastic life. That is, he is molded into a "subject" of a certain
kind — one very different from the subjectivity he possessed when first agree-
ing to enter the monastery. At the same time, he is "subject" to a strict set of
"governmental" controls that both limit his options and develop his capacities, thus enabling him to participate competently in a structured existence
that gives his life meaning.[14] The powers of this individual are certainly developed, but only in a specific direction. In addition, the intent is that the powers
the individual develops will be put at the service of the order.

At the beginning of this process, remember, the individual gave consent.
But when looking back on his years of training, the monk hardly recognizes
the young man who agreed to enter the monastery. He is simply not the same
person that he was then. He may have given his consent to the rigorous training of the monastery, but in a very real sense the relevant individual was not
present when that consent was given. It is only after one is "disciplined" in a
certain way — only after one's subjectivity has been shaped and certain powers
developed, while others are pushed to the side, that individuals can meaningfully give consent to what the structures of power will do to them.

The power exercised over the monk falls somewhere between "consent" and
"coercion" and can be neither captured nor criticized using those terms.[15] The
result is an oppositional dilemma. If we take the liberal tradition seriously, it
is only when the need for consent is ignored that power acts illegitimately. An

act of "regicide" is required in political theory and practice precisely because it is not equipped to describe—much less provide critical criteria for—this important "growth industry" in the area of power formations, which Foucault calls disciplines.

At one time, perhaps, the sovereignty model might have more closely approximated the actual operations of power than it does today. The question for Foucault is not how anyone could ever take the sovereignty model seriously. Rather, he asks: "In a society such as ours, where the devices of power are so numerous . . . in this society that has been more imaginative, probably, than any other in creating devious and supple mechanisms of power, what explains this tendency not to recognize the latter except in the negative and emaciated form of prohibition? Why are the deployments of power reduced simply to the procedure of the law of interdiction?"[16] The sovereignty model presents itself as an exhaustive description of the nature and functioning of power. In turn, every conceivable form of opposition to power is said to wait on the transgression of the border separating consent from coercion and oppression. The inadequacy of this model, on Foucault's account, is that its poles of consent and coercion fail to capture the existence of "power at the extreme points of its exercise, where it is always less legal in character."[17] By "less legal" Foucault means those exercises of power that are not captured by rights and their violation or recognition. The emergence of this kind of power is a relatively recent event: "In the seventeenth and eighteenth centuries, we have the production of an important phenomenon, the emergence, or rather the invention, of a new mechanism of power possessed of highly specific procedural techniques, completely novel instruments, quite different apparatuses, and which is also, I believe, absolutely incompatible with the relations of sovereignty."[18]

Disciplines do not function through consent—they do not derive their legitimacy or their goals from the individuals who come into contact with them. What disciplinary power does is *normalize*.[19] As an example, Foucault points to the invention of the nineteenth-century classroom. Rectangular desks arranged in a rectangle allow for the formation of "a single great table, with many different entries, under the scrupulously 'classificatory' eye of the master." The student's "progress, worth, character, . . . application, cleanliness and parents' fortune" would all be reflected in the pupil's position on the table.[20] As a result, a mass of individuals is dispersed, individualized, and organized. The goal, however, is not to maintain a static distribution. Instead, a standard of performance is set. Individuals are evaluated and arranged according to that standard but also subjected to exercises that will move them closer to the norm. As students' performances improve or decline, their position on the "table" changes accordingly.

In guiding individuals to strive for optimum performance relative to some norm, disciplines cannot be said to employ coercion in any straightforward sense of the word.

> Disciplinary power . . . refers individual actions to a whole that is at once a field of comparison, a space of differentiation and the principle of a rule to be followed. It differentiates individuals from one another, in terms of the following overall rule: that the rule be made to function as a minimal threshold, as an average to be respected or as an optimum towards which one must move. It measures in quantitative terms and hierarchizes in terms of value the abilities, the level, the "nature" of individuals. It introduces, through this "value-giving" measure, the constraint of a conformity that must be achieved.[21]

A power that achieves its goals through the "constraint of a conformity that must be achieved" is simply a different kind of power that cannot be understood as a traditional model of political power. For the latter, if some act or organization is consented to, then the operations of power are legitimate and unobjectionable. If, on the other hand, power acts without securing consent from the relevant subjects or in violation of the terms whereby government and the law have been legitimized, then power has acted illegitimately and may be opposed. As Locke comments, "When Men by entering into Society and Civil Government, have excluded force, and introduced Laws for the preservation of Property, Peace, and Unity amongst themselves; those who set up force again in opposition to the Laws, do *Rebellare*, that is, bring back the state of War, and are properly Rebels."[22] This kind of clarity—one is tempted to add "unfortunately"—is lacking in a disciplinary regime. Locke presents a picture of self-conscious agents who seek to protect recognized attributes through the establishment of government. Disciplinary power, however, does not protect preexisting "properties" of the individual; rather, it *inserts* such qualities into individuals. "Individuals" do not precede disciplinary power—they are produced by it.

A double meaning informs Locke's use of "Property" in the passage just quoted. In addition to external possessions of land, crops, and gold, the individual's possession of *self* is also included.[23] The ability to fish, hunt, or cultivate the earth is a "property" or capacity which the individual holds and which helps to legitimate the possession of the products of labor. By cultivating these powers, individuals come to possess themselves in much the same way as the fruits of a cultivated field belong to the farmer. In protecting the external possessions of a person, society at the same time respects the independent personality that produced them. Disciplines, however, take over the task of the individual's cultivation. Disciplines are to individuals what the individual in Locke's account is to the land cultivated by that person—a means of inculcating properties in the individual that were not there before. As we see with Locke, however, such capacities are central to what makes a human personality, and so Foucault is led to the claim that disciplinary power "manufactures" individuals.[24] Yet while the exercise of power is unmistakably present with disciplines, it is impossible to conceive it in the way Locke does *political* power. Individuals at the founding of a discipline do not possess a form of power that will be combined to create it—rather, the process works in somewhat the reverse manner. There is no way to give consent to the erection of a disciplinary power before becoming part of that discipline. But once that happens, the issue of consent is moot. Nor is one coerced in the sense of that word as used by rights theorists. Instead, the individual is placed in an environment that evaluates, corrects, and encourages responses according to a norm.

In the sovereignty model, "*Wherever Law ends Tyranny begins,*"[25] but this clear-cut dividing line is not present in the disciplines. There are no rights at issue. Of course, actions could be taken in a disciplinary setting that *would* violate an individual's rights. An individual could be unjustly restrained or assaulted. But properly speaking, these acts are outside the province of the exercise of power specific to the disciplines and fall instead under the rubric of the political power mentioned above by Locke.

Foucault characterizes the exercise of power associated with disciplines as "dangerous."[26] One source of this danger is that, in comparison with the operations of sovereignty, their operations are much more dispersed and anonymous. In the "classic, juridical theory, power is taken to be a right, which one is able to possess like a commodity, and which one can in consequence transfer or alienate, either wholly or partially." The theory concentrates on "that concrete power which every individual holds and whose partial or total cession enables political power or sovereignty to be established."[27] The functioning of power in the sovereignty model is relatively clear and simple. The functioning of disciplinary power, on the other hand, is notoriously difficult to follow. For instance, to extract labor power of increasing value from the human body, the body is subjected to a "political technology," really a broad grid of disciplinary powers.

This technology is diffuse, rarely formulated in continuous, systematic discourse; it is often made up of bits and pieces; it implements a disparate set of tools or methods. In spite of the coherence of its results, it is generally no more than a multiform instrumentation. Moreover, it cannot be localized in a particular type of institution or state apparatus. . . . In its mechanisms and its effects, it is situated at a quite different level. What the apparatuses and institutions operate is, in a sense, a microphysics of power, whose field of validity is situated, in a sense, between these great functionings and the bodies themselves with their materiality and their forces.[28]

Difficult to localize, hard to formulate, and pulled together from diverse bits and pieces, such exercises of power are, as a result, resistant to analysis and focused opposition. This very difficulty we have in conceiving the exercise of power in terms other than those of the sovereignty model allows the exercise of disciplinary power to go undetected.[29]

Part of the strategic grid into which disciplines fit, it turns out, is this incapacity to imagine power being exercised in terms other than those provided by the sovereignty model. The invisibility of this kind of power is aided from another side. We easily become suspicious of those who hold power, but at the same time we put our trust in those possessing knowledge. Because knowledge is assumed to be innocent of power, we believe that knowledge is disinterested. Of course, we all know of cases where those possessing knowledge serve power interests and modify the knowledge they provide to suit the requirements of power. In this case, however, knowledge is said to be corrupted and distorted—not to be true knowledge at all. The goals, conclusions, and methods employed are disqualified once the damning link to power interests is revealed.[30] But it is not in this sense that Foucault establishes the link between knowledge and power. Foucault agrees with Nietzsche that knowledge can never be of an absolute or final nature but is instead a selecting out, among the many readings and possibilities present in a concrete instance, of those characteristics and aspects that will promote the goals of the individual or group doing the selecting. On one level, knowledge already is a form or expression of a will to power because it represents "this" and not "that." By picking out what to emphasize and what to present positively or negatively, knowledge shapes the world it "describes." Knowledge is linked to power not as a result of some perversion of its true function or essence (the blame for which can be found in some error or corrupting influence) but as the unavoidable result of its own activity.[31] Foucault makes this same point with reference to science, saying it is "not so much a matter of knowing what external power imposes itself on science, as of what effects of power circulate among scientific statements, as it were, their internal regime of power." [32]

Now, it might seem that the Frankfurt School would be committed to abandoning the dualism of the coercion-consent model in favor of something more subtle. And certainly a great deal of its work does manage to capture a broader range of power's operations. [33] But precisely in response to the oppositional dilemma referred to above, the Frankfurt School returns to the coercion-consent dualism. In the social contract model, potential contractees are aware of their interests and seek to protect them through the political association they agree to form. The problem with modern Western societies, according to the Frankfurt School, is that individuals and classes *make mistakes* about what their *true* interests are. We are (more or less) subjectively convinced that our own best interests are served by a capitalist economic system, diluted by significant doses of welfarism (for all classes), repressive culture, and so on, but in this we are misled. Our true interests reside elsewhere, and it is the task of critical thought to make those interests an object of study and public debate so that they can gradually oppose and ultimately replace our mistaken view of our interests. [34]

In effect, the consent that we give to the societies we inhabit is "uninformed" and so not true consent at all. In this way, the "consent-coercion" dualism familiar from liberalism is reintroduced. There may be a certain internal logic to this move, and it may root our opposition to modern power in more familiar terrain, but it is riddled with difficulties. Who, for instance, is to decide what a true as opposed to a false interest is? In what is this true, more human interest rooted, if it is not to be found in any of the actual ways humans concretely live?

Although he recognizes the value of the Frankfurt School's work on the link between domination and technology, [35] Foucault does not see much hope for an oppositional strategy that rests on the distinction between true and false interests. But while this may save Foucault from some of the untenable positions the Frankfurt School found itself forced to adopt, it does nothing to dissipate the problem that originally motivated the School, namely, where to locate opposition in a social world that has managed to blur the line separating the operations of power from the consent that, on the liberal model, was intended to check its abuses.

At first, Foucault seems merely to intensify this problem. At least, he has a reputation in some quarters for describing a social world that resembles, at best, a "prison without walls." Foucault appears to rehearse all the familiar themes from the Frankfurt School: individuals are products of a power they do not control and cannot oppose, whereas the social contract is just a convenient legal fiction that masks the functioning of an omnipresent power. What seems to strengthen the reader's despair in confronting Foucault's account of all this is that something that was there in the Frankfurt School is left out of Foucault's work. Foucault points to no transcendent, repressed interests that could act as a lever to oppose the kind of power he describes so well. If anything, Foucault's world is darker than that of the Frankfurt School and darker still than that of the Prince of Darkness, Theodor W. Adorno.[36] The high watermark of this bleak view of Western society is reached, appropriately enough, in *Discipline and Punish*, where Foucault tells us that in our societies "it is not that the beautiful totality of the individual is amputated, repressed, altered by our social order, it is rather that the individual is carefully fabricated in it, according to a whole technique of forces and bodies. We are much less Greeks than we believe. We are neither in the amphitheater, nor on the stage, but in the panoptic machine, invested by its effects of power, which we bring to ourselves since we are part of its mechanism."[37] So much for the "false interests" strategy. The question is, with what does Foucault replace it? Or does he replace it with anything?

What Foucault does is separate opposition and critical thought from claims about the right kind of human nature and the social forms needed to realize it. This move is marked, in part, by the well-known "knowledge-power" sign. On the one hand, by bringing these two terms close together, Foucault dismisses the idea that some form of knowledge (of our true nature, true interests, and so forth) can act as the platform from which we can denounce power. On the other hand, by refusing to collapse them into one big ball of domination, he points to the oppositional possibilities present in the tentative and shifting nature of their alliance.[38]

We have seen that scientific knowledge is a kind of power that allows us to manipulate nature and extract its energies to serve our needs. Foucault wants to extend the unremarkable connection between knowledge and power in people's relation to nature to the ways in which human beings are constituted. They too are manipulable, plastic variables. Foucault's argument has its forerunners here, as well. Certainly the Marxist tradition has long asserted that individuals and societies are products of the social environments in which they grow up and work.[39]

At this point, it is Foucault who stops and Marxist theorists who take a further step: despite what the world has made of us today, there is nevertheless a better one waiting in the wings. The source of this better world can be located in history and its dialectical progression, in the inherent and identifiable contradictions of today's social order, in a faith concerning the ultimate character of human nature, or in all these things together. Singly or together, these emancipatory visions are said to constitute a kind of knowledge — of what our true interests are, of what human nature really requires before it can flourish, and so on. Knowledge of our true and essential nature may be weak in the face of a dominant social power, but at least it is not corrupted into power's tool.[40]

For Foucault, however, this separate, emancipatory kind of knowledge does not exist. The role that knowledge usually plays, including in many cases the kind that claims to be emancipatory, is that of companion to the constructs of power which shape our world. For instance, practitioners of the human sciences such as psychiatrists, social workers, and demographers provide the wielders of power with both crucial information about the objects of its exercise and knowledge about how to shape and transform human material. Jeremy Bentham's architectural trick, the Panopticon, is a good example. Designed for prison use, the aptly named design allows a guard in a centrally located tower to observe the inmates without himself being seen. This not only improves social control but allows for the collection of information about the inmates — their habits, their responses to corrective practices, and so on. This knowledge is not simply accumulated. Instead, it is used to refine structures of power so as to optimize controls and adjust the handling of human material.[41] The inmates' true selves are not repressed; rather, their "true selves" are created, manufactured by one or several technologies of power.

As the example of the Panopticon shows, Foucault wants to dismiss essentialist notions of human nature. There is, for him, no final emancipated human condition that society should realize — nor, to be more modest, is there a vision of human nature that can be appealed to when assessing today's faulty approximations. These things do not exist. Thus, there can be no knowledge of them that can act as an effective bar to the encroachments of power. Again, it is just this denigration of an emancipatory, "powerless" knowledge that surprises and disappoints the "critical theorists" among Foucault's readers.

It is easy to see why this picture of the relationship between knowledge and power would not be enthusiastically affirmed by critical thinkers. To use another term for knowledge of humanity's true interests and nature, where is the *normative* criteria for Foucault's work? Habermas puts the complaint this way: "Foucault . . . replaces the model of domination based on repression (developed in the tradition of enlightenment by Marx and Freud) by a plurality of power strategies. These power strategies intersect one another, succeed one

another; they are distinguished according to the type of their discourse formation and the degree of their intensity; but they cannot be *judged* under the
aspect of their validity."[42] That some kinds of knowledge act as forms of power
and that knowledge and power work together to produce certain kinds of environments—thus far can critical theorists and Foucault walk together. But
the moment Foucault refuses to acknowledge the existence of a different order
of knowledge—one that allows us to determine beforehand what is good or
bad about a particular exercise of power, one that allows us to "judge its validity"—at that moment, a rather exasperated dispute begins. What, after all,
is Foucault up to as a critical thinker if he refuses to tell us what kind of world
to work toward? Or, at least, what is it about the world we live in that is unacceptable? Responses to such questions would involve some minimal claim
about the essential part of human nature that must be respected in constructing social arrangements.

The first thing to be said about this common criticism of Foucault is that it
does not address Foucault's claims. Is Foucault right about how power operates? Is he right about the essentially *creative* functions of power as opposed
to the more familiar *repressive,* coercion-based model? Foucault's critics skip
this stage of the discussion and go on to ask about the consequences of Foucault's view if he *is* right—namely, what oppositional possibilities does Foucault specify? The answer, they wrongly conclude, is "none." They then use
this unpleasant conclusion to denigrate, through association, Foucault's description of power's operations.

The second point that is missed by Foucault's critics is the possibility that
instead of describing an omnipotent form of power with an unbreakable hold
on our subjective states, the "power-knowledge" sign marks a kind of weakness in the construction of modern power. An unnoticed consequence of Foucault's observations on the relation between knowledge and power is the increased importance of knowledge. If power and knowledge are intertwined,
it follows that one way to understand power—potentially to destabilize it or
change its focus—is to take a firm hold on the knowledge that is right there at
the center of its operations.

But it might be asked what possible use knowledge that is already implicated
in power could be to one seeking to reverse, neutralize, or even merely understand power relations. If knowledge and power imply each other so intrinsi-
cally—so the argument might run—knowledge could never offer the critic a
target to attack or a staging area from which to launch an assault on the workings of power. Foucault's point, however, is that while power and knowledge

imply each other, one cannot be *reduced* to the other. "You have to understand," Foucault argues in one of his interviews, "that when I read—and I know it has been attributed to me—the thesis, 'Knowledge is power,' or 'Power is knowledge,' I begin to laugh, since studying their *relation* is precisely my problem. If they were identical I would not have to study them. . . . The very fact that I pose the question of their relation proves clearly that I do not *identify* them." [43] The fact that a relation and not an identity exists between knowledge and power means that there must be some distance separating them. And it is this distance that must be traced and exploited for critical purposes. [44]

Thus, what at first glance appears to be a subjugation of knowledge to power turns out to be an empowerment of knowledge. Why else, indeed, would Foucault work so hard to give us so much information if this knowledge could not be used to oppose forms of power thought to be dangerous? But, again, this knowledge does not concern the nature of our essence and the related theme of emancipation. Rather, it concerns coming to grips with those precise rationalities and bodies of knowledge that have played a crucial role in forming individuals and the social structures they inhabit. Foucault (as we shall see) has good reason to believe that access to this kind of knowledge will present options and expose political possibilities.

On one level, we can think of the power-knowledge sign as a kind of hermeneutic circle. [45] In "What Is Critique?" Foucault recommends the power-knowledge approach over a reliance on "the perspective of legitimation" familiar from the classic and recent critical traditions in political theory. Instead of relying on knowledge of our true nature to ground a criticism of domination, we should study the play of forces at work in a field of power and knowledge.

> One sees . . . that this grid is not composed of two categories of elements foreign to one another, those of knowledge on one side and those of power on the other. . . . For nothing can appear as an element of knowledge if, on the one hand, it does not conform to an ensemble of rules and constraints characteristic, for example, of some kind of scientific discourse in a given epoch, and if, on the other, it is not endowed with effects of coercion. . . . Inversely, nothing can function as a mechanism of power if it is not exerted according to procedures, instruments, means, or objectives that can be valid in more or less coherent systems of knowledge. [46]

Traditional critical approaches—including, here, the Frankfurt School—try to find a site outside the domain of power from which to attack its effects and excesses. Foucault's more hermeneutic approach directs us to the structural flaws and unexpected crevices within a particular power-knowledge dynamic. Foucault believes we have a problem that we have yet to confront, much less solve — namely, how to oppose a form of power that, as part of its exercise, manufactures and molds our subjectivities. He does not think that the familiar oppositional tools associated with rights, consent, legitimacy, and so on are adequate to the task, arguing that we have reached a kind of oppositional impasse:

> Against these usurpations by the disciplinary mechanisms, against this ascent of a power that is tied to scientific knowledge, we find that there is no solid recourse available to us today, such being our situation, except that which lies precisely in the return to a theory of right organized around sovereignty and articulated upon its ancient principle. When today one wants to object in some way to the disciplines and all of the effects of power and knowledge that are linked to them, what is it that one does, concretely, in real life . . . if not precisely appeal to this canon of right?[47]

Foucault insists that such appeals are ultimately ineffective, however much their familiarity attracts us. But where Foucault sees a weakness in our ability to confront power in modern society, his critics see a weakness in *him*. Foucault is approached as though he wishes to *promote* a world in which consent, rights, and so on are irrelevant rather than as someone who *describes* a world where these tools are less and less efficacious. That done, we are then subjected to a lot of profound discussion about the lack of a normative basis for Foucault's oppositional activities, whereas Foucault's whole point is that "normativity" no longer functions as an adequate basis for oppositional activity.

Arguing from his perception of how power operates, Foucault calls for a new kind of politics. The elements of this politics will contain some familiar terms (freedom, opposition, government, individual), but Foucault's vision accounts for the novel and increasingly complex ways in which these terms function. The chapters that follow — on the individual and disciplines, society and government, freedom and opposition — will provide an outline of that politics and an opportunity to review the kinds of questions Foucault posed and the adequacy of his own responses to them.

ⅠⅠ Disciplines and the Individual

Political theory begins with the individual. It takes the individual as its starting point regardless of which of the two traditional tasks it pursues: (1) explaining empirically how societies function on the basis of what principles and "truths" one accepts about human nature, or (2) arguing normatively about how societies should be structured so as to respect some fundamental characteristic of human nature as embodied in the individual.[1] For Aristotle, humans are political animals; political institutions should respect this. According to Hobbes, we are infinitely desirous beings: if we get something we want, we immediately want something else.[2] Given this picture of human nature, institutions radically different from the kind discussed by Aristotle are recommended.[3] Again, Kant provides us with a quasi-teleological argument about the unique capacity of human beings to will moral laws consciously rather than being driven by instinct, like other animals, and asserts that only those institutions respecting this faculty can be justified.[4]

Foucault also wishes to begin with a discussion of individuals, but with a difference. Both empiricists and normativists describe a static or fundamental human nature. Neither Aristotle's comment that we are political animals nor Hobbes's assertion that, as far as humans go, happiness *means* "the continual progress of desire" is to be understood historically.[5] What they claim about the humans of their day is true of humans everywhere and at all times. Foucault, on the other hand, wants to historicize the creation of the human subject.[6] If human beings are made in the way Foucault suggests, the traditional tasks of political theory become irrelevant. Political *philosophy* endeavored to describe the appropriate nature of political and social institutions based on a specific description of human nature; political *science* attempted to provide general laws that would make human interaction predictable. However different, both approaches require a stable human nature from which to argue their claims and put forward their prescriptions. Foucault describes an unstable, malleable human material that requires a shift in focus away from political philosophy and political science. Instead of briefly indicating the properties of our human nature and then describing what social arrangements are appropriate, political theory should concentrate in large part on those forces that go into producing diverse psychic states.

Two consequences follow for political theory. First, understanding and describing human nature becomes a torturous process of creative interpretation. As long as human nature is mutable, discovering the movement and quality of the forces that constitute it becomes a never-ending task. Second, the customary focus on legitimate versus illegitimate institutions that refer back to an unproblematic and static human nature is undermined. Outlining the kinds of institutions that do or do not respect human nature can no longer be a primary task in a world where the forging of that human nature is precisely what is at issue.

Political theory, Foucault argues, has been centered up until now on the "sovereign," where that term refers not only to the summit of political society in the form of a monarch or a state but also to the sovereign nature of each individual.[7] Both the desirous Hobbesian and the Kantian pursuing her goodwill by the light of the categorical imperative know what kinds of human beings they are. The only question is, will they be lucky enough to live in a world in which they can flourish? For the Hobbesian, a hospitable political world is one that orders the plurality of competing desires via an all-powerful Leviathan, and for the Kantian, one that respects our capacity to make laws for ourselves. But for Foucault these pursuits must appear wildly speculative. We need a political philosophy, Foucault says, that is not focused on the sovereign, in part because the individual is *not* sovereign over himself in the way political philosophy has argued up until now. No single, nonhistorical answer can be given in response to the question of what the individual is, what he needs to flourish, what rights he has, and so on. A political theory that does not assume a given human nature, that seeks to understand how humans have been fashioned and even how they can be refashioned, would be one that moved beyond political philosophy and political science as commonly practiced. Just such an approach informs Foucault's efforts to understand the origins of prisons and the disciplines that emerge from them—or the emergence of "biopower" or his description of Greek sexuality.

Discipline and Punish and the Art of Government

Discipline and Punish (*DP*), originally published as *Surveiller et punir,* is best understood as one *part* of a broader effort that Foucault makes to depict the mix of forces and phenomena that arose in the context of the industrial revolution. To put it another way, it is best not to view *DP* in isolation. It is true, however, that as Foucault's books were published, they were not presented as parts of a broader picture. Several times near the end of his life, Foucault did give a retrospective unifying assessment of his efforts, and each time he made it clear that *DP* must be seen as part of a broader investigation of the ways in which Western society functions.[8]

If we were to put *DP* in the context Foucault favored, how would that change the way we read it? Foucault believes that beginning in the sixteenth century, new opportunities presented themselves to those exercising power. The result was that a new kind of power arose with novel tactics and new strategic objectives.

At the heart of this change was a displacement in the theory and practice of statecraft away from the sovereignty of the monarch and toward a concern for "government," where the latter refers not only to the person governing but also to a wide variety of efforts in both the "public" and "private" spheres to shape the human material at one's disposal. Governance as a theme assumed an importance it would not otherwise have had as a result of its link to the problem of salvation that had been raised with renewed vigor during the Reformation and Counter Reformation.[9] Individuals and the groups they joined sought to govern themselves (both their thoughts and acts) in such a way as to secure their eternal salvation. Those involved in statecraft sought to "govern" the actions of subjects in a way that would strengthen the state in the context of an increasingly hostile international environment. To achieve this kind of governance, the concept of a sovereign who imposed his or her will on a community of subjects was no longer adequate. The subjects within one's jurisdiction must not be so much "ruled" or ordered about as "guided" to achieve desired ends. Learning how to guide subjects in this way became "the art of government," and this art is by no means restricted to the sovereign as traditionally conceived but is practiced also by a wide variety of powers of different sizes and with varying purposes (the head of a family, of a monastery, and so forth).

The origin of this shift away from a concern with sovereignty and toward governance can be found in an empirical change in the way power functions and the development of a new kind of knowledge about what it means to govern and how one should undertake governance. Governance, it turned out, had less to do with forcing people to do what the sovereign wanted and more to do with steering them in the desired direction without coercion. The advantages of this approach were twofold. First, the actions of the individuals so guided were voluntary and so were executed with less reluctance. Second, the actual goals pursued in a scheme of governance differed from the ones that were announced. This gap between the intentions of those governing and those governed meant that the goals of a particular policy could avoid public scrutiny.

We can begin to appreciate the difference in the new tactics of "governance" by looking at some of Jeremy Bentham's ideas on the subject. There are, he tells us, two means of preventing harmful actions. The first is to forbid them outright and threaten violators with punishment. Bentham calls this "direct legislation." "Indirect legislation," on the other hand, "has recourse to oblique methods": "In the first case [direct legislation] the legislator openly declares war against the enemy, announces his approach, pursues the foe, fights him hand to hand, and scales his batteries in broad day. In the second [indirect] case he does not make known his plans. He lays mines, sets spies to work, seeks to frustrate the designs of the enemy, and to secure an alliance with those who might otherwise have harboured hostile intentions."[10] Direct legislation has all sorts of disadvantages but perhaps the most important is that it "has no adequate grip upon many mischievous acts which evade justice, either by reason of their extreme frequency, or owing to the difficulty of definition."[11]

Indirect legislation will supplement the direct form of penal sanction by providing tools for the "art of influencing and directing the inclinations."[12] Instead of outlawing the sale of liquor, for example, a government would be wiser to increase the relevant taxes. "In proportion as the price is raised beyond the means of the large mass of the community, people are deprived of the opportunity of yielding to the vice of intemperance." In general, legislators need to come to grips with the psychology of the human will, so as to guide it in directions that are socially useful or at least not socially harmful.[13]

Indirect legislation can take a variety of forms. Instead of outlawing a particular class of actions, the legislator can remove the means necessary to commit them: "In this matter the policy of the legislator may be likened unto that of a children's nurse. The iron bars for the windows, the guards around the fire, her care to remove sharp and dangerous implements from the hands of her charges, are measures of the same kind as forbidding the sale or manufacture of dies for minting money, of poisonous drugs, of arms easily concealed."[14] Or the legislator can work to "augment the strength of . . . less dangerous desires," which can then struggle with the more hazardous, socially inappropriate appetites. As examples Bentham mentions promoting the consumption of tea (to replace alcohol) and the dissemination and encouragement of card games and other trivial amusements, such as the theater, music, and literature.[15]

Though Bentham does not pursue this idea himself, it is obvious that the same means can be used not only to keep individuals from doing what their governors do not want them to do but also to encourage them to develop habits and behavior patterns conducive to the welfare and strength of the community. Overall, the thought behind indirect legislation is to replace (or, better, supplement) laws that express the plain will of the sovereign with regulations that play on the known psychological inclinations of the subjects. The advantage of this method, as mentioned earlier, is that it achieves its ends without debate and without arousing misgivings among the subject population.[16]

It is in the context of this developing "art of government" — Bentham says it is "still a new subject"[17] — that the disciplines need to be situated. The guidance of a nation's population in directions conducive to the public welfare is the gross or macro level on which governance occurs; disciplines can be thought of as the micro level. One way to think of *DP*, then, is as part of a broader argument about the art of government that arose in the context of the profound changes that remade European society from the sixteenth century onward. How should all these people be governed? reformers and administrators asked themselves. This was not a normative question concerning the legitimacy of the power to be exercised but a practical problem of means and ends.

How do disciplines work? And how are they similar to and different from the kind of governance Bentham was discussing? With both governance and disciplines, the goal is to persuade groups of individuals to behave in a certain way without provoking them into thinking critically about what they are being asked to do. In governance, this goal is accomplished through what can reasonably be called manipulation. The legislator is not forthcoming about the reasons for the tax on alcohol. It is done to reduce the consumption of alcohol, but the legislator does not admit this because it would provoke an argument over and even resistance to the policy.

With governance, the already existing conscious motivations of the subjects are steered in this or that direction. Once those motivations are known, rules are structured in such a way as to extract optimum kinds of behavior. Disciplines do not work in the same way. The objective of a discipline is to create a particular capacity among a group of individuals. In other words, in governance the existing inclinations of individuals are manipulated, whereas with disciplines, capacities and inclinations are created. Of course, there is nothing wrong—quite the contrary—with inculcating useful skills into groups of individuals. But disciplines work to transmit capacities to subjects in a way that increases their powers (and thus their productivity) without at the same time enhancing their autonomy: in schools, rote memorization; in factories, precise movements dictated by assembly line requirements; in armies, endless drills. The method for inculcating these abilities is simultaneously the model for how they will be put to use in the examination, on the shop floor, and during battle.

With governance, then, inclinations are managed in such a way as to avoid dissent. Disciplines instill capacities and enhance the productivity of individuals while promoting docility. Disciplines are part of the answer to the question, How are all these people to be governed?

Disciplinary Prisons

Foucault's starting point in *DP* is the origin of the prison. Why was this form of punishment chosen over others available in the eighteenth century? Foucault distinguishes three approaches to punishing criminals: that of the ancien régime, a representational mode, and the modern period of the prison. The first kind of punishment was designed to reassert the power of the sovereign on the body of the condemned. Every offense against the king's law was not simply the violation of a code but an attack on his majesty as well. The criminal, along with the people who gathered to witness the punishment, was reminded of the king's power through the use of branding, disfigurement, or even ritual reenactments of the crime followed by torture and death.[18]

Those who called for reforms, however, were not interested in combating the barbarity of these practices—so at least Foucault maintains, even though these reformers said clearly enough that they, like any modern reader, were horrified by the stories of torture from the ancien régime. "Who does not shudder with horror when reading in history of so many terrible and useless torments," Foucault quotes the Italian penal-reformer Beccaria as exclaiming, "invented and coldly applied by monsters who took upon themselves the name of sage?" Foucault is suspicious: this "recourse to 'sensibility' . . . bears within it a principle of calculation."[19] The problem for the reformers, Foucault maintains, is not the suffering of the criminal but the potentially negative consequences his or her suffering will have on the spectators or judges, who, alternatively, may themselves become hardened and vicious at the sight of so much state-approved torment or may begin pitying the wrong person—the criminal.[20] In the period following the French Revolution, reformers turned first to a representational mode of punishment which involved "a sort of general recipe for the exercise of power over men: the 'mind' as a surface inscription for power, with semiology as its tool; the submission of bodies through the control of ideas; the analysis of representations as a principle in a politics of bodies that was much more effective than the ritual anatomy of torture and execution."[21] These new "semio-techniques of punishments" would replace the king's vengeance with "the transparency of the sign to that which it signifies."[22] To this end it will be important to avoid utilizing the same punishment for different crimes—which would be like using the same word to say different things. Instead of putting lazy vagabonds in prison, put them to work.[23] Fanatics have a high opinion of themselves—subject them to public ridicule. Punishment should be a "school," a "legible lesson," where everyone will learn to read the public signs pointing out how profitless the specific crime is via the very punishment assigned to it.[24] Not long after it was proposed, this representational mode of correction was abandoned in favor of the prison, which served as a general punishment for all crimes save the worst and the least.[25] From attempting to fashion punishments into signs that would warn away potential violators, reformers turned instead to the enclosed space of the prison.

What was it that attracted reformers, finally, to the model of the prison? Why was it chosen over other alternatives? Foucault believes that even posing this question accomplishes something: Instead of viewing the prison as the brute and irreducible fact of all social existence, it is shown to be a choice that is made—one that might not have been made. Why was *this* path chosen?[26] The answer had to do with the opportunities for bending and shaping human beings in new ways. Behind walls the prisoner could be observed, knowledge accumulated, and a file created that could then be compared with others. The extent of depravity could be assessed and a program for reform worked out. Through various architectural tricks the possibility of constant observation could be created, leading prisoners to act as if they *were* being observed at all times—thus forcing them to govern their behavior constantly. In this closed environment characterized by the exercise of unrestricted power, prisoners' habits, attitudes, personalities, and gestures all became objects of manipulation and coercion. For such a power to be effective, it must be constant and so both absolute and independent of other powers.[27]

The sovereign, then, uses awesome power to mark the criminal through ceremonial punishment as a vanquished enemy, which results in a tortured or mutilated body. The representational reformers wanted to institute a system of signs to establish a compelling image of the crime and its consequences, so as to work on the "soft fibers of the brain" of the population.[28] The prison-centered reformers propose, on the other hand, an administrative apparatus that would, as Foucault puts it, deposit its traces directly on the body of the individual. Get a firm grip on the body and its forces, bend them to your will, and the mind will follow. Its method is the subjection of the individual to the coercive environment of an enclosed space to produce a body that has been subjected to strict training.[29]

Foucault not only is interested in the origin and development of prisons but also wants to show how the disciplines, as they were implemented or even only imagined, were applied to a broader social setting. The true objective of the movement to reform the practice of justice associated with the monarchy was to "set up a new 'economy' of the power to punish, to assure its better distribution, so that it should be neither too concentrated at certain privileged points, nor too divided between opposing authorities; so that it should be distributed in homogeneous circuits capable of operating everywhere, in a continuous way, down to the finest grain of the social body."[30] No doubt a distinction should be made between the goals and dreams of these reformers and their capacity to give effect to them. Failure to make such a distinction—and Foucault's writing sometimes encourages just such a lapse—dupes us into reading *DP* as the description of a fully realized and inescapable disciplinary society. As we proceed, we will see why this is an implausible conclusion. To mention just one problem here, such an account would leave out the element of contingency and chance that Foucault elsewhere makes such a central part of his writings on genealogy.[31]

The central purpose of *DP* emerges when Foucault describes the shift from the prisons themselves and the disciplines within them to their application in society at large. At the end of part 2, Foucault summarizes the purpose of the new disciplinary procedures developed behind the prison walls in a way that will illustrate the possibility of a general application. "Ultimately," Foucault says, "what one is trying to restore in this technique of correction is not so much the juridical subject . . . but the obedient subject, the individual subjected to habits, rules, orders, an authority that is exercised continually around him and upon him, and which he must allow to function automatically within him." [32]

As Foucault goes on to point out, however, such a total subjection can be fashioned only in very specific contexts. The discipline must involve imposition of a full timetable of activities if it is to succeed in forcing the individual to change behaviors and adopt certain habits. Especially required is what Foucault calls "a very special relation between the individual who is punished and the individual who punishes": "The agent of punishment must exercise a *total power, which no third party can disturb;* the individual must be *entirely enveloped* in the power that is being exercised over him. Secrecy is imperative, so too is autonomy, at least in relation to this technique of punishment: it must have its own functioning, its own rules, its own techniques, its own knowledge; it must fix its own norms, decide its own results." [33]

Early in part 3, Foucault moves the disciplines out from behind the prison walls: "In the course of the seventeenth and eighteenth centuries the disciplines became general formulas for domination." The disciplines "constantly reached out to new domains," tending "to cover the entire social body." [34] But how could the disciplines retain their effectiveness outside the prison? Clearly, in a broader social setting, the disciplines could no longer count on "the very special relationship" between the punisher and the punished. Outside the prison, individuals cannot be "entirely enveloped" by a "total power." Both secrecy and autonomy, which Foucault insists are "imperative" for the functioning of the disciplines in the prisons, are difficult to achieve outside it — and so too the guarantee of nonintervention by third parties. Another possible intervention is also more difficult to avoid outside the prison — that of the individual subjected to disciplinary constraints, the "second" party, who may revolt against the coercions associated with the disciplines. One could go further and affirm that the omission of this factor — that is, the possibility and consequences of *individual* resistance — detracts from Foucault's account of the effects of disciplines within as well as beyond the prison walls.

Many readers find in *DP* a dystopian vision of society that either reinforces their own rejection of Western society or their rejection of Foucault. This reading is seemingly underlined in the section on Bentham's Panopticon. "On the whole," Foucault observes there, "one can speak of the formation of a disciplinary society in this movement that stretches from the enclosed disciplines, a sort of social 'quarantine,' to an indefinitely generalizable mechanism of 'panopticism.'" The conclusion seems clear: Foucault is describing a society that has become fully "disciplined." Foucault then begins to summarize the views of one N. H. Julius, a German prison reformer who wrote in the early 1830s. It is Julius who "gave this society its birth certificate."[35] Foucault goes on to paraphrase Julius: In ancient Greek societies, the architectural problem was how to make a small number of individuals—at the circus, in religious festivals, for political oratory, plays, and so on—visible and audible to a large number of people. The predominance of public life was assured by the very setting in which these activities were conducted. But now we have moved from a society in which the principal elements are no longer the community and public life but rather private individuals on the one hand and the state on the other. The architecture, as well as the spirit of society, goes through a significant change in the process. Rather than amphitheaters that allow multitudes to observe the play or spectacle, the multitudes are broken up into discrete units on the model of the Panopticon. The multitude is thus individualized and made observable, quantifiable, manipulable. The individuals are not only the products of a particular mechanism of power but also the very agents of its exercise. Conclusions such as this concerning the relationship between individuals and disciplines have perhaps an overly dramatic effect. If we as individuals are "carefully fabricated" in the panoptic machine, which "we bring to ourselves since we are part of its mechanism,"[36] what hope can there be that we might discover a way out of the disciplinary maze?

But for our author, asking the way out of the maze is the wrong way to think about opposition. There is no outside. As Foucault says at one place of the disciplinary model, individuals are the effect of power but are also its *vehicles*.[37] This comment is similar to the one about individuals being part of the mechanism of the discipline. Both comments—individuals as vehicles of the disciplines and as part of their mechanism—can be read in two ways. The usual reading is that individuals are the wholly determined and dependent creatures of the disciplines. As products of the disciplines, persons are unable to identify and thus incapable of criticizing or opposing them. Far from opposing the disciplines, the individual as one of the cogs in its wheels actually supports their operation.

The second and probably truer (certainly more useful) reading of such comments is that precisely because individuals are part of the power mechanism of the disciplines, they are in a better position to challenge it. It is not, in Foucault's view, from some place "outside" of power (in this case, a disciplinary mechanism) that individuals acquire the resources they need to oppose it, whether this "outside" is access to some powerless "truth" about humanity's telos or even from some opposed power formation. The fact that we are *vehicles* of disciplinary power reveals, according to the second interpretation of the passages we are now examining, not the omnipotence of power but its fragility. Such vehicles might go off the designated path in directions that frustrate the purpose for which they were originally developed.

Foucault's claim that modern power formations are often fragile does not conform to the usual treatment of him as a prophet of closed and effective systems of power. One attempt to raise and then discount this ingredient of Foucault's theory is found in Steven Best and Douglas Kellner's *Postmodern Theory*. They admit that "Foucault's own interventions into political struggles and debates would make little sense if he felt that the deadlock of power was unbreakable."[38] In this context, they point to Foucault's claims about the contingent origins of power as well as its fragility. They go on to argue, however, that talk of contingency and fragility is "rare," and they see the "overriding emphasis of Foucault's work" as being "the ways in which individuals are classified, excluded, objectified, individualized, disciplined, and normalized."[39] First, it is hardly correct to say that Foucault discusses the "fragility" or "contingency" of power only rarely. These terms are mentioned frequently, and if we leave quantitative analysis behind, the subjects they represent play a central role throughout Foucault's work.[40] Second, it is wrong to say that Foucault's sense of oppositional possibilities is wholly contained in the terms "fragility" and "contingency," important as they are. The whole point is missed if we say that opposition makes no sense if the "deadlock" of power is "unbreakable." The "unbreakability" of power does *not* constitute a "deadlock" for Foucault. Rather, it is in the context of a specific power relation like a discipline that opposition becomes conceivable in the first place.

DP looks much different if we approach it not as another installment of the Frankfurt School's "administered society" series but as a Nietzschean reflection on the ways in which individuals are indeed created—though not definitively *determined*—by a plurality of social forces. The result is a much more interesting book. This Nietzschean treatment of individuality and social forms becomes more pronounced in Foucault's later work and provides the basis for rethinking the possibilities of oppositional activity.

Those interested in dismissing Foucault—such as the translator and interpreter of Jürgen Habermas, Thomas McCarthy—work hard to present him as a member of the pre-Habermasian Frankfurt School. In his essay on the subject, McCarthy approvingly quotes another critic of Foucault, Nancy Fraser, as follows: " 'Foucault writes as if oblivious to the existence of the whole body of Weberian social theory with its careful distinctions between such notions as authority, force, violence, domination, and legitimation. Phenomena which are capable of being distinguished via such concepts are simply lumped together. . . . As a consequence, the potential for a broad range of normative nuance is surrendered, and the result is a certain normative one-dimensionality.' "[41] But it seems criticisms such as these fail to meet Foucault's argument. What was the whole point of Foucault's exercise in DP, just to take that example? It was to show that there were some very important forms of the exercise of power that could not be effectively understood or criticized using the "careful distinctions between legitimate, consensual forms of authority and illegitimate, violent forms" mentioned by Fraser.

What does a discipline do? It shapes individuals—neither with nor without their consent. It does not use violence. Instead, individuals are trained. In addition, this method of training—its originators and practitioners hope— will not only impart skills but will do so while reducing the political efficacy of the individuals involved. If violence has not been used, the discipline cannot be criticized using the normal liberal rhetorical devices. The "careful distinctions" discussed by Fraser and supported by McCarthy are *too gross* to capture the phenomena at hand. Foucault is certainly not the first theorist to refer to this kind of operation of power. Marx, for example, explains how workers become "acclimated" to the routine of factory life and as a result lose any sense of being imposed on. They have been "disciplined."[42] Every second-year graduate student—and plenty of intellectuals in and out of the academy—*knows* this. So why is Foucault being treated as the messenger who must be killed?

What can one do if current practices, if the social world as it is, cannot be effectively critiqued from within using the standard liberal rhetorical tools? For that *is* the problem Foucault and Marx confronted. The answer—adopted in part by Marx and rejected by Foucault—is very old: push the world you want out to the exterior of the world you inhabit. The past or the future are the usual proposed sites. We children of the twentieth century know what such millennial expectations have led to, but Fraser and the others write "as if oblivious" to this history and the pause it has given to responsible and thoughtful critical theorists.

What needs to be considered and is missed by thinkers such as McCarthy is that Foucault's rejection of normative ethics is not merely the perverse, wholly individual and willfully voluntarist consequence of a sometimes brilliant but immature caprice.[43] The profound sense of comfort and reassurance that such criticisms of Foucault seem to produce in their authors should have warned them that they were on the wrong track. Foucault did not write, as surely Fraser herself suspects, in ignorance of Weberian distinctions concerning power or in ignorance of the well-worn line of products issued by contemporary neo-Kantian ethics. Nor was he merely bored by such ethical accounts—though boredom would be a secondary consequence of Foucault's true objections. Really, it is writers such as Fraser who write "as if" and perhaps actually in ignorance of the impasse that critical thought has reached in the late twentieth century.

Foucault's approach to the disciplines will be better distinguished if it is contrasted with a broadly construed Kantian critique of them. From a Kantian or generally liberal perspective, it is easy to say something critical about the disciplines. Their effect on individuals appears to be almost entirely negative. Individuals are used purely as means to some ulterior end rather than as creatures with ends of their own. In the process, the capacity of individuals to shape their own lives is compromised. The Kantian is able, in terms of his or her own ethical universe, to say what is unacceptable about the world Foucault describes. A number of irritants intrude at this point, however, just when it might seem that Foucault and some of his critics are able to join hands. Foucault makes it clear that he does not share and indeed rejects the Kantian criticism of the disciplines. First irritant, then: How has Foucault managed to describe a world so well that so manifestly violates Kantian ethics without sharing those ethics or even *while* rejecting them?

A suspicion emerges that is tied to a second irritant: Does Foucault in fact disapprove of and reject the disciplinary world he describes? The answer is yes and all Foucault's critics say it for him. But they also go on to say that Foucault lacks a normative basis for this affirmative response they have supplied on his behalf. The possibility is then left open that Foucault does not really oppose the disciplines—at least that he cannot be said to oppose them until he takes the helping hand offered by Kantian ethics. Until then, Foucault's opposition to the disciplines is ineffective, merely personal, arbitrary, decisionist.[44] Moreover, not only does Foucault describe a world Kantian ethics would reject while rejecting Kantian ethics, but he then also returns the compliment paid him by his Kantian critics by suggesting that elements of the very "normative" criteria so regrettably absent from his own work have played a part in the "normalizing" society described in *DP.* And this is a third irritant.

The result is a fractious tone in much of the critical commentary on Foucault. Foucault's critics work from an ethical basis whose validity Foucault does not acknowledge. The critics know this, but instead of seeking in Foucault's writings a different approach to the phenomena he describes, they assume he has adopted a strangely uncritical perspective. The assumption is that if Foucault does not have recognizably liberal, normative objections to disciplinary practices, he could not have anything else to say about them. It is at this point in the argument that the critics are in error.[45] But this error can be recognized only if we shift perspective and think about disciplines, where they come from, and how they might be opposed, all from a Nietzschean position. Foucault does indeed have a critical perspective on at least some of the disciplines some of the time, but this perspective is also to be distinguished from a liberal or Kantian one. It is possible, after all, to oppose effects associated with the disciplines from more than one perspective, just as it is possible to support individual rights and freedom from state intervention in our personal lives for reasons other than the liberal ones with which we are most familiar.[46]

Disciplinary Projects

Foucault at times gives the impression that disciplines originally found in prison settings were successfully extended to a broader social world, where they established a disciplinary society. Let us admit that this is an exaggeration and go back to consider the true purpose and operation of disciplines. Why were the disciplines devised? What motivated their originators? What made the transfer of disciplines from the prison to a social setting an attractive option for some?

As we have seen, Foucault is careful to relate the functioning of the disciplines to their social context. The "large demographic thrust of the eighteenth century; an increase in the floating population. . . ; a change of quantitative scale in the groups to be supervised or manipulated" all called for a new kind of exercise of power.[47] Disciplines promised to organize, distribute, and individualize this growing mass as a way of reducing the threat that it posed. Taken as a simple collective mass, the people were unpredictable and dangerous. At the same time, the disciplines sought to integrate this newly organized mass into a complex production apparatus as part of the industrial revolution. In other words, the outline of the story Foucault tells us is similar to an account of the industrial revolution. Foucault's contribution is to examine more closely some of the projects that were brought into being in response to the problems and opportunities created by a massively realigned social system. What he finds is that disciplines make two promises: they claim to be able to take an unorganized, untrained, and potentially disruptive—at best, useless—population and inculcate and enhance its productive capacity, and at the same time ensure its political docility.[48]

Several levels of thought in this presentation of the tasks of the disciplines must be distinguished if Foucault is not to be misunderstood. First, there are the actual programs of the reformers, the inventors of the disciplines. Because these were rather numerous, Foucault tends to present their features at a distance from their actual operation. From this same distance, Foucault at times writes in a retrospective mode about the effect the disciplines came to have once they were fleshed out. A further distortion to which we have already been introduced is Foucault's literary habit of using language that at times appears to present the disciplines as fully realized modes of power that not only exist but do so in a pure state, in near complete accordance with the designs of their creators. The need to generalize from multiple instances, the desire to present the reader with a certain retrospective look at the disciplines from a vantage point far in their future (namely, our present), and a literary device designed to reveal the full impact of the disciplinary exercise of power have led one reader after another to conclude that Western societies—in Foucault's account—are nothing more than an interlocking system of disciplinary mechanisms.[49]

Foucault must take his share of the blame for this reading. It is, however, the wrong reading—certainly the least profitable one. When Foucault describes the "disciplines" to us, what slice of social reality is he attempting to describe? Modern society as a whole? Certainly Foucault encourages this view by describing his work rather paradoxically as a "history of the present."[50] But this idea cannot be allowed to persist in this vague way—we need a much better idea of how such a book as *DP* functions—*how* it succeeds (if it does) in providing critical insights apart from the usual discourse about norms and rights.

Let us first settle this matter of the object Foucault describes and then proceed to consider how his description contributes to a critical assessment of "our present." In one place, Foucault tells us what the book is *not* about: "In this 'birth of the prison,' what is the question? French society in a given period? No. Delinquence in the eighteenth and nineteenth centuries? No. The prisons in France between 1760 and 1840? Not even that."[51] All three of the possible times and places that Foucault mentions are, of course, perfectly valid subjects of historical concern. The task of presenting the reader with an account of "the prisons in France between 1760 and 1840" is to show how the work of the prisons was actually conducted. If the thesis is that French society as a whole—and not just its prisons — became "disciplined" during a particular period, then the writer's task would be to show the specific events that marked this transformation. But these strips of reality are not the objects of Foucault's analysis.

If, however, the disciplines Foucault describes are not a description of "reality," then what are they? They are descriptions of *programs* of action.[52] In *DP*, Foucault uses the words "schemes" and "dreams" to denote the projects leading up to and culminating in the Panopticon. Major elements of these programs either failed to see the light of day or were confronted by oppositional factors that forced modifications in their implementation. But none of this is to say that the projects in question were idle or wholly disconnected from the world they sought to order. These schemes were always created in response to some actual and often pressing social need. All are concerned with the tasks of managing, controlling, and ultimately directing masses of people that both pose a threat to social stability and present an opportunity for magnifying the power of the state.

Foucault explicitly cites the social origins of the disciplinary schemes. Disciplines are "techniques for assuring the ordering of human multiplicities."[53] All of a sudden schools and hospitals, to take two of Foucault's examples, were flooded with unprecedented numbers of people seeking education and health care and there were no established procedures for handling them. At the same time, some of the newer creations of the period, such as the modern army and the factories, required the efficient management of large numbers of soldiers and workers. New economies of scale and quite different uses for the human body created the conditions in which a new type of power could come into being.

The fact that new needs now existed did not mean that the organization of power the disciplines demanded was either automatically accepted or that it was the only conceivable response. In the area of punishment, for instance, Foucault shows at length that the "disciplinary" option, though ultimately successful, was not the only one to which the reformers turned.[54] Disciplines were not some inevitable secret at the heart of European capitalism but schemes developed by certain authors, thinkers, often practitioners in various fields, administrators, and so on. They were one way of dealing with the problems and opportunities associated with a demographic, industrial, and military environment that was in a state of flux.

An example used by Foucault is the French naval hospital located in the port city of Rochefort. It was simultaneously a site of "embarking and disembarking, diseases and epidemics — a place of desertion, smuggling, contagion . . .

a crossroads for dangerous mixtures, a meeting-place for forbidden circulations."[55] The hospital was certainly dedicated to the treatment of its patient population, but to perform its duties it had to be a filter, a mechanism that "pins down and partitions; it must provide a hold over this whole mobile, swarming mass, by dissipating the confusion of illegality and evil. The medical supervision of diseases and contagions is inseparable from a whole series of other controls: the military control over deserters, fiscal control over commodities, administrative control over remedies, disappearances, cures, deaths, simulations. Hence the need to distribute and partition off space in a rigorous manner."[56] This is one side of the disciplines, one aspect of the task that they took up: populations that mushroomed in an absolute way had to be managed, while the new uses to which people were put also led to new concentrations of individuals.

No one likes prisons, and so it is easy to describe in negative terms the disciplines Foucault finds in them—but what about a naval hospital? Shall we denounce the hospital administrators? But anyone who would allow the contagiously ill to mingle with the wounded is simply not doing his or her job. Nor in this context does it make sense to condemn the effort to develop files on individuals that allow doctors to track the progress of disease, cures, and death. In fact, Foucault does not consider all forms of discipline bad. They do not imply some fundamental violation of the human personality that we are all morally bound to condemn. But taken together with the variety of attempts to "microgovern" human populations that is characteristic of our societies, disciplines can be seen as an instance of the "excess governance" that can develop into something limiting and objectionable.

Instead of dividing the world into good and bad exercises of power, Foucault prefers the "flat and empirical" question, "What happens?"[57] From this perspective, a broader treatment of power is made possible. On the one hand, we do not like prisons, and on the other, it is hard to criticize the administrators of the naval hospital for their handling of a difficult situation. If we insist on a moral evaluation, it is easy to disapprove of what occurs in the prison at the same time as we affirm the policies of the hospital administrators—"good" and "bad" exercises of power have been described. For Foucault, however, this concession ignores the procedures and tactics that unite the prison reformers and hospital administrators: the fixing and ranking of human multitudes, the development of files that track "progress," the invention of procedures to bend human material in predetermined directions. Once that is done, Foucault will not have provided us with absolutely good and bad kinds of power that all moral or rational individuals are constrained to recognize as such. On the contrary, differently situated individuals will have very different perspectives on the phenomena he describes. Avoiding abstract evaluative judgments on power "as such," then, allows Foucault to discuss the disciplinary project in a more usefully ambiguous way—not as something bad or good so much as "dangerous" or "double-edged" in its effects.

By itself, the use of power in the naval hospital model is unobjectionable, but when applied to a broader setting the effect may not be so trivial. The "political dream of the plague" is just such a society-wide application of the lessons learned at Rochefort. The special circumstances of the plague had often led to undesirable political and social consequences for the communities in which it raged. Hierarchies were overturned and conventions flouted in the presence of arbitrary threats of death. At the same time, the plague-stricken town was often the site of unprecedented social controls that worked to reverse the rejection and caricature of social life traditionally associated with the plague: "not the collective festival, but strict divisions; not laws transgressed, but the penetration of regulation into even the smallest details of everyday life through the mediation of the complete hierarchy that assured the capillary functioning of power; not masks that were put on and taken off, but the assignment to each individual of his 'true' name, his 'true' place, his 'true' body, his 'true' disease." [58] In *DP,* Foucault provides the reader with an example of this program or dream. [59] The strict control of the city afflicted by plague was the subject of a broad array of proposals and regulations. The immediate goal was, of course, similar to that of the naval hospital: control the contagion as much as possible through a military conduct of social life. And as with the hospital, the intent or object is difficult to criticize. But Foucault believes that something else besides this immediate goal is either in the minds—the "dreams"—of those who propose such strict social controls or is an unforeseen consequence of the implementation of these controls.

> The plague-stricken town, traversed throughout with hierarchy, surveillance, observation, writing; the town immobilized by the functioning of an extensive power that bears in a distinct way over all individual bodies —this is the utopia of the perfectly governed city. The plague (envisioned as a possibility at least) is the trial in the course of which one may define ideally the exercise of disciplinary power. In order to make rights and laws function according to pure theory, the jurists place themselves in imagination in the state of nature; in order to see perfect disciplines functioning, rulers dreamt of the state of the plague. [60]

Certainly the plague is a unique opportunity for experimenting with diverse techniques of social control—but, again, Foucault does not make clear who has this dream and to what extent its realization is ever accomplished or even attempted. Perhaps part of the difficulty in understanding Foucault has to do with the level of intellectual activity addressed in his reconstruction of disciplinary projects. Political philosophy usually deals with ideal institutions and idealized forms of argument. Foucault deals with the social imagination of actual practitioners of power and with the techniques of organizing and producing power.

The writers that Foucault investigates are "practical," little concerned with theoretical systems or disputes over human nature. More often they are administrators, heads of police, and advisers to rulers. In this last category, rather exaggerated programs of social control and sovereign omniscience were put forward, but less as part of the actual workings of a proposal and more as an advertisement, a bit of hyperbolic self-promotion. Others—administrators and writers of manuals on political administration, such as Turquet de Mayenne, whom Foucault discusses in his 1979 lectures on political reason—simply try to come up with schemes for effectively managing the problems and potentials of an emerging modern world. They develop what Foucault calls "schemes" (often translated into English as "projects"). They do not use a state of nature or some other imagined account of society's origin to explain where political life comes from or what justifies its existence. Their dream is not of an origin that might help transform or criticize today's world so much as a dream about how to make today's world function more effectively.

In other words, the people who actually work up the social world into the place where we live our lives are, like Foucault, concerned with the *how* of power: how to manage large populations, how to isolate people with infectious diseases, how to inculcate useful skills into groups of individuals. Sometimes this "how" produces relatively large-scale programs of action, such as Bentham's Panopticon; at other times, more immediately practical, piecemeal, and technical solutions are improvised.[61] In a sense, the "political dream" of the plague-stricken city is precisely a reduction of politics to as close to the zero point as possible with a concomitant open field for a "public-administrative rationality."

Foucault's field of study might also be characterized like this: His administrators and police chiefs have little to do with political philosophy and so cannot act as authors of works that promote a vision of a political utopia. Administrative handbooks, not philosophical treatises, are more often the products of their pens. On the other hand, the world they dream of more often sees the light of day.

This discussion of technical innovations and dreams conveys a more modest appreciation for what Foucault is trying to accomplish in *DP.* The tradition of political philosophy associated with the Frankfurt School would, perhaps, see Foucault's discussion of military dreams and plague cities overrun by bureaucrats as instances of a broader and irreversible rationalization of society. But this is not at all how Foucault uses these texts. He is not attempting to show us that all society is a prison, a military camp, or a plague city thoroughly penetrated by bureaucratic surveillance. He is not trying to work within the field of political philosophy that supports and expects such extravagant conclusions.[62] Nor, on the other hand, does he see himself working as a pure historian intent on describing a certain slice of reality at some time in our past. He is not a historian of ideas, a historian of discrete social forms, or a participant in the activity of political philosophy that draws on one or more of these intellectual pursuits. As Foucault argues in a debate over *DP:* "It is, perhaps, necessary to question the principle, often implicitly admitted, that the sole *reality* which can pretend to be history is 'society' itself. A type of rationality, a manner of thinking, a programme, a technique, an ensemble of rational and coordinated efforts, with defined and pursued objectives, along with instruments for attaining them, etc., all that is real, even if it does not pretend to be '*the* reality' itself, nor 'the' entire society."[63] Rather than attempting to describe "all" society yesterday or today as a single reality, Foucault explicitly rejects such a conception. The presence of that requirement as a background assumption has led many readers to fit *DP* into a certain political slot in accordance with certain expectations of what a "political," "historical," and "critical" work should be.

Disciplines, Individuals, and Norms

"Discipline 'makes' individuals; it is the specific technique of a power that regards individuals both as objects and as instruments of its exercise."[64] For many, it has been simply impossible to read this sentence without snapping into place the last lock on Foucault's vision of the modern iron cage and throwing away the key—or the book, depending on one's sympathies. If individuals are literally *made* by disciplines, how would it ever be possible for them to turn around and meaningfully confront their makers? If the objects that society administers are its own products, even creations, then such a society is, almost by definition, a "fully administered" one. But, as we shall see, Foucault's "individuals" are much less unitary than is usually believed. Disciplines may make individuals, but not completely or finally. This leaves plenty of room for change and opposition.

Disciplinary power, like the kind in the Rochefort Naval Hospital, " 'trains' the moving, confused, useless multitudes of bodies and forces into a multiplicity of individual elements — small, separate cells, organic autonomies, genetic identities and continuities, combinatory segments. Discipline 'makes' individuals."[65] Thus transformed from a swarming mass into an organized grid, other possibilities emerge for the manipulation of the human material. From the vantage point of the crowd a dispersal and fixing of individuals appears to be the "cellular" effect of the disciplines. But once individualized on this — as it turns out — "gross" level, the disciplines can go on further to divide the body of the individual into "subindividuals."

First, the normal are segregated from those who are abnormal: those who are insane are placed in hospitals, and the criminals are put in jails. Once there, experiments will be performed to test programs for manipulating human material. This is done with a view toward producing more acceptable behavior among social "misfits." In addition, some of these programs might be made applicable to other settings as well. Such an institutional setting as Bentham's proposed Panopticon will take away the corrupting subculture of prison life — which had its own set of pressures and constraints — and replace it with a set of checks and coercions designed to produce compliant, productive citizens. The "discovery" behind the Panopticon, as Foucault presents it, was a double one: Moral appeals, religious sermons, and the like had no effect by themselves. Rather than rely on such "normative" appeals, the Panopticon made possible the operation of a set of uninterrupted exercises and activities. These worked to "turn" the gross, empirical social offender by inculcating more socially acceptable habits and dispositions. Not the "moral sense" of the already socially shaped human unit but a community of *subindividuals* was the object and creation of this punitive rationality. The successful implantation, growth, and increased influence of these created subindividuals were ensured by the omniscient surveillance that is the best-known feature of the Panopticon. That part of the prisoner not created by the discipline, the part brought with the individual into prison, is not allowed to interrupt or somehow check the spread and growing influence of the implanted subindividuals, owing to the unblinking light that shines on it from the panoptic eye. Of course, each individual prisoner is not watched twenty-four hours a day, but the Panopticon is designed in such a way so that whether one is being watched is impossible for the prisoner to tell. This turns out to be the essential "mental" correspondence to the disciplinary infusions. Never sure when they are being watched by someone in the central tower—or even if there is anyone in the tower at all—prisoners come by degrees to watch themselves, to make sure on their own that exercises and tasks are performed in the correct manner, that no word or gesture escapes that is other than part of the prescribed routine.

Given enough time, enough exclusive working of the disciplines on prisoners, a "gross," "everyday" individual is produced who is first prepared to appreciate a religious lecture and finally to rejoin society. That, at least, is the claim of the "scheme." Again, the motto of the disciplines might be: Get hold of their bodies—their hearts and minds will follow.

As I said earlier, once human populations are distributed in a cellular manner, they become subject to transformative techniques that, it is hoped, will make the individuals and the transformed collectivities in which they participate both more useful and more docile. According to Foucault, individuals are reduced as a political force and augmented in terms of certain skills.[66] How does this happen? Part of the answer has to do with what Foucault describes as "normalization," which, along with surveillance, "becomes one of the great instruments of power at the end of the classical age."[67]

The term "normalization" is not to be seen in an immediately negative light. A norm is a standard of some kind that a multiplicity of individuals must reach and maintain to perform certain tasks. Though Foucault is obviously playing a word game here, disciplines on this level have "norms" in a non-"normative" (or nonmoral) sense. If members of a group are to be trained to do something, one way to do it is to establish standards that will act as performance goals for each individual. A number of the tasks that Foucault shows the disciplines requiring are, at first, simple but demanding. The act of raising a rifle to the shoulder to aim and fire is broken down into as many parts as possible. Each step is simple, but all together they demand the full attention and commitment of the individual.[68] As time goes on, less concentration is required as the activity becomes automatic. In this way the individual is subordinated to this play of fragmented gestures repeated by rote, which makes the individual psychologically (and politically) something less and economically something more than the sum of its parts.[69]

In the course of training large numbers of individuals to perform various activities, other senses of "norm" become evident. First, there is "the normal," meaning the average or the mean: Different individuals display varying aptitudes in learning and executing a series of hand-eye motions that make up the smooth performance of almost any occupational task. This allows a ranking to be traced around a norm of performance. Some do it faster, without mishap, whereas others are slow or clumsier; few are actually normal. This norm then contributes to a conception of the "natural" (thus normal) human body. During its performance of specific tasks, it becomes clear that the natural body can do certain things and not others. In learning to raise a rifle to the shoulder, the body resists certain motions and responds easily to others, thus forcing the inventors of disciplines to adjust their exercises and establishing a mean set of physical capacities, which is both natural and normal, with both of these last terms setting the mark for another set of distinctions: healthy and sick, normal and abnormal.

As the above distinctions and valuations accumulate, a particular conception of the "truth" about human beings emerges, a term that shares and intensifies many of the ambiguities of "normal." The first kind of truth generated by the play of disciplines is a descriptive, objective, and even scientific one. Around the tasks that the disciplines design, a certain biological set of truths emerges. The "natural" body is capable of repeating exercises for specific periods of time; the mind ("on average") is capable of absorbing only so much instruction; and as already mentioned, the body resists or allows certain movements. A group of capacities and motions establishes the truth of the human being as an object of a certain kind. But it goes without saying that the natural human being and the mind discovered by the disciplines are natural only in relation to the tasks set by the disciplines. In other words, what counts as natural and thus normal depends on the kinds of things the sciences decide to measure, which in turn reflect specific economic, military, and social needs. The disciplines decide what is natural and then measure individuals to see whether they are normal. Individuals, as Foucault asserts, are created by power. So too is the "truth" about them.

Now, if some outside agency imposes its will on a human agent, such an action is often called *coercion,* or even violence. For Foucault, in the case of disciplines, this categorization is unsatisfactory because it fails to specify the much more complex processes by which individuals come to recognize themselves as subjects in the context of the experience provided by a grid of power relations. "Bad" or "violent" coercion is replaced, in Foucault's account, by an elaborate and indeterminate interplay between the object of disciplinary power and the discipline itself. Disciplines "produce" the individual, and this statement does indeed stand against the various liberal views of the individual as a unified, presocial monad. But it also works against the claim that a *unified* subject is *socially* produced. Disciplines produce individuals in the same way that the rules of a particular sport such as baseball "make" an individual who both obeys and plays with these rules to create a certain individuality, or character—a certain set of mobile intersection points that is recognizable, real, and transitory. To make Foucault's point clear, we might outline it this way: (1) this individuality is real, actual, "true"; (2) it does not refer to some preexistent, unified, or essential self; and (3) it does not exclude the existence within the *empirical* individual of other "individuals"; these obey other rules in other games, though of course there are intersection points and interactions between one (sub)individual and another.

Thus, the clause "disciplines create individuals" is not at all to be read as a denial of oppositional, creative, or random possibilities. Such a reading would assume, as Foucault does not, that individuals are unitary, single psychic structures. If they were, then the claim that some kind of power relation such as a discipline *created* the individual would foreclose the possibility for opposition. But for Foucault, both disciplines and the individuals they create are plural. No gross individual is ever wholly enclosed by one discipline, just as baseball players are never just baseball players but other kinds of individuals as well.

In addition, the rules and products of disciplinary power, along with all other kinds of power relations, are themselves sites of varied interpretations and uses. The soldier who learns how to shoot in a "disciplined" and efficient manner is given a skill. Let us grant for a moment that one element of the program involved in the exercise of disciplinary power is the reduction of the soldier as a disruptive political force while increasing his or her value as an efficient cog in a military machine. We can also admit that this program has had its moments of success: in World War I, large masses of newly trained individuals were disposed of in battle without mutinies or other ill consequences associated with arming and training hundreds of thousands of individuals to function as military units. (No doubt, this success was not automatic, permanent, or without exceptions.) The *program* of the disciplines was to create politically weak and economically (or militarily) powerful combinations of masses of individuals. But the move from the drawing board to varied points of application in social contexts is a story of successes, failures, unforeseen interactions with other factors, and so on. It is simply not Foucault's intent to describe a "normalized" or "disciplined" society. That is not, as I have said elsewhere, the *object* of his study, not his "referent." Because the "normalized" or "fully administered" society is not Foucault's object of analysis, he is not required to indict the usual list of those suspected of causing such phenomena: capitalism, socialism, rationalism, and so forth.

To understand Foucault's true objective, let us return to his account of the disciplines in *DP*. In the first instance the disciplines disperse a mass of un-organized persons into a discrete, cellular complex attached to the bed, cell, desk, and the like. The mass is dispersed, but a "hold" on the persons is never-theless retained. Thus organized, individuals become objects of training, the inculcation of skills, which gives rise to an organic, natural body. Of course, this average is relative to the multiplicity in which the individual is situated — relative too to the specific demands made by the discipline in question.

By organizing masses of individuals in particular ways, new truths emerge: truths that were not there before that disposition of forces; truths that are not somehow false relative to something deeper; real, actual truths, which, ironi-cally to our way of thinking, lack a foundational ontological status. But if these are truths, absent both dismissive quotation marks *and* essentialist pre-tensions, then they cannot be challenged by a deeper human nature, "genuine" interests, and so forth. Instead of discounting supposed truths as false, Fou-cault engages in a reflection on the nature of the particular truths involved and their consequences, an intellectual activity made possible by the very claim that the truth in question is not of an essential or foundational kind and thus "untouchable."

Out of training comes hierarchization — the ranking of individuals along the "advanced" and "backward" continuum, which itself makes reference to the natural, organic, or "healthy" human being. This ranking, however, does not remain static, as we have seen: "Disciplines have for their function the reduc-tion of gaps."[70] Through repeated exercises all individuals are moved closer to the norm, though it is also true that the position of the norm has a tendency to climb slowly up the scale to accommodate a shifting mean of performance.

A variety of inducements and coercions are employed to force this move-ment in the direction of the norm. In one passage, for example, Foucault talks of how the architectural design of a building can make a mass of individu-als more visible and controllable. It is a poorly designed disciplinary structure that merely fixes individuals in their places. The very fact of being continu-ously watched, combined with activities that must be performed because sur-veillance is unceasing, allows an alteration or bending of individuals accord-ing to a preconceived program. Foucault's use of school manuals makes this point clearly. Students who perform their exercises poorly, are unprepared, and so on are not simply ranked low on the scale relative to the norm but are also given "bad points," which can often be worked off only through repeti-tive drilling. But these "demerits," as they are popularly known, "are only one element of a double system." Indeed, as argued in one manual, the teacher "should avoid as much as possible the use of punishments. On the contrary he should make his benefits more frequent than his punishments, the slackers being more encouraged by the hope of being regarded in the same way as the diligent students than the fear of chastisements. This is why it will be a very great benefit when the teacher will restrict the use of punishments, in order to win if possible the heart of the child."[71] The "slackers" will then wish to achieve and surpass the norm. The subjective *desire* to achieve superior status is a far more effective impetus to improvement than the coercion associated with punishments. Rather than forcing or somehow threatening the individual into compliance with external demands, the teacher creates a receptive psychic environment. The child will be normal only when she or he learns to form the letters correctly.

Foucault compares the disciplinary system of punishments to criminal justice: In the latter, punishments result if a violation of the law is discovered. With disciplines, on the other hand, subjects are distributed along a line with a "negative" and a "positive" pole: "All conduct falls in the field of good and bad marks, good and bad points."[72] In other words, "normal," along with perhaps "surpassing the norm," which originally had reference to a "natural" and "organic" body, shades off into the value judgment "good," which both transforms the sense of normal while also intensifying the reference to the natural and empirical object. Concomitantly, "falling short of the norm," "subnormal," shades off into the value judgment "bad," "abnormal," "retarded." The "normal" becomes *normative.*

> By this game of quantification, of this circulation of credits and debits, thanks to the permanent calculation of good and bad points, disciplinary apparatuses hierarchize "good" and "bad" subjects in relation to one another. Through this micro-economy of perpetual penalty there operates a differentiation which is not one of acts, but of the individuals themselves, of their nature, their potentialities, their level or their value. Discipline, in penalizing acts with precision, judges individuals "in truth"; the penalty that it puts into operation is integrated into the cycle of knowledge of individuals.[73]

We are once again reminded of a point made by Nietzsche. Will to power, as he describes it, is expansionist: "Every drive is a kind of lust to rule; each has its perspective that it would like to compel all the other drives to accept as a norm."[74] Even in a prison it is difficult to imagine the circumstances under which a set of exercises—the graduated implantation of a skill relative to a standard of performance — can wholly occupy the space of an individual so as to accomplish the double goal of reducing it as a political force and enhancing it as an economic one. And, as it turns out, it is not the location of a discipline in a prison or some other exclusive site that is the key ingredient in the success of the discipline. (If that were true, it might drive one more nail into the coffin of the idea that Foucault is offering us a picture of society as a complex of interlocking prisons.) The central element in compelling all the other forces, actual and potential, to accept a disciplinary perspective as a norm is its association with truth. This association is made up of a double "juridico-natural reference."[75] Disciplines establish a natural "organic" body, one about which "true" — in the sense of "objective" — statements can be made. This is done in the context of handling human multiplicities, with the result that these "objective" truths make reference to a norm or standard that has to do with a mean, an average. All the individuals that make up a multitude are measured alongside this norm, which seen from one angle is simply a statistical average, merely descriptive, whereas from another it acts not in a descriptive sense but a prescriptive one. Appropriately ranked relative to the "mean-norm," individuals are judged according to two criteria: (1) where they are situated relative to the mean or natural set of capacities typical of humans; and (2) their ability to advance or propensity to fall behind in the training designed to pull individuals up to and beyond the norm. In different but related ways, both criteria rely for their effectiveness on persuading individuals to accept an expanded conception of truth about themselves. The first sense of truth — one having to do with the "natural" body — allows for exclusions, segmentations, differentiations of the populace according to what is normal and what is not. The second sense — the one having to do with success or failure relative to the performance standards set by disciplines — superimposes a good-bad distinction on what was at first only a mean distribution of individuals. The "truth" of the individual at first identified objectively on an arbitrarily established scale of performance turns into a *valuation* of the individual. "Truth," then, straddles and mediates between the individual as an empirical object and as a moral being.[76] In both senses, the individual is invited to expand the purely observational truth according to arbitrary criteria into a substantive truth about what is good and bad about an individual, what deserves to be excluded, confined, or marked off; what is to be praised or admired, discouraged or disparaged.

  If the discipline can succeed in persuading individuals to tie a substantive sense of truth — another term might be "morality" — to what are, after all, very restricted manifestations of human activity and potential, it will have made good on its promise to reduce the individual as an efficacious political subject while enhancing its value as an economic one. Properly speaking, disciplines should be competent to judge whether individuals are able to perform certain functions, or what Foucault calls "acts." But in terms of the dual goal (of reduced political and increased economic power), this is not sufficient. The object of assessment is expanded from the restricted area of "acts"—that is, how well an individual loads and fires a weapon—to "individuals themselves" and their "value," as to whether they are "good or bad subjects."[77] This would be Foucault's most emphatic criticism—perhaps "warning" would be a better word—regarding disciplines: each discipline acts as a will to power which demands that its norm-based distinction between good and bad act as the orthodox evaluation of the humans in question.

Criticism and Experience

There is for Foucault undoubtedly something demonic about the blurring of these two senses of truth: the normal body as observed scientific fact and the normal individual as a standard of valuation. As a standard of valuation, of course, this set of "scientific truths" about human beings is mobilized to achieve a variety of exclusions from the human community, of which Foucault highlights two in his discussion leading up to that of Bentham's Panopticon: lepers and plague victims. Two very different ways of dealing with these populations, based on their own peculiarities, were developed. For the leper there was what Foucault calls a rejecting confinement. Lepers were herded onto boats and sent to islands to die. For plague victims, as we have already seen, a more strictly disciplinary approach is taken: all individuals in a city were pinned down and exhaustively accounted for in a life-or-death battle with the disease. "The leper was caught up in a practice of rejection, or exile-enclosure; he was left to his doom in a mass among which it was useless to differentiate." No need for disciplines here. Victims of the plague, on the other hand, "were caught up in a meticulous tactical partitioning in which individual differentiations were the constricting effects of a power that multiplied, articulated, and subdivided itself."[78] Complete separation from the community for the leper; creation of a visually penetrable space for the plague city, like a beehive that has been cut away, allowing the observer to see what happens in each cell without exception. The first group is marked and set aside, and the second, held and squeezed in the tightening fist of social control.

These are different projects, Foucault says, that reveal "two ways of exercis-

ing power over men, of controlling their relations, of unravelling their dangerous blendings." They also correspond to different political dreams: the pure
community produced by exclusion and the disciplined city produced by unimpeded observation. But while different, these projects were not incompatible.[79]
Lepers and all others symbolized by the lepers could be subjected to discipline
in a way that would intensify their exclusion even if this no longer included
actual banishment (though this practice was by no means dropped). Rather
than leaving the manifestly abnormal to remain in an unorganized and un-
differentiated state, the excluded are themselves individualized. And this very
individualization continues the task of excluding and separating.

From the other side, individuals in a disciplinary setting find themselves
subject to practices of exclusion. The plague victim is turned into a leper.
The soldier who cannot aim and fire the rifle properly is deformed, an idiot,
unnaturally slow; the same is true of a worker who cannot meet "normal"
assembly line speeds or a student who cannot learn a lesson after three repeti-
tions of an exercise. "On the one hand, the lepers are treated as plague victims;
the tactics of individualizing disciplines are imposed on the excluded; and, on
the other hand, the universality of disciplinary controls makes it possible to
brand the 'leper' and to bring into play against him the dualistic mechanisms
of exclusion. . . . All the mechanisms of power which, even today, are disposed
around the abnormal individual, to brand him and to alter him, are composed
of those two forms from which they distantly derive."[80] It is just at this moment in DP that Foucault introduces Bentham's Panopticon, the "architectural
figure" of this combination of marking lepers and distributing individuals.[81]

Having reviewed Foucault's account of the disposition of human material
by the disciplinary mode of power, we are led once again to consider those aspects of the process Foucault rejects and on what basis. What Foucault does
not mean to reject about the disciplines is some supposedly inherent moral offense involved in shaping human material to conform to a standard. Although
Foucault is perfectly willing to take advantage of the negative connotations
associated with "normalization" in presenting his account of the disciplines,
his deeper view has nothing to do with denouncing the formation of individuals in general. To make sense of such a denunciation would require some
kind of background Kantian or more generally liberal assumption about a
preexisting subjectivity that was being violated. Because Foucault rejects this
premise, he can hardly complain if disciplines "bend behavior towards a ter-
minal state."[82] For the philosophical tradition in which Foucault operated, all
meaningful or effective experience involves a certain amount of shaping of the

individual according to new criteria that are supplied by the experience itself.[83] These, at least, are the kinds of experiences Foucault describes individuals going through in his books on "social practices" — *Madness and Civilization, The Birth of the Clinic, Discipline and Punish*, and the series on sexuality. In the first three — as well as the first of the sexuality series — Foucault describes experiences from which he would like to distance himself and his readers. But that does not mean that all experiences and, with them, all shaping of human material are inherently evil. For Foucault, the "experience" and the kinds of values, structurings of social life, and so on that accompany them are inevitable. By themselves they are not good or bad. It is rather the way they are used and the — sometimes unforeseen — consequences they produce that are to be assessed.

> According to Nietzsche, Blanchot and Bataille, experience . . . accomplishes the "tearing" of the subject from itself, transforming it into something different from what it was, or completely other than itself, achieving its annulment, its disassociation, as a result. This enterprise of de-subjectification, the idea of a "circumscribed experience," that tears the subject from itself, is the fundamental lesson that I have taken from these authors. . . . The way I do my books, I have always conceived them as direct experiences "tearing me" from myself, to prevent me from always being the same.[84]

The disciplines operate through the use of experiences — practices, exercises, punishments, examinations — that will accomplish just such a tearing of the subject from itself to create something new. (See Foucault's description of the creation of the soldier, who must first have the "peasant" chased out of him.[85]) And there might be something about the particular products of that specific kind of tearing and shaping that we might want to criticize and repudiate. But that all such dissociation and re-creation are to be rejected on general grounds is a view Foucault would not endorse. As we see at the end of the quotation above, a similar kind of self-annulment and refashioning through experience is at the heart of his own most important personal goal in writing books.

Foucault expands on this last theme in his introduction to *L'usage des plaisirs*, a book that many commentators see as a sharp break with Foucault's earlier concerns. Whereas previous works focused on power, domination, and the individuals created by them, the last two volumes of the sexuality series act as a surprising and somewhat contradictory reexamination of the self and subjectivity — so the reviewers' comments usually run. Foucault's own view is quite different. The task of studying subjectivity did indeed require a different approach, but previous researches acted more as background material than as mistakes that must be corrected so as to advance. For him, "the analysis of power relations and their technologies made it possible to view them as open strategies, while escaping the alternative of a power conceived of as domination or exposed as a simulacrum."[86] For a subjectivity that was tied to sexuality, Foucault felt it was necessary "to analyze the practices by which individuals were led to focus their attention on themselves, to decipher, recognize, and acknowledge themselves as subjects of desire, bringing into play between themselves and themselves a certain relationship that allows them to discover, in desire, the truth of their being, be it natural or fallen."[87] At the very least, such a study requires materials different from those Foucault employed in *La volonté de savoir*, the volume immediately preceding *L'usage des plaisirs*, as well as from those used in *Discipline and Punish*. But at a certain level of abstraction, all three are concerned with the same question: How do experiences of diverse kinds destroy and create the plurality of subjectivities of which we are made up of at any particular moment? "After first studying the games of truth in their interplay with one another, as exemplified by certain empirical sciences in the seventeenth and eighteenth centuries, and then studying their interaction with power relations, as exemplified by punitive practices—I felt obliged to study the games of truth in the relationship of self with self and the forming of oneself as a subject, taking as my domain of reference . . . what might be called 'the history of desiring man.' "[88] This necessitated a shift away from a focus on sexuality as it was perceived and practiced in the eighteenth and nineteenth centuries (the object of study in *La volonté de savoir*) and toward ancient Greek and Roman sources. But this does not mean that Foucault's project loses all unity. Each of his studies can be seen as an element in the study of "the games of truth and error through which being is historically constituted as experience; that is, as something that can and must be thought. What are the games of truth by which man proposes to think his own nature when he perceives himself to be mad; when he considers himself to be ill; when he conceives of himself as a living, speaking, laboring being; when he judges and punishes himself as a criminal? What were the games of truth by which human beings came to see themselves as desiring individuals?"[89] Experience, truth, being—despite changes in focus, topic, and perspective, these are the true objects of Foucault's work.[90] One kind of being (take as an example the peasant) is shattered through experience, in the process of which a new kind of truth emerges, leading to a new style of being (the soldier). The purpose of such studies is not to prove to us that nothing can change but rather "to learn to what extent the effort to think one's own history can free thought from what it silently thinks, and so enable it to think differently."[91] The *critical* possibilities are very much tied to an argument about how "subjectivity" comes about in the first place.

Change, however, will not come about in a way that is radically different from the dynamic of "experience-truth-being" that critical thought initially sets out to describe. In his books, Foucault does not try to provide historical proof that the things he describes — psychiatric institutions, prisons, disciplines — should be denounced. (Which is not to say that he never denounces these entities.) Foucault's true ambition is for his books to act as an "experience" for his readers that will make it possible for them to stand in a different relationship to the objects he describes. As he comments in one interview:

> [*The History of Madness*] constituted for me — and for those that read or utilized it — a transformation of the relationship (marked historically, theoretically and also from the point of view of ethics) that we have with madness, the psychiatric institution, and the "truth" of that discourse. There is then a book which functions as an experience, much more than as an observation of historical truth. . . . That which is essential is not found in a series of verifiable historical observations: rather it is as an experience that the book makes it possible to do something. And an experience is neither "true" nor "false": it is always a fiction, something that is constructed, that exists only after it is made, not before; it is not something of "truth," but it is made a reality.[92]

Foucault coins the term "book-experience" to distinguish his work from "truth-books" and "demonstration-books."[93]

What the plurality of forces such as the disciplines with *their* experiences have made of us is always a tangled and knotted string of events to keep track of. There is no single-event, disciplinary creation of this or that set of individuals that one can pin down. Even as we become aware of some forces and reject or seek to modify their effect on us, others take their place, or those previously in the background come to the fore. We are never completely transparent to ourselves, either as individuals or as a society. We grow up in a mostly unreflective state with regard to the influences that shape us.

In *DP*, Foucault describes a variety of normalizing practices not so he can prove to us that we have been cast in stone, followed by a smirk and a shrug at our discomfort. Rather, he tries to give us an experience of a certain kind of rationality that could help change our relationships with ourselves and call into question the particular kind of truths associated with that rationality. Our relationship with ourselves will change when powers that have worked secretly are revealed. They can never have the same kind of force, even if they continue to influence us.

Foucault's highest aspiration, however, was to create a situation in which we could participate in determining — though not dictate — the direction and shape of the "next truth." Drawing on what has already been made of us, combined with a knowledge of how that came about and the matrix of forces that maintain it, Foucault thought it would be possible to enter into the game of "experience-truth-being" in a more reflective and conscious manner. In this way, Foucault leaves "critique" as traditionally conceived behind as the central aim of philosophic activity.

> We must stop regarding as superfluous something so essential in human life and in human relations as thought. . . . There is always a little thought even in the most stupid institutions, in the most silent habits. Criticism, then, is a matter of flushing out that thought and trying to change it. . . . Practicing criticism is a matter of making facile gestures difficult.[94]

▌ ▌ ▌   Governmentality and Population

We have defined "disciplines" in Foucauldian terms as those micromecha-
nisms of power whereby individuals are molded to serve the needs of power.
Discipline in a factory produces skilled workers; in an army, efficient fighting
units; in the classroom, receptive students. When he speaks of "government"
Foucault extends the exercise of power from the individual to the populations of political units large or small. To frame a clear picture of the social and
political context that Foucault intends to portray and analyze, both the reformation and reeducation of individuals (by "discipline") and the management
of populations (by "government") must be described. Then we should be able
to perceive and evaluate Foucault's oppositional strategies in the precise terms
he intended in writing *Discipline and Punish*.[1]

Foucault's intention is to recast the political forms of Western society. There
are three elements to this account. First, the most important and creative inventions concerning the uses of power have taken place in the development of
local, site-specific mechanisms for handling (and producing) individuals and

groups. Second, historical research shows that the origins of these new techniques are conflictual and political. As we shall see, an examination of that history produces two insights useful for critical reflection: (1) the emergence of a particular exercise of power (or form of rationality) occurs at the intersection of disparate influences and projects, the scrutiny of which can undermine the confidence of both practitioners and subjects of a power relation; and (2) from a tactical standpoint, the contingent and even makeshift character of power constructs suggests lines of attack. Taken together, the production of individuals through disciplinary mechanisms and the management of populations through the "art" of government produces an image of power that is formidable, to be sure, but hardly monolithic or impervious to critical reflection. But—and this is the third element—this critical orientation must free itself from the myth of "the Revolution," with its overtones of millennial transcendence. The way power is actually configured in the West leaves plenty of room for countermoves, but these can be considered only once the mythology of the Revolution is put to one side and replaced by a sober analysis of the specific characteristics of power constructs.[2]

One way Foucault criticizes the myth of the Revolution concerns the emphasis often placed on the state as the "absolutely essential . . . target to be attacked" and taken over.[3] This narrow focus on the summit of political power in society derives from the view that only a complete revamping of economic and political conditions (that is, a revolution) can improve humanity's situation. "But the State," Foucault argues, "does not have this unity, this individuality, . . . nor, to speak frankly, this importance: maybe, after all, the State is no more than a composite reality and a mythical abstraction whose importance is a lot more limited than many of us think."[4] We need to break with the myth of both the State and the Revolution that will overthrow it, decompose the complex reality that in fact constitutes the social world, and substitute a *political* ethos of critique for one that aims to transform society according to a transcendent vision of fully liberated human nature: such are the preconditions for effective oppositional thought in a post–Berlin Wall world.

Biopolitics and "Raison d'état"

In volume 1 of *La volonté de savoir,* Foucault discusses the link forged in the nineteenth and twentieth centuries between the human sciences and medical practices designed to keep populations healthy, on the one hand, and government policy on the other—a combination that he refers to sometimes as "governmentality" or as "biopolitics." These terms connote the merging of two historical developments: the industrial and agricultural revolutions of the nineteenth century and the birth and expansion of a variety of human sciences.[5] Foucault's entire argument about the emergence of a form of knowledge conducive to the acquisition and maintenance of power must be interpreted in light of the historical circumstances surrounding the industrial revolution.[6]

The rise of "power-knowledge" can be traced to the period of the French Revolution when starvation, plague, and other causes of early demise "ceas[ed] to torment life so directly."[7] This relative surcease from the constant preoccupation with death—brought about by, among other factors, increased agricultural productivity—meant that for the first time Western societies could contemplate the conditions of existence as "forces that could be modified." Life was extricated from the "randomness of death," with the result that some conditions of life could be expected to submit to "knowledge's field of control and sphere of intervention." Foucault uses the term "biopower" to "designate what brought life and its mechanisms into the realm of explicit calculations and made power-knowledge an agent of transformation of human life."[8] On this view, "power-knowledge" is not a constant feature of power's functioning. There are, no doubt, significant instances of power's interaction with knowledge that predate the industrial and agricultural revolutions. Thus, as Foucault points out, the power of the sovereign once took the form of torture to extract "knowledge" from a suspected criminal. In certain religious disciplines, the monitors of orthodoxy have the authority to demand confessions—and thus knowledge of internal psychic states—from penitents. But as it will be described here, power-knowledge did not *characterize* the functioning of power in those preindustrial contexts. To take a parallel point from Marx, an important distinction exists between capitalist societies, which are based on commodity exchange, and precapitalist societies, in which commodity exchange occurs but does not characterize the economic life of the society.[9]

In contrast to a power organized around the sovereign, the events clustered at the beginning of the industrial revolution meant that "power would no longer be dealing simply with legal subjects over whom the ultimate dominion was death, but with living beings, and the mastery it would be able to exercise over them would be applied at the level of life itself; it was the taking charge of life, more than the threat of death, that gave power its access even to the body."[10] One consequence of the above development was the "emergence of 'population' as an economic and political problem."[11] Fertility, diet, death rates, and a dozen other variables could be studied, followed by the adoption of policies intended to effect "a positive influence on life" that would "administer, optimize, and multiply it" while "subjecting it to precise controls and comprehensive regulations."[12] We can see why this kind of power is a *knowledge-power*. Various kinds of knowledge about the population must be gathered to determine the most efficient ways to manipulate the relevant variables. Once organized in this manner, specific courses of action can be adopted to promote some variables, create more favorable ones, and truncate or eliminate adverse ones. At times the policies adopted as a result of the accumulation of knowledge are simply the propagation of information in distilled, popularized form. Knowledge is provided that will encourage the population to act in a certain manner, respond to selected stimulants in certain ways, and so on.[13]

In his 1979 Tanner lectures Foucault ties the rise of "knowledge-power" to the evolution of the European system of states.[14] He points out that one of the chief ways states could increase their power and influence in a hostile international environment was to promote the health, morals, fecundity, and attitudes of their populations. This was possible only after the threat of imminent demise had loosened its grip—precisely the result of the economic revolutions of these times. Given these developments, the goals of health, fecundity, and so on were not simply to be promulgated as dictates. Rather, the state saw to it that they were actively promoted and the policies associated with them materially inserted into the lives of people. The development of these policies and their implementation, Foucault tells us, became the subject matter of a branch of knowledge—*Polizeiwissenschaft*. This "police science," however, was not at first concerned only with the criminal but rather with the whole array of factors making up a healthy, productive population. To the extent that these efforts were successful, substantial advantages would accrue to the state: "As a form of rational intervention wielding political power over men, the role of the police is to supply them with a little extra life; and by so doing, supply the state with a little extra strength."[15]

Biopolitics, then, is made possible by certain advances in the struggle against death. It seeks to consolidate and extend those advances through a broadly understood science of policing. This biopolitics is in turn part of the specific means-end rationality associated with the maintenance of states popularly known as "reason of state."[16] On the one hand, reason of state is thought of as the rationale that elevates state interests over those of the individual. The most obvious example is the right to declare war and send citizens to their deaths to ensure the state's survival or enhancement of its power position.[17] Thus, in the rationality particular to reason of state, "it is clear that governments don't have to worry about individuals; or government has to worry about them only insofar as they are somehow relevant for the reinforcement of the state's strength: what they do, their life, their death, their activity, their individual behavior, their work, and so on."[18] In fact, however, states must be concerned about individuals since the aggregate health and productivity of individuals are consequential for the maintenance of the state's strength. This concern is not for the individual as such but rather as one unit in the multitude that makes one state stronger than a hostile neighbor.

None of this is to say, however, that every initiative proposed to improve the health of the population was subsumed under the interests of the state: "Health and sickness, as characteristics of a group, a population, are problematized in the eighteenth century through the initiatives of multiple social instances, in relation to which the State itself plays various different roles. On occasion, it intervenes directly."[19] At times the state's interventions are thwarted, while at others the state is "the object of solicitations which it resists."[20] What needs to be imagined is a wide array of forces seeking to confront the illnesses of the social body—straightforward diseases as well as pauperism and other maladies—with their own projects for reform, often independent of one another. What is true for Foucault is that general societal concerns, some of which emphasized the state's need for a healthy and productive population, provided the opportunity for a variety of experiments in "power-knowledge."

Thus a number of ways exist to interpret this reading of "reason of state" and its attendant biopolitics. On a certain level it is even popularly acknowledged that states have interests different from and sometimes conflicting with those of the individuals that make them up. Yet these differing interests often manage to reach agreement. Therefore advocates for the unemployed want government funds to help idle workers avoid poverty. From the side of the state, Keynesians promote the same policy but for a different reason—as part of an effort to establish demand-side pressures that will aid a weakened economy. Because different interests happen to coincide, partisans of one interest may take up the rationale belonging to another: thus, advocates for the unemployed may point to the national interest served by providing those who are out of work with a temporary income. Such an arrangement is not all bad. Fortunately, the promotion of individual and group welfare promotes the separate interests of the state. The individual and group are instrumentally important to the state—only on that basis does the latter concern itself with the former.

The only difficulty with this response is that reason of state does not always promote the health and prosperity of the population. War is only the outer limit or ultimate expression of this divergence. It may not always be true that the full development of the population is necessary for the state — an optimal point might be found beyond which the state is unable to exploit the continued development or even security needs of the individual. Or it may be that not every section of the population needs to be brought up to a general level of health, education, longevity, and so on for the state's needs to be met.

With governance, the goal is to dispose of the resources at hand so as to extract a maximum of energies through an artful combination of natural elements (geography, soil, water, and the like) and human powers. This particular rationality does not work alone, however. A different rationality with its own history and purposes is available for an alliance with "governmentality."

The Care of Others: Pastoral Power

This other rationality is referred to by Foucault as a *pastoral* power.[21] The rationality characterizing this exercise of power is not only different from but also perhaps the direct opposite of reason of state. In contrast to the latter, pastoral power is directly concerned with the welfare of the individual. In its ecclesiastical form, this care centered both on the physical well-being of the individual and on the group — as well as the state of the soul of each individual. Each individual was required to reveal the secret thoughts that alone could testify to the soul's health.

Foucault believes the practices and ethos of pastoral power have survived the long, slow decline in the influence of religion in Western life. In its secular variant, where leading the flock safely to the next world is no longer at issue, pastoral power continues to concern itself with the health and psychic states of the individual in this world. Thus psychologists and psychiatrists, as well as others with a less professional facade, diagnose and attempt to address the miseries of modern life. At the same time, social workers and state agencies do their best to shape their programs in a way that will promote the health and even the happiness of individuals they come into contact with. Often they find themselves using the methods — or at least adopting the assumptions — associated with psychology.

When "reason of state" and "pastoral power" are placed next to each other, there seems to be a sharp conflict between their respective modes of relating to the individual. Indeed, taken at face value, these two rationalities appear to stand in a hostile relationship. For the first, the vigor of the state is the desired end, with services for individuals expended as a means to that end, whereas for the second the well-being of the individual is what is anticipated, with the state viewed only as a more or less adequate environment in which to pursue this goal.

For Foucault, however, these seemingly counterpoised rationalities came together in ways that benefited both. Professions investigating individual psychic states could be extremely useful to a biopower construct intent on managing the variables associated with population. But it is not Foucault's argument—as we shall see—that pastoral power has become nothing more than a servant of state needs. Rather, biopower and pastoral power have been pulled together to create something else while at the same time retaining a separate existence in their own spheres. Their independence—their opposed ends and separate histories—is indeed part of what makes their integration into a strategy possible in the first place.

An illustration of the intersection of state and pastoral interests is found in the 1978 address "The Dangerous Individual."[22] As we saw in *Discipline and Punish*, the eighteenth century witnessed a shift from a form of exemplary punishment that used the body of the criminal to demonstrate the power of the sovereign to a technology of power designed to reform lawbreakers: "In the older systems, the horror of punishment had to reflect the enormity of the crime; henceforth, the attempt was made to adapt the modalities of punishment to the nature of the criminal."[23] With the development of urban centers, demographic studies, and the whole subject of human populations, "The social 'body' ceased to be a simple juridico-political metaphor . . . and became a biological reality and a field for medical intervention. The doctor must therefore be the technician of this social body, and mediate a public hygiene."[24]

In this context, the criminal was an obvious focus of attention as a manifestation of a pathological condition in the population. In the old regime, the law had the straightforward task of attributing specific criminal acts to a specific individual, who was then punished. In the eighteenth and nineteenth centuries, however, the criminal came to stand for a social malady that signified a broader threat to society than the criminal act itself. Such a disease might spread. Could it be stopped, perhaps reversed, both in the individual criminal and in society at large? To answer that question, psychiatry introduced the issue of motivation. In other words, a troubling affliction in the population—the province of biopower—provided the secular pastorate with an opportunity to expand its field of action dramatically: "At the turn of the nineteenth century psychiatry became an autonomous discipline and assumed such prestige precisely because it had been able to develop within the framework of a medical discipline conceived of as a reaction to the dangers inherent in the social body. . . . Nineteenth century psychiatry was a medical science as much for the societal body as for the individual soul."[25]

Today, it is a matter of course that a magistrate should order a psychiatric examination before sentencing certain categories of individuals or when opposing sides in a trial produce contradictory expert psychiatric testimony. But what is now taken for granted has a history. As Foucault describes it in "The Dangerous Individual," psychiatry in the 1830s and 1840s used a particular tactic to establish itself as an important contributor to the health of the social body and to justify its intercession on one side or the other in criminal proceedings. It fastened on those instances of motiveless, monstrous, and passionless crimes that defied comprehension and for that very reason seemed to threaten the social fabric that much more ominously. A theory of "monomania" was introduced.[26] This form of insanity, psychiatric experts explained, was extraordinarily intense, while remaining "invisible until it explodes." Monomania was an instance of "insanity in its most harmful form": "A maximum of consequences, a minimum of warning. The most effects and the fewest signs. [It] thus necessitates the intervention of a medical eye which must take into account not only the obvious manifestations of madness but also the barely perceptible traces, appearing randomly where they are least expected, and foretelling the worst explosions."[27] Despite the apparent normality of those afflicted, psychiatrists argued that monomania was a form of insanity. Those committing crimes under its influence could not be found guilty. Only trained professionals, however, could tell the court whether an individual suffered from monomania or was simply a cold-blooded murderer. At the same time, having discerned the causes for the passionless murders they investigated, psychiatrists—or others deferring to the expertise of psychiatrists— could devise remedies for this disease on both an individual and a social scale. Here, then, we have an example of two distinct, even opposed rationalities intersecting and establishing ties as each found conditions for growth in the other. A biopower tethered to state needs and a secularly oriented "pastoral" power in the form of psychiatry met on the ground of social hygiene to form a union—what we today call "forensic psychiatry."

Foucault multiplies examples of the cooperation between human sciences focused on the individual and the needs of society. Among his best-known illustrations is the emergence of "sexuality" as a matter of concern in the nineteenth century. At that time, Foucault says, a discourse on sexuality emerged that centered on the "analysis, stocktaking, classification, and specification" of the sexual practices of a population for the same reason that the mental health — "motivational state" might be a more precise term — of criminal elements became a matter of concern. As with criminals, the desire to peer behind sexual practices to the variety of motives that (it was assumed) produced them was prompted by the hope of exerting an influence on those motives. Rather than "condemned or tolerated," sexual activity now had to be "managed, inserted into systems of utility, regulated for the greater good of all, made to function according to an optimum. Sex was not something one simply judged; it was a thing one administered. It was in the nature of a public potential; it called for management procedures."[28]

The state was now interested in measuring its national resources in the coin of population numbers. It is then a short step from wanting to quantify this resource to influencing it, modifying, redirecting, and remolding it. Above we saw the perception of criminality as a social disease provide the opening for the entry of psychiatric "experts on motivation" into the criminal justice system. Similarly, the classification of reproductive activity under the heading of "public potential" provided sexologists with the operational niche they required to expand their activities.[29] Foucault does not wish to argue, however, that these forms of knowledge were called into existence by a centralized power concerned to improve social controls. Once again, these knowledges had their own history and rationality. It is also true, however, that these disciplines do not remain unchanged through their association with biopolitics. Nor are the policies and self-understanding of those executing government programs unaffected by the fact that the information they want and the policies they pursue are filtered through the interpretive grid of the social sciences.

A double-edged conclusion seems to follow from Foucault's argument that a plurality of distinct forces goes into shaping modern forms of power. On the one hand, it seems more difficult to discover the dynamics of a power relation made up of a number of different, autonomous forces; on the other, there is the hope that a power built up out of a number of distinct entities will be less omnipotent and more subject to change than it would be if constructed as a "totality." When society is viewed as a "totality," greater explanatory power is produced — but too often theorists of this term talk themselves (and the rest of us) into an escape-proof prison. An account of modern power that focuses on its contingent and makeshift structure leaves open more opportunities for change but at the expense of a comprehensive explanatory scheme.

One way to think of the relation between distinct rationalities is in terms of the overall strategies into which they fit—what Foucault calls the "rule of double conditioning."

> No "local center" . . . could function if . . . it did not eventually enter into an over-all strategy. And inversely, no strategy could achieve comprehensive effects if it did not gain support from precise and tenuous relations serving not as its point of application or final outcome, but as its prop and anchor point. There is no discontinuity between them, as if one were dealing with two different levels (one microscopic and the other macroscopic); but neither is there homogeneity (as if the one were only the enlarged projection or miniaturization of the other); rather, one must conceive of the double conditioning of a strategy by the specificity of possible tactics, and of tactics by the strategic envelope that makes them work.[30]

Thus, as we have seen, the historical emergence of population as a tractable variable gave rise to a kind of social hygiene. Psychiatrists saw an opportunity to fill this need and did so in ways that affected both psychiatry and the criminal justice system.

There is nothing "natural" or inevitable, in Foucault's view, about such a confluence of interests. Perhaps the need on the part of the state to investigate, control, and redirect criminal activity could have been satisfied other than by a recurrence to the motivational experts of psychiatry. In addition, there is nothing guaranteeing that the "fit" between the strategic setting and the chosen tactics (remembering here that the latter are not conceptualized and created at some strategic center or headquarters) will be particularly smooth or permanently well adjusted. As Foucault points out in the case of psychiatry, "Probably it was not realized, at least at first, that to add the notion of psychological symptomatology of a danger to the notion of legal imputability was not only to enter an extremely obscure labyrinth, but also to come slowly out of a legal system which had gradually developed since its birth during the medieval inquisition."[31] There are, in other words, "side effects" associated with the integration of distinct rationalities into a strategic deployment.

An example of these side effects can be seen in those "sciences" of sexuality that arose in response to the state's need to monitor and manipulate the reproductive practices of national populations. It might be the state's interest in population control that provides the practitioners of such sciences with access to the tools, money, centers of knowledge, and social respectability necessary to pursue their aims. But this fact does not allow us to reduce the work of sexologists to a mere functional relation to state needs. On the contrary, owing both to their subject matter and their independent status, researchers on sexuality tended to pursue their own agendas. Indeed, their independence fit into the strategy being devised: knowledge, especially knowledge claiming to be scientific, had to be independent and free of external controls to be counted as such. Certainly, a field of work and its practitioners can be swallowed up and become subservient to a particular interest. This is a far cry, however, from a prerequisite for usefulness. Truly independent research is widely recognized as an essential requirement for producing reliable—hence useful—results.

The new sciences of sexuality confronted an already existing social structure in the form of the family. Once again, we see Foucault illustrating the complex interaction between discrete historical objects with different histories and rationalities that move in different directions. At the time of the rise of biopolitical concerns, the family, according to Foucault, was characterized by a kinship system that he describes as a *"deployment of alliance."* [32] The "alliance"-oriented family structure interacted with the broader society through "a system of marriage, of fixation and development of kinship ties, [the] transmission of names and possessions." This organization of the family sought to duplicate a hierarchical, homeostatic social body. Thus, "the important phrase for it is 'reproduction.'" In contrast, the sexologists of the nineteenth century introduced a "deployment of sexuality." This deployment saw the relations among family members not as a multiplicity of structural supports for the re-creation of a hierarchy but as a promising way to incite a discourse of truth within the family that would reveal its secrets. And what was the object of these new investments of the family? The suppression of sexuality had nothing to do with these maneuvers. Nor is the ultimate value of the family's discourse of truth concerning sex to be found in the specific terms in which it comes to be described—though this may, of course, be the immediate goal of those practitioners pursuing this field of study. The true worth of those "revaluations" of familial relations, according to Foucault, is that they put family relations in motion. The family became a dynamic and evershifting ensemble of forces and so more easily susceptible to observational scrutiny. But if the creation of new experiences opened the family up to observation, the nature of these experiences was not without some relation to the biopolitics of the period. Whereas the old deployment of alliance (basically, kinship) was tied to the broader social system by facilitating the ordered circulation of wealth and the reproduction of an elite, the new deployment of sexuality helped to intensify awareness of the body and its rhythms of production and consumption: "The deployment of sexuality has its reason for being, not in reproducing itself, but in proliferating, innovating, annexing, creating, and penetrating bodies in an increasingly detailed way, and in controlling populations in an increasingly comprehensive way." [33]

We must be careful, though, not to see the control of populations as a goal immediately present in the minds of every practitioner of sexual science in the nineteenth century. (On the other hand, there is nothing inherently evil about such a goal, and it could very well have been an intended consequence for some.) Sexuality's "reason for being" as described by Foucault in the passage just quoted must be understood in the sense of the overall strategy with which it could integrate. From the perspective of the state, there was an interest in the accumulation of information about the population. This interest easily shifts over into an attempt to manipulate the variables one has discovered in order both to maximize their observability and to find ways in which they can be molded into more productive shapes. To the extent that the new sexual knowledge was uniquely equipped to bring the family out into the open, it was useful. But it by no means follows that every element of the family's sexualization is mirrored by some need openly proclaimed by the state and its managers of public policy. While not ignoring the practical, public usefulness of their researches, experts in the new sexology no doubt followed their research wherever it led. An important cautionary note that Foucault introduces in all his work is that elements of a strategy cannot be functionally reduced to the overall strategy in which they end up participating. [34] As already emphasized, there is no single, all-encompassing rationality that determines the shape and content of historical objects. Rather, different rationalities meet in a determinate historical landscape and establish coalitions for the pursuit of aims that, for a time at least, complement one another. The picture of a contingent and even makeshift alliance of numerous forces is what stands behind Foucault's well-known comment that "power relations are both intentional and nonsubjective": "There is no power that is exercised without a series of aims and objectives. But . . . let us not look for the headquarters that presides over its rationality. Neither the caste which governs, nor the groups which control the state apparatus, nor those who make the most important economic decisions direct the entire network of power that functions in a society." [35] Thus, it cannot be said, for instance, that all—or even very many—doctors treating hysterical women were unconcerned with their plight and sought only to use their distress to transform the family into a willing subject for the imposition of social disciplines. Nor were these symptoms merely the ex nihilo creation of the sexologists themselves—though they certainly had a hand in their creation. But the intentions of the practitioners aside, the deployment of sexuality in the family called into being a host of educators, doctors, and psychiatrists who in turn identified and labeled the symptoms of "the nervous mother, the frigid wife, . . . the perverse husband, the hysterical . . . girl, the precocious and already exhausted child," and so on.[36]

As Foucault points out, none of this medicalization completely replaced the deployment of alliance, which retained a diminished but still discernible function as a social prop. Consequently, a real tension existed between "sexuality" and "alliance";[37] by no means did patterns of familial relations provide an even playing field for the sexuality that was superimposed on the former. The resulting strains served to intensify the appeals to experts, doctors, and psychiatrists.

> From the mid-nineteenth century onward, the family engaged in searching out the slightest traces of sexuality in its midst, wrenching from itself the most difficult confessions, soliciting an audience with everyone who might know something about the matter, and opening itself up unreservedly to endless examination. The family was the crystal in the deployment of sexuality: it seemed to be the source of a sexuality which it actually only reflected and diffracted. By virtue of its permeability, and through the process of reflections to the outside, it became one of the most valuable tactical components of the deployment.[38]

The tensions between the "deployment of alliance" and the "deployment of sexuality" contributed to the success of the latter by furthering the process of opening up the family to the gaze of experts. But these same tensions represented a risk. Just because the new sciences of sexuality really were independent and not merely the creatures of the overall strategic configuration in which they nevertheless did play a role, they tended—from the point of view of the *strategy*—to overshoot their mark, transforming each element of the family into "an active site of sexuality."[39] This, according to Foucault, explains the undiminished stringency of the ban on incest in modern societies. In societies organized around kinship and alliance, such a ban plays a strictly functional role. With the rise of the deployment of sexuality, this ban takes on a double significance: first, it reaffirms the continued importance of the family as a system of marriage and kinship ties in the face of the assault represented by the family's sexualization, and second, the ban serves the deployment of sexuality by turning incest into the secret that must be unveiled. Thus, incest "is manifested as a thing that is strictly forbidden in the family only insofar as the latter functions as a deployment of alliance; but it is also a thing that is continuously demanded in order for the family to be a hotbed of constant sexual incitement."[40] This instability had to be, as it were, pinned down: the deployment of sexuality had to be kept in check if the deployment of alliance were to avoid being swallowed up by the former. Thus, "the strong interest in the prohibition of incest" is viewed by Foucault as

> a means of self-defense . . . against the expansion and the implications of this deployment of sexuality which had been set up, but which, among its many benefits, had the disadvantage of ignoring the laws and juridical forms of alliance. By asserting that all societies . . . were subject to this rule of rules, one guaranteed that this deployment of sexuality . . . would not be able to escape from the grand and ancient system of alliance. . . . For this is the paradox of a society which, from the eighteenth century to the present, has created so many technologies of power that are foreign to the concept of law: it fears the effects and proliferations of those technologies and attempts to recode them in forms of law.[41]

Elements of a strategy, then, are not always created or controlled by that strategy. Their effects are not turned on and off at the convenience of the broader entity into which they fit. That is why, in the case of the deployment of sexuality, special "restraints" must be devised to keep it from following out its *own* rationality to the end.

The Plurality of Power in the West

There are two lessons to be learned from the examples of criminal psychiatry and the deployment of sexuality in Foucault's work. First, we are putting together a picture of the specific dynamics, as Foucault saw them, of modern Western societies. This will help us make sense of and assess the oppositional devices Foucault at times seemed to suggest were appropriate to these special dynamics. At the same time, those specific examples can act as illustrations of Foucault's more theoretical descriptions of the functioning of power in general. For instance, it is easy to read Foucault's general claim that strategies are "intentional and nonsubjective" as an unfortunate example of the Continental appetite for obscure and irritating epigrams. I believe, however, that the examples accompanying this claim help to revise that perception.

With the introductory volume to *The History of Sexuality*, then, a work written at almost the same time as *Discipline and Punish*, we have an approach to modern power that fully respects several principles. Power constructs — or we could say broad strategic configurations—are made up of coalitions or alliances of discrete power-knowledge circuits. One way of thinking of this is as a cautionary note against functionalism: the fact that a quantum of knowledge or scientific endeavor fits into a broader strategy does not mean that the knowledge in question can be reduced to a mere manifestation or product of the strategy. Strategic configurations are not cut whole from a single cloth. With the emphasis on the plural, Foucault describes his work as the attempt to analyze "forms of rationality: different foundations, different creations, different modifications in which rationalities engender one another, oppose and pursue one another."[42]

Another such principle is that the discrete elements of a strategy have their own rationality—that is, their own means and ends. This is why Foucault cautions against focusing critical attention on the general process of rationalization in Western societies and instead counsels us to study the process of rationalization in a number of fields of activity.[43] Thus, the history of psychiatry's involvement with the criminal justice system may lead us to question whatever uplifting, heroic story psychiatry may want to tell about its work in that system. But at the same time the revelation of the fortuitous composition of historical constructs can lead to a perhaps more fundamental insight: "The things which seem most evident to us are always formed in the confluence of encounters and chance, during the course of a precarious and fragile history."[44] The things in question are precarious and fragile precisely because they are not unitary. The effects they achieve are comprehensive to the extent that they draw on a variety of resources—that is, substrategies with their own rationality, their own goals—to cover a broad field: "What reason perceives as *its* necessity, or rather, what different forms of rationality offer as their necessary being, can perfectly well be shown to have a history; and the network of contingencies from which it emerges can be traced."[45]

These contingencies can be traced—but that does not guarantee that they will be. This conditional phrasing explains a somewhat puzzling fact about Foucault: despite his reputation as a thinker who presents power as difficult to oppose, he often refers to the *fragile* character of modern power.[46] Its fragility is, for him, an objective and demonstrable fact. For instance, as we saw above, there is the example of the application of the sciences of sexuality to an often quite resistant family structure. This activity is carried out in the context of certain aims of the broader state structure. It goes without saying, however, that the interests and aims of these two distinct areas of concern—those of the state, on the one hand, and of the sexologists, on the other—do not always coincide. In fact, this whole construct of the deployment of sexuality is a rather unstable house of cards. At the same time, we are ill-equipped to observe the delicate balancing act that actually characterizes the interaction of different rationalities. "The relations of power," Foucault says in one place, "are perhaps among the best hidden things in the social body."[47] Their true strength, their seeming unassailability comes from this concealment rather than from some inherent imperviousness to critical judgment. Once the veil is pierced, Foucault subscribes to an optimism which points to the "many things [that] can be changed, fragile as they are, bound up with more circumstances than necessities, more arbitrary than self-evident, more a matter of complex, but temporary, historical circumstances than with inevitable anthropological constraints."[48]

The assumption in this context that power is a unitary substance tied to a universal rationality or appropriated and monopolized by a particular class or by the state is one condition of power's invisibility in modern societies. As the foregoing examples have shown, modern power is based on the interaction of at least two quite different rationalities. One is a secularized pastoral power, which traces its origin back through a long history of Christian confessional practices.[49] Pastoral power focuses on the individual's needs and state of mind and the internal movements of the soul. The secular "pastor"—in the form of psychoanalyst or social worker—sets himself or herself up as a spiritual adviser and confidant to whom the individual is invited to "open up."[50] It is a "form of power that cannot be exercised without knowing the inside of people's minds, without exploring their souls, without making them reveal their innermost secrets. It implies knowledge of the conscience and an ability to direct it."[51] But the conditions for the expansion of this extraecclesiastical pastorate were found in the context of a rationality that was headed in an almost opposite direction: "reason of state" (as discussed above) was in principle unconcerned with individuals except as a potential resource. Psychiatry was able to prove itself useful in both assessing and potentially reforming the emotional lives of the individuals it treated.

At this point, we come to the real heart of Foucault's concern about the nature of modern power and the dilemmas he believes are created by efforts to oppose it. The state's need to calculate and manipulate one of the most important resources at its disposal—its people—combined with the methods and skills of the secular pastorate produces what Foucault describes as a "demonic" configuration: "Our societies proved to be really demonic since they happened to combine these two games—the city-citizen game and the shepherd-flock game — in what we call modern states."[52] In what sense does Foucault use the word "demonic"? Foucault believes that individuals in modern societies have a difficult time becoming mature, which is understood in terms of the ability to participate in directing the forces that determine one's makeup, including one's subjectivity: "From the idea that the self is not given to us, I think that there is only one practical consequence: we have to create ourselves as a work of art."[53] At this point we should not allow ourselves to be distracted by the characterization of the self as a work of art. Instead we should focus on Foucault's claim that maturity cannot be achieved until individuals develop a complex relationship to the self, a relationship that is all the more necessary because the self is neither immediately present in all our acts nor waiting to be discovered somewhere in our psychic depths. In the context of these external authorities appropriating the task of self-constitution, one sense of the word "demonic" comes to mind — it suggests possession: "For Christians the possibility that Satan can get inside your soul and give you thoughts you cannot recognize as Satanic but that you might interpret as coming from God leads to uncertainty about what is going on inside your soul."[54] In this case, the Christians are better off than modern subjects — at least they recognize the possibility that some ideas might come from external sources of which they might not approve. In the modern setting, the "experts on motivation" have a fairly free reign when it comes to persuading us to recognize ourselves in a wide array of foreign implantations. The first sense in which modern societies are demonic is their capacity to shape subjective experiences that we nevertheless believe are uniquely our own. In other words, what is demonic about the union between pastoral and state power is that it acted as an independent dynamic that tended to claim for itself the whole field of the relation between individuals and broader social structures (such as the state). The battle to define what an individual is and what her or his proper relation to society might be is taken out of the hands of actual individuals and treated as the possession of experts.

A demon is capable of speaking to us with the voice of God. It is capable, that is, of presenting itself as its own opposite, when in reality both of the faces it turns to us represent the same entity. This is a second sense in which modern biopower is demonic: it has built into it a seeming opposition between the needs of the individual and those of the state. And what "seems" to be an opposition is in fact, in one sense, an opposition. It is true, to make this point once again, that the rationality characteristic of pastoral power stands directly opposed to that of the state. The point is that this very opposition has been put to use in the specific context of modern "biopower." The conclusion Foucault reaches is that it is very difficult to appeal successfully to one or another of the two poles of biopower when attempting to disengage from the effects of power in modern societies. Indeed, sometimes he argues it is simply impossible to confront power in these terms.[55] It is Foucault's response to this dilemma that gives him the reputation of a pessimist when it comes to imagining oppositional forms. Neither the principle of sovereignty, which guarantees individual rights in the context of a certain organization of state power, nor the special focus on individuals associated with the disciplines and pastoral power provides the leverage needed for effective oppositional activity.[56]

It could be argued that Foucault's refusal to appeal to a "theory of right" is somewhat misguided. After all, one of the reasons contemporary power relations are (presumably) fragile is that they are constructed from diverse, autonomous, and thus separable entities. That is, if "discourse can be . . . an effect of power, but also a hindrance . . . a point of resistance," then why not appeal to one side of the demonic configuration of modern power (such as pastoral versus state interests)?[57] Foucault appears to harbor conflicting views about which oppositional tactics are effective and desirable. If discourses can circulate into an opposing strategy without even changing their form, then what objection can there be to opposing pastoral (or a particular disciplinary) power with the principle of right that is associated with the sovereignty model?[58]

Instead of seeing Foucault as contradicting himself, however, a more productive reading might be that he is describing different kinds — or even levels — of oppositional activity. "In real life," oppositional groups appeal to rights in their struggles against institutions and disciplines.[59] A certain amount of critical power can be expected from such appeals, just because there are "different and even contradictory discourses within the same strategy."[60] But in the medium and long term, the fundamental fact about these opposed discourses is going to be that the general condition for their growth and development is found in the overall strategy into which they fit. Even more: the fact that some discourses in a strategy may contradict each other may not be extraneous to the separate but integrated functions they play relative to each other in that strategy. Above we have seen the example of pastoral power and reason of state, what Foucault elsewhere calls the "individualizing" and "totalizing" aspects of modern power.[61] Their opposed stances are essential to the specific fields of activity they concern themselves with. In the case of pastoral power, a deep concern for the individual's welfare is the precondition for the opening up of the individual to the probings of psychiatrists and social workers.

There can be no cynicism here. It is not a matter of psychiatrists merely acting as though they care about their patients while extracting clues about motivational states helpful for the purposes of mass manipulation. This is the image conveyed in certain literary dystopias, where the state has total control over the individual both as a producing body and as a configuration of subjective states that it is able to control — indeed a horrifying prospect. But these chilling stories are not the kind that Foucault wants to tell. Not only is it possible that disciplines and the effects of "biopolitics" will be opposed, but it is *inevitable* as well, a virtual law of life.

I V   Genealogy in the Disciplinary Age

Foucault urges that two points be kept in mind when assessing and describing modern power formations:

(1) The essential function of knowledge of specific kinds—knowledge about population trends or the wide variety of diseases (both psychic and physical) that plague the social body as well as the internal psychic states of individuals

(2) The multifaceted and local origins of power in the West, which has meant that diverse strategies—distinct and even opposed rationalities—may come together, often through chance, to form particular power constructs Foucault claims that we lack conceptual tools for opposing the operation and expansion of this more diffuse and opportunistic kind of power.[1] His first task is to develop a clearer picture of how power operates outside the conventional sovereignty model. The second is to develop a critical apparatus adequate to that power.

Genealogy is one of these tools. By genealogy, Foucault refers to the historical investigation of the origins and rationality of specific power formations. In this chapter, I follow a brief discussion of the purposes and methods of genealogy with a more detailed study of its use by Foucault.

Genealogy and the Uses of History

Genealogies are historical studies whose purpose is to produce critical effects in the present. Foucault has used the genealogic method to investigate prisons, clinics, schools, hospitals, criminal psychiatry, and sexuality. What is it about the history of the technologies of power in such settings that supports a critical project? And what is it about the critical value of these histories that is particularly applicable to our study of the structures of power as Foucault has described them?

Foucault is a student of Nietzsche, and it is from that philosopher that he acquires his ideas on genealogy as a method of historical inquiry. In his *On the Genealogy of Morals,* Nietzsche tells the story of the birth of what he calls *ressentiment* among the persecuted Jews of the late Roman Empire.[2] To make a long story dangerously short, Nietzsche argued that Christianity should not be seen as a timeless body of moral principles valid for all humanity. But he made this point indirectly—what he did not do was "polemicize" against Christianity by laying out its moral principles (submission to God, love of one's neighbor, and so forth) and then proceeding to dispute them as one would do in a debate.[3] Instead, Nietzsche shows us what he claims are the conditions under which the Christian religion developed in the hope that we will come to the conclusion that such an artifact as Christianity is not, in all probability, applicable to our conditions of existence centuries later. Christianity was the product of an oppressed group. The moral precepts and beliefs presented in Christian dogma bear the clear marks of this oppression. Thus, the belief in a world beyond this one where the meek and poor in spirit will be raised up, whereas the powerful will be thrown into the pit, is neither an accidental feature of Christianity nor a plausible basis on which to ground a universal morality. It is not an accidental feature of Christianity because the early Christians were unable to gain access to a kingdom in this world, and so to make their way through an impoverished existence, they provided themselves with both a little hope (for a kingdom in the afterlife) and an imagined revenge on their proud Roman lords. It is not a basis on which to ground a universal morality because the conditions that produced the Christian dogma seem too local and contingent. Christianity may or may not have been beneficial to the Jews who took it up at the time, but how—so at least Nietzsche wants to argue—can we take it seriously today?[4] Nietzsche as genealogist does not argue that the principles of Christianity are "wrong" in any ultimate sense. Qua genealogist, Nietzsche wants to confront us with the fact that a certain morality is, at best, a local and time-centered phenomenon that does not apply to us.

In general, Foucault adopts Nietzsche's strategy in his historical writings, and probably less admixture of the genealogical with the polemical mode exists in Foucault's version than in Nietzsche's. The first critical task of genealogy, then, involves distancing oneself from the institution, morality, or worldview that is investigated. If we accord Nietzsche's account of Christianity its intended relevance for our time, its moral precepts will cease to have transcendent status and will be legitimate objects of critical scrutiny.[5] At the same time, however, the genealogist will come in closer contact with the object of investigation as a concrete historical reality with all the twists, turns, accidents, and human passions characteristic of this world. From both sides, a "disillusionment" takes place.

A frequent misconception concerning genealogy should be addressed before moving on to consider Foucault's use of Nietzsche's genealogical method. Nietzsche is the philosopher of power.[6] It is sometimes thought that the critical force of Nietzschean genealogy rests on his unveiling of the role of power in the development of important cultural artifacts. And there is, indeed, a sense in which this is the case. To the extent that we thought Christianity was a pure essence unsullied by the power position of those involved in its creation, we are no doubt disabused of that view in the process of genealogical investigation. But it is not Nietzsche's position that *the reason* there is something wrong with Christianity is that "power" was involved in its formation, as if the presence of power implied a coercive and unjust resolution of the issue between the Roman lords and the oppressed Jews. Similarly, Foucault's book on the prisons is not at its deepest level a denunciation of the prison system based on its roots in the exercise of power. That claim, for both Nietzsche and Foucault, would seem outright trivial. This point about the ubiquity of power is tied to the argument, implicit in Nietzsche and explicit in Foucault, that power is a productive rather than (primarily) a repressive force in the shaping of the social world. The idea that one could object to the prison or some other object of genealogy solely on the basis of the part played by power in its formation would lead the reader, via a seemingly "Nietzschean" detour, back to a view that both authors have argued is insufficient for an understanding of how power works.

For example, in his insightful article on genealogy, Arnold Davidson argues that "genealogy does not try to erect shining epistemological foundations. As any reader of Foucault learns, it shows rather that the origin of what we take to be rational, the bearer of truth, is rooted in domination, subjugation, the relationship of forces—in a word, power."[7] That conclusion is too gross to yield critical effects for either author. Again, to the extent that we are misled into believing that some truth or moral precept has a "powerless" history, Davidson's point stands, but this assertion can be only preliminary. Taken as the core of genealogical critique, the claim that power is at the heart of various phenomena, when made by philosophers who claim that power can be found everywhere, lends itself to the ever popular self-referentiality response on the part of Foucault-Nietzsche critics: you (the genealogist) want to complain about the power present in the formation of cultural artifact X, but because your own critique is just as reliant on "power" as what you criticize, how can you denounce it without condemning yourself at the same time?[8]

The answer is that the critical effect of genealogy does not consist in revealing the presence of power—coercive, repressive, or otherwise—in our institutions and practices. Instead, it is designed to transform what was, in Heidegger's terms, "ready-to-hand" and thus unexamined into something that is "present-to-hand" and a proper subject for critical reflection. Too often, critical accounts of Foucault rely for their persuasive power on a significant dumbing down of his notion of power, combined with a distortion of the means and ends of the genealogical method. In his "Critique of Impure Reason," Thomas McCarthy, in terms very similar to those of Charles Taylor and Jürgen Habermas, argues that Foucault cannot account for his own project in other than "actionist terms." Genealogy is "simply another power move," just "another intervention meant to alter the existing balance of forces."[9] But is there another purpose for interventions beyond altering the existing balance of forces? The strongest objection that can be made against such arguments is that they do not go up against the heart of the position articulated by Foucault. The feeling of bad faith one gets when entering into the world of the critical response to Foucault is produced by this evasion. For instance, there is absolutely no attempt to refute Foucault's claim that power is productive. Is this or is this not an advance in our understanding of the functioning of power? If Foucault is actually right, then the lack of a normative, a priori critical stance with reference to power formations is less something Foucault himself desires or argues for as it is a problem with which we all must deal.

The same mistake—reading Foucault and his genealogical studies as exposés on "power" as a general category—is made from a more sympathetic perspective by Judith Butler in Gender Trouble: "To expose the foundational categories of sex, gender, and desire as effects of a specific formation of power requires a form of critical inquiry that Foucault, reformulating Nietzsche, designates as 'genealogy.'"[10] Here I think that Butler—along with many other feminist appropriators of Foucault—reproduces an approach to power that Foucault worked to supplant. It was not Foucault's view (nor was it Nietzsche's) that to say some cultural artifact was produced by power is the same as to say there is something illegitimate or a priori objectionable about that particular cultural artifact. Power is not "bad" or immoral, nor is the inevitable shaping and constraining that goes with it. Critique that relies on the "exposure" of the operations of power relies on a superficial and frankly classically liberal conception of power.

"Reversal" of Discourse

As I suggested in the first chapter, the key role played by knowledge in modern power formations makes knowledge a potential site of resistance. Near the end of *The History of Sexuality*, Foucault warns us not to regard the discourses that make up disciplines as "once and for all subservient to power or raised up against it." Instead of visualizing a "world of discourse divided between accepted discourse and excluded discourse," we must imagine "a multiplicity of discursive elements that can come into play in various strategies. . . . Discourse transmits and produces power; it reinforces it, but also undermines and exposes it, renders it fragile and makes it possible to thwart it."[11] Such is possible because "discourses are tactical elements or blocks operating in the field of force relations; there can exist different and even contradictory discourses within the same strategy; they can, on the contrary, circulate without changing their form from one strategy to another, opposing strategy."[12] And Foucault provides us with an example of how this "reversal" tactic with regard to discourses might work.

> There is no question that the appearance in nineteenth-century psychiatry, jurisprudence, and literature of a whole series of discourses on the species and subspecies of homosexuality, inversion, pederasty, and "psychic hermaphrodism" made possible a strong advance of social controls into this area of "perversity"; but it also made possible the formation of a "reverse" discourse: homosexuality began to speak in its own behalf, to demand that its legitimacy or "naturality" be acknowledged, often in the same vocabulary, using the same categories by which it was medically disqualified.[13]

Apparently the repressive hypothesis dies hard![14] For what is homosexuality's attempt to speak on its own behalf, to refer to itself as legitimate and even natural, if not a demand that homosexuality no longer be *repressed?* Earlier in *The History of Sexuality,* urging individuals to speak — on their "own behalf," of course — was described as the essential material for the constitution and advance of disciplines.[15] Furthermore, attempts to criticize the medicosexual regime were described by Foucault as a mere ruse of power that encouraged individuals to "open up."[16] But now we seem to have a completely different, even opposite treatment of the same material. Instead of being "part of the same historical network of the thing they denounce," those who demand that the naturalness of their homosexuality be recognized are effectively utilizing the insight that while discourse can be an "instrument and effect of power, it can also be a hindrance, a stumbling-block . . . a starting point for an opposing strategy."[17]

Perhaps Foucault wishes to argue that there remains an important distinction between his "reversal" model and the repressive hypothesis. Once again, it is necessary to consider the matter on two levels. *Theorists* of repression (Wilhelm Reich, Freud) believe that an unbroken, subterranean, tyrannized discourse must be enabled to break through to the surface. This surfacing is then equated with a final form of freedom, which refers back to a prior and essential human nature. On this level, Foucault maintains his opposition to the repressive *hypothesis.* Foucault's discussion of reversal does show, however, that homosexuals could achieve a tactical advantage through the use of the same terms as those of the medicosexual regime.

Foucault walks a thin line here. Those who use what Foucault describes as a tactic probably do not conceive of it as such. Homosexuals who adopt and revalue psychomedical characterizations regard their moves in terms of a liberation of human nature. Is it, after all, possible to battle oppression without some commitment to a scheme of "human liberation," however conceived?[18] Foucault's argument might be that by using the same terms to refer to itself as does the medicosexual regime that constituted it, homosexuality (to stay with that example) concedes too much terrain to the power that constructed "homosexuality" as a category in the first place. The categorization is not questioned — all that is desired is to hurl a resounding "No" at the negative moral valuation given to it. At the same time, the fundamental claim of the discourse swirling around sexuality — that the liberating truth about oneself is realized through an emphasis on and verbalization of sexuality — is enthusiastically affirmed and allowed to spread.

Despite these objections, "reversal" is still an important form of opposition, frequently used and often effective. It also points to the power of discourse and knowledge in the disciplinary age. Foucault's worry is that although it can be "provisionally useful, to change the perspective from time to time and move from *pro* to *contra,* these reversals . . . are quickly blocked, being unable to do anything except repeat themselves. . . . As soon as we repeat indefinitely the same refrain of the anti-repressive anthem, things remain in place; anyone can sing the same tune, and no one pays attention. This reversal of values and truths . . . has been important to the extent that it does not stop with simple cheers (long live insanity, delinquency, sex) but allows for new strategies." [19] The "reversal" tactic, then, which relies on the circulation of bits of a dominant discourse for opposing strategic purposes, is not the "solid recourse" Foucault says we need in the disciplinary age. [20]

Knowledge of various kinds plays a key role in the formation and constitution of disciplines: categorizing knowledges, which divide the sane from the insane; productive knowledges, which invent and stimulate sexuality; confessional knowledge, which gives power access to individuals' inner lives. Because of the importance of knowledge in the functioning of modern power, it is perhaps natural that genealogy—which provides its own kinds of knowledge—should be looked to as an important element in developing strategies that will counter the knowledge-based forms of power dominant today.

In "Nietzsche, Genealogy, History," Foucault discusses the nature of "rules" and the manner in which they may be used. We can think of the uses all sorts of individuals with disparate ends made of the theory of sovereignty as a kind of (serious) game being played by those contending for power at the time. The theory of sovereignty was used by aristocrats and parliamentarians and then by monarchs and nobles to justify and conceptualize their battles with each other. [21] This example shows that "rules are empty in themselves, violent and unfinalized; they are impersonal and can be bent to any purpose. The successes of history belong to those who are capable of seizing these rules, to replace those who had used them, to disguise themselves so as to pervert them, invert their meaning, and redirect them against those who had initially imposed them; controlling this complex mechanism, they will make it function so as to overcome the rulers through their own rules." [22] Today's set of rules centers around the status and effects of the various kinds of knowledge made possible in the wake of the industrial revolution. The claims made and, if you will, "prestige" enjoyed by those possessing knowledge must be transformed into objects of critical reflection if modern power is to be effectively confronted. Genealogy helps make this possible.

If one of the goals of genealogy is to change the way rules of discourse are given effect, we can refer to the "reversal" tactic discussed thus far as "reversal genealogy." It could be defined as the attempt to turn elements of a governing discourse around, to revalue some or all of them in such a way that what was previously disqualified or marginalized in a discourse is instead valorized and legitimated, often using the same terms and categories as the discourse that previously disqualified it.

The other sorts of genealogy to be discussed here are all based on historical investigation. One type of genealogy is aimed at making us question the unconscious gestures and assumptions that make up so much of our world. Another version of genealogy points to a possible future kind of politics that would remain based in historical investigations. I will call the first kind of genealogy to be dealt with here "historical genealogy," and the second, "political genealogy."

Historical Genealogy

Foucault describes philosophy's task as describing "the nature of the present." The most effective tool for this portrayal of our present lies in a "recourse to history." For Foucault, "history serves to show how that-which-is has not always been; i.e., that the things which seem most evident to us are always formed in the confluence of encounters and chances, during the course of a precarious and fragile history." The things that make up our present world "have been made, they can be unmade, as long as we know how it was that they were made."[23] Indeed, finding out how something was made and unmaking it are often both accomplished at the same time: "Experience has taught me that the history of various forms of rationality is sometimes more effective in unsettling our certitudes and dogmatism than is abstract criticism. For centuries, religion couldn't bear having its history told. Today our schools of rationality balk at having their history written, which is no doubt significant."[24] Foucault presents a number of illustrations of the kinds of potent effects he believes history — or genealogy — can provide. In his many writings and talks, however, he does not distinguish among them, leaving the techniques and goals of genealogy ambiguous. Foucault insists a number of times that "the intellectual no longer has to play the role of an advisor. . . . What the intellectual can do is to provide instruments of analysis, and at present this is the historian's essential role."[25] If this is indeed the historian's task, then we will want to have a sharper picture of the use and effects of genealogical researches. A logical place to begin is the recognized urtext in the field: "Nietzsche, Genealogy, History." I do not intend to discuss this obscure work as a whole but instead want to dip into it and pull out versions or elements of genealogy.

A Genealogy of Battle Lines

A first kind of genealogy, then, "seeks to reestablish the various systems of sub-jection," the "hazardous play of dominations" that make up the real history of humanity.[26] The social systems, morals, and habits that fill up our world are not the product of some ideal historical progression from barbarism to civili-zation but rather the offshoots—Foucault calls them an "emergence"—of cer-tain relations of forces. "The analysis of *Entstehung* [origin] must delineate this interaction, the struggle these forces wage against each other or against adverse circumstances."[27] In tracing out these encounters, genealogy will show that the emergence of an institution or concept from a determinate relation of forces will be significant less in terms of the operation of the institution or the moral content of the concept than as the "scene where [the combatants] are displayed superimposed or face to face. It is nothing but the space that divides them, the void through which they exchange their threatening gestures and speeches." Concomitant with the transformation of relations of forces into historical ob-jects of various kinds are accompanying valuations and interpretations that reflect and support the "domination of certain men over others."[28] These inter-pretations are, in turn, transformed into targets of struggle so that the devel-opment of humanity itself can be viewed as "a series of interpretations." In this context, "the role of genealogy is to record . . . the history of morals, ideals, and metaphysical concepts, the history of the concept of liberty or of the ascetic life, as they stand for the emergence of different interpretations, they must be made to appear as events on the stage of the historical process."[29] The crucial historical period for our time is "the great nineteenth century effort in disci-pline and normalization." For this period, "it will be necessary to construct a history of what happens in the nineteenth century and how the present highly-complex relation of forces—the current outlines of the battle—has been ar-rived at through a succession of offensives and counter-offensives."[30]

One example of the capacity of new interpretations to affect current power relations and even produce new ones can be found in Foucault's *Madness and Civilization*. During what he calls the "Classical Age"—from about 1650 up to the French Revolution—those considered "mad" were confined in institu-tions, which were not, however, solely for such individuals. Instead, people thought to be mentally disordered were locked up with all those guilty of "idleness" — the unemployed, beggars, unattached former soldiers, and so on. Such a grouping might seem heterogeneous to us, but Foucault argues that this age did not experience it this way. In the prevailing view of that time, the idle were guilty of irrational behavior and should be grouped together. Those considered "mad" chose their irrationality. Society condemned and isolated them while defining itself as rational by confining them. Treatment was either nonexistent or reduced to the same forced labor to which all idlers were subject.[31]

Around the time of the French Revolution, a new interpretation of madness by reformers such as Philippe Pinel in France and Samuel Tuke in England began to take hold. Individuals considered mad were now diagnosed as ill, removed from the company of idlers and criminals, and housed in special institutions, soon to be called asylums. As Foucault goes on to show in this case, more subtle distinctions among the "useless" and surplus population of Europe allowed for more precisely focused and calibrated experiments in normalization.[32] For our purposes here, however, the important point is that a new interpretation — a new knowledge — leads to new institutions, new structures of power, and new justifications for them.

A genealogy of this type — one focused, to be brief and incomplete, on the emergence of new interpretations and new forms of domination associated with them — will produce two beneficial consequences. First, we will be disabused of a false story that held us in thrall. As Foucault points out in *Madness and Civilization,* the usual account of the "liberation" of "mad" people from the houses of confinement by reformers centers on the humanitarianism and heroism of individuals such as Tuke and Pinel versus the brutality of the jailers at such institutions.[33] Such a hagiography blinds us to the material operations of power associated with a novel interpretation. A second benefit of this first style of genealogy has to do with revealing the possibilities for a counteroffensive — the most likely and effective points of attack.

Genealogy of Contingency

But not all genealogical research uncovers effaced battle lines. One kind of traditional historical scholarship, according to Foucault, is the "attempt to capture the exact essence of things, their purest possibilities, and their carefully protected identities." Rejecting the metaphysics associated with this approach, the genealogist "finds that there is 'something altogether different' behind things: not a timeless and essential secret, but the secret that they have no essence or that their essence was fabricated in a piecemeal fashion from alien forms. . . . What is found at the historical beginning of things is not the inviolable identity of their origin; it is the dissension of other things. It is disparity."[34]

Two critical lines of thought are associated with this approach to genealogy. First, the institutions and morals that present themselves as natural end products of a comprehensible and progressive history are revealed as a cobbled patchwork of heterogeneous elements. Second, very closely associated with the patchwork theme but conceptually distinguishable is the claim that "we must accept the introduction of chance as a category in the production of events. There again, we feel the absence of a theory enabling us to conceive the links between chance and thought."[35] The world in which we live "is a profusion of entangled events," and we must learn that "the forces operating in history are not controlled by destiny or regulative mechanisms, but respond to haphazard conflicts."[36]

At first glance this critical angle may not seem to be very promising. And yet this genealogy of chance or contingency is one for which Foucault has very high hopes. The unique character of power in the disciplinary age, it will be remembered, is that it is constructed from the bottom up out of diverse elements.[37]

If we investigate the growth of disciplinary power in this genealogical "ascending" manner, what do we gain for our trouble? In an earlier chapter, we noted that Foucault outlined the development and interaction of pastoral and state power, neither having much to do with each other at first.[38] The outstanding characteristic of pastoral power is its individualizing effect. The functional model for the pastor is the shepherd and flock. Pastors are responsible both for the collective destiny of their flock and that of each member, whose lives, actions, and thoughts were legitimate matters of concern if the congregation was to be led successfully to the next life. The knowledge required of each individual consisted of the surface details of her or his life — outward sins, material state, and so on — but, of course, also included knowledge of what went on in the soul.[39] To gain access to this internal kind of knowledge, pastors required their charges to engage in extensive self-examination and to let their consciences be guided through the practice of confession. When combined with the state's need to understand and shape the populations under its control, pastoral power proved to be a central element of modern power.[40] Foucault feels this insight is key for orienting and redirecting the strategy and tactics of opposition. One style of thought Foucault is criticizing here is that of the Frankfurt School. Thinkers such as Theodor Adorno and Max Horkheimer argued that the state and all subordinate circles of power are dominated by an instrumental reason driven — at least initially — by capitalist economic forms. This rationality spreads over and penetrates into the entire social body. Individuals are treated as means not ends, which turns out to be especially dangerous in the context of the growth of powerful and efficient technological means for handling them in just such a functional manner. An unleashed instrumental rationality accounts for the primary features of modern societies — from the functioning of large state bureaucracies to the operation of mental hospitals, schools, the culture industry, and so on.[41] For Foucault, such an account gives us too much and too little: "Rather than wonder whether aberrant state power is due to excessive rationalism or irrationalism, I think it would be more appropriate to pin down the specific type of political rationality the state produced. . . . It's not 'reason in general' that is implemented, but always a very specific type of rationality."[42] The reliance on Reason with a capital *R* to account for a modern plague of normalizing institutions leads to the shielding of disparate phenomena behind a single cloak — too much is explained. What is missed is both an account of what the different kinds of power that make up our society are and how and when pastoral power and police power "happened" to run into each other — too little is explained. This accidental convergence did not have to happen, it might not have happened, and it is not destined to shape all possible forms of social organization.

Let me briefly specify the advantages that Foucault believes derive from this more accurate account of the origin and functioning of modern societies. First, an unwarranted pessimism or fatalism is associated with accounts of power that emphasize the global effects of a technologically based instrumental rationality.[43] Power is "unmasked" at the expense of effective challenges to it. Modern states must join the rest of the things that populate our world: "They can be unmade, as long as we know how it was that they were made."[44] Call this a reason for optimism. Second, the deleterious effects of Western rationalism will not be confronted with a focus on its supposed nonconsensual or even violent effects. Such an approach, Foucault seems to believe, locates the struggle against political rationality in a sphere both outside its own domain and inadequate for the purposes of countering its effects — that is, within the sphere of right. It also will not do "to cast the blame on reason in general" — this is a critical filter whose pores are too large to capture the kinds of phenomena specific to political rationality.[45] Instead of an opposition based on the principle of sovereignty or a denunciation of rationalism, Foucault directs our attention to the historically contingent formation of political rationality — the accidental convergence of pastoral and policing forms of power — as the true ground for the exercise of this power. This leads Foucault to an important conclusion: "Opposing the individual and his interests [to the state] is just as hazardous as opposing [the state] with the community and its requirements."[46] The specific hazard involved is the erection of new institutions based once again on one or the other of these poles of modern power. It is not that modern power is able to absorb every form of opposition but that it is specifically geared to accommodating and co-opting resistance that centers either on the individual or the community, since these are complementary terms of its own constitution. The "inevitable effects" of political rationality "are both individualization and totalization. Liberation can come only from attacking not just one of these effects but also political rationality's very roots.[47] Call this second advantage of Foucault's analysis the prerequisite for opposition's genuinely radical and critical effects.

The combination of political rationality and pastoral power provides an example of the operation of *chance* in bringing together disparate elements — that is, the disciplines of punishment and psychiatry, each with its own "history . . . trajectory . . . techniques and tactics" to form a historical object that still has profound meaning for us today. The value of such a genealogical analysis is that it "fragments what was thought unified" and "shows the heterogeneity of what was imagined consistent with itself."[48]

The two kinds of genealogy discussed so far — those of battle lines and of contingency — do seem to have their own character and distinct critical effects. It should be kept in mind, however, that what is analytically distinguished here is experienced as a much more complex interplay in the real world. Taken by itself, the description of historical events as the creation of battle lines between opposed interests that are then blurred in the interests of the dominant party is too close to a quasi-Marxist account to be acceptable to Foucault. Too much emphasis on the element of strategy also results in what Foucault insists is a false overestimation of the unity and even the existence of a ruling class. The impression easily forms that a "bourgeoisie" or some other centrally located agent dictates all the tactics and goals of the disciplines, from panoptic surveillance towers to precisely crafted sexual perversions, in accordance with a predetermined plan. At the same time, however, a pure description of historical events as the product of contingency would overlook the quite conscious operation of specific "wills to power" (to adopt Nietzsche's term) who do make use of strategic tools to achieve their goals.

The picture Foucault wants to promote is not one or the other but a mix of both. This blend is not arbitrary, however. He believes the conscious strategic element is almost always local and restricted to specific concerns. A generalized strategic effect is nonetheless achieved when these discrete wills to power seek to secure and improve their position in the surrounding environment through tactical alliances with other structures of power. Perhaps the best example of this account of power in Foucault's work is his discussion of the union achieved by psychiatry and criminal law in the nineteenth century.[49]

Disciplines and other local forms of power certainly attempt to adopt rational plans that will advance their goals. On this level, strategy is conscious. But no strategy is able to take full account of the ever shifting relation of forces resulting from a plurality of diverse power centers. The *conditions* of growth and survival, that is, will never be fully predictable, and from this angle, contingency is the primary factor. The resulting interaction of a multitude of wills to power, although producing far less than a seamless and total power, will nevertheless have general effects across the entire social body. As Foucault puts it, "The rationality of power is characterized by tactics that are often quite explicit at the restricted level where they are inscribed. . . , tactics which, becoming connected to one another, attracting and propagating one another, but finding their base of support and their condition elsewhere, end by forming comprehensive systems: the logic is perfectly clear, the aims decipherable, and yet it is often the case that no one is there to have invented them." [50]

But if contingency plays such a key role in this account, how do such "comprehensive systems" result? Foucault explains that the strategic, purposive account of power formations is primarily a retrospective one. For instance, "judiciary and psychiatry join hands, but only after such a mess, such a shambles! . . . My position is as if I were dealing with a battle: if one isn't content with descriptions, if one wants to try and explain a victory or a defeat, then one does have to pose the problems in terms of strategies and ask, 'Why did that work? How did that hold up?' That's why I look at things from this angle, which may end up giving the impression the story is too pretty to be true." [51]

Comparative Genealogy

Another variant of genealogy can be referred to as "comparative." Part of the shift in subject matter between volumes 1 and 2 of *The History of Sexuality* is from a genealogy of "battle lines/contingency" in the first volume to a comparative mode in the second. The first volume is concerned with the question of sexuality and the techniques of power disposed around it in the context of the emergence of population in the nineteenth century. The second is situated in a completely different epoch: it considers the formation of codes of ethics and their relationship to the formation of the self in ancient Greece. In turning, for instance, to Greek sexual ethics, Foucault discovered what he argued was an ethics not bound to a specific code and to which one must conform. Rather, each (free, adult male citizen) conducted his own "economy" of pleasures — was in charge of his own ethical existence — with reference to the kind of life he wanted to lead. Thus, if there were restrictions on the frequency, timing, and intensity of a Greek adult's sexual contact with a boy — and even if total abstinence was practiced — it was not because a church or society had listed a set of formal or informal rules forbidding or regulating such behavior, and still less because someone had designated such activity as evil or unnatural. For the free Greek male, the elemental and powerful drive linked with sexual pleasures was the closest one could come to the dividing line between the animal and the human worlds. It was thus viewed in the context of a battle for mastery over oneself and for the dominance of reason over passion. This "internal" battle had broad implications for the Greek citizen's capacity for playing his role in the polis as a whole. For the Greeks in Foucault's study, "self-mastery and the mastery of others were regarded as having the same form; since one was expected to govern oneself in the same manner as one governed one's household and played one's role in the city, it followed that the development of personal virtues . . . was not essentially different from the development that enabled one to rise above other citizens to a position of leadership."[52]

In this codeless practice among the Greeks that Foucault investigates, sexual pleasure was a dangerous drive that needed to be carefully controlled and adjusted in the effort of self-stylization. It may be contrasted, for instance, with Augustine's concern over the kind of desire he had for a young friend.[53] Did his friend represent a terrestrial glimpse of heavenly beatitude? Or was this a sinful desire implanted by the Devil and designed to lead Augustine away from God? Among the Greeks, then, a suspicious attitude toward pleasure resulted in an ethos of self-discipline. The successful practice of this ethos was necessary for the government of oneself and of others. With early Christian thinkers, there was a shift to a hermeneutics of desire that utilized forms of confession which were directed by spiritual superiors and which were designed to detect and uproot ungodly thoughts. By pointing to this mutation in the central reference point for ethical questions — what Foucault calls the "ethical substance" — the general point can be made that the axis of moral behavior is historically relative.[54]

But Foucault has a more specific use in mind for the comparison between Greek ethics and contemporary reality. What is interesting about the distinctive ethical substance of the Greeks is that, existing as it did before the codes of behavior associated with Christian teaching, it mimics to a degree the ethical predicament of the modern era — so at least Foucault claims.[55] Very well, then: can a return to an understanding of "ethical substance" as constituted by the Greeks help provide a solution to our problem, which is, after all, so similar to that of the Greeks? For Foucault, asking a question like this is the wrong way to go about using the possibilities offered by comparative genealogy. One cannot simply "find the solution of a problem in the solution of another problem raised at another moment by other people."[56] There is for Foucault "no exemplary value in a period which is not our period. . . . But [in the Greeks] we do have an example of an ethical experience which implied a strong connection between pleasure and desire. *If we compare that to our experience now,* where everybody — the philosopher or the psychoanalyst — explains that what is important is desire, and pleasure is nothing at all, we can wonder whether this disconnection wasn't a historical event, one which is not at all necessary, not linked to human nature, or to any anthropological necessity."[57]

It is not that the products of comparative genealogy tell us what to do or how to act or provide us with easy answers or models for our behavior. Instead they, like the knowledge provided by other varieties of genealogy, point to the contingent, historical character of the "problem" we confront today. We are not furnished with alternatives as the result of a comparative genealogical study but with a destabilization or denaturalization of the kind of individuality (and ethics connected with it) that dominates us now. Summing up the method and intentions of comparative genealogy, Foucault writes, "Among the cultural inventions of mankind there is a treasury of devices, techniques, ideas, procedures, and so on, that cannot exactly be reactivated, but at least constitute, or help to constitute, a certain point of view which can be a very useful tool for analyzing what's going on now — and to change it."[58]

So far I have reviewed two forms of opposition to the kinds of knowledge-power constitutive of power in the modern disciplinary era. The reversal or revaluation of discourses is not strictly a kind of historical study, and so its relation to genealogy is tenuous. I have broadly labeled the second level of opposition "Historical Genealogy." This level makes up genealogy proper and contains three subdivisions: battle lines, contingency, and comparative. Up to this point, we can identify two sources for the specific usefulness of genealogical research in a disciplinary setting.

First, as Foucault mentions several times, "The relations of power are perhaps among the best hidden things in the social body."[59] A decisive first step
in confronting and perhaps changing power relations is simply to reveal them
and their mode of operations. A misunderstanding must be avoided, however:
the exercise of power itself is often not a secret. After all, in the Panopticon,
everyone can see the tower. What remains hidden is the cumulative effect of
so many discrete influences. If there is a cloak for this activity, it can be discovered in the influence of two traditions: (1) that which insists on seeing the
individual as a unified, monovocal subject — no matter to what experience the
individual is subjected, the subject remains prior and ontologically superior to
the experiences that mold it; and (2) the view, attacked directly by Foucault a
number of times, which tells us that "power makes men mad, and those who
govern are blind; only those who keep their distance from power . . . shut up
in . . . their room, their meditations, only they can discover the truth."[60] In
this view, in other words, power crushes individuals, whereas knowledge sets
them free — partly by limiting the exercise of power, partly by telling them
what their true nature is. But in Foucault's description of the operation of disciplinary power, knowledge of what makes up individuals and characterizes
populations shapes them in essential ways. As long as knowledge is regarded
as innocent, the ways in which it shapes us will remain undetected. Genealogical research is the distinctive means for broaching the question of the influence
of knowledge-power on the constitution of individuals, as well as the prior
unity of the subject. Having seen, for instance, the actual circumstances of psychiatry's first participation in criminal proceedings, we might be suspicious
of psychiatry's claim to be a disinterested body of knowledge of the human
psyche, while wondering what such human sciences as psychiatry make of us
when they "describe" us.

Second, genealogy is also specifically geared to a disciplinary setting owing
to the ascending character of power constructs. Disciplinary power, it will be
remembered, is "capillary" in two senses: it attempts, not always successfully,
to govern the "details" of our existence, down to gestures and thoughts; and
the techniques and knowledge that make up disciplinary power are not directed from on high by a central power but develop on their own in the inter-
stices of society. Techniques developed by a discipline in one area can be com-
mandeered and employed in broader strategies. Now, it is obviously absurd
to imagine that such a pattern exhausts conceivable configurations. As a look
at "Nietzsche, Genealogy, History" has shown, genealogy is exceptionally well
equipped to map out the disparate elements that have been welded together.

Political Genealogy

All the forms of genealogy we have schematized thus far approach similar goals by using varying tactics of historical research. Each prods us to become aware of unquestioned assumptions, thoughtless gestures, seemingly legitimate institutions, and unexamined modes of thought by revealing their contingent and (sometimes) violent foundations. But it is immediately apparent that, useful as these tools are and valuable as their results might be, all the forms of genealogy sketched here have the restricted goal of disturbing the present. None seek to move beyond unsettling our practices to propose (for example) new kinds of power relations to replace disciplines.

Nothing requires Foucault to advance beyond introducing disorder in our lives and thoughts. On a number of occasions Foucault explicitly rejects the intellectual's role as a prophet who shows the ways to some bright future. Rather than inform progressive movements of the true goals for which they are fighting, the actual forces they should combat, and in what manner, all of which "can only have effects of domination," Foucault suggests that intellectuals strive "to present instruments and tools that people might find useful."[61] The forms of genealogical analysis summarized above can be counted as Foucault's contribution to the creation of instruments and tools useful at this particular moment.

Foucault seems to have made two attempts to use his genealogical researches as a means to move beyond the kind of limited disruptive effects we have seen so far. To distinguish them from what has gone before, we can refer to these two forward-looking efforts as "political genealogy," or the political uses of genealogy.

Political Genealogy I

In "Nietzsche, Genealogy, History," Foucault makes clear his disdain for claims of "objectivity" made by those conducting historical work. Whereas "historians take unusual pains to erase the elements in their work which reveal . . . their preferences in a controversy," genealogy is "explicit in its perspective and acknowledges its system of injustice."[62] That is, the genealogist interrogates the past from an openly biased position: "I am well aware that I have never written anything but fictions. I do not mean to say, however, that truth is therefore absent. It seems to me that the possibility exists for fiction to function in truth, for a fictional discourse to induce effects of truth, and for bringing it about that a true discourse engenders or 'manufactures' something that does not as yet exist, that is, 'fictions' it. One 'fictions' history on the basis of a political reality that makes it true, one 'fictions' a politics not yet in existence on the basis of a historical truth."[63]

The above quotation presents a more ambitious program than the provision of "tools and instruments" we saw earlier under the category of historical genealogy. Using the latter, we can make our way to the insight that, for example, asylums were constructed in a piecemeal fashion from alien forms, with the critical and distancing effects associated with such a study. This critique of origins, however, does not by itself produce forces that can effectively challenge or replace the specific matrices of power-knowledge that dominate us today.

In contrast, what I label as "political genealogy" works to incite the creation of new power-knowledge circuits that can compete with and supplant old ones. An example is Foucault's own work (and that of others) on madness, which made it possible "to establish a 'we' . . . that would . . . form a community of action" concerning the treatment of the mentally ill. This new "we" was characterized by a distinct manner of looking at the problem of mental illness that sought to do battle with and supersede the dominant perspectives of the day.[64]

It seems, then, that we have the following picture of the first of two kinds of political genealogy: As a response to a problem in the present, a history is narrated that makes possible and even propels the formation of a community of action that will address the issue at hand. But this new "we" has (and was meant to have) effects of power—how else was the previous form of power to be challenged? In the case of asylums, faith in the humanitarian motives and scientific methods of their founders gives way to doubt, then repudiation. The asylums are emptied, their treatments discarded. New institutional forms (community half-way houses) and therapies (self-administered psychotropic drugs) are introduced. No doubt, the truth- and power-effects of the anti-asylum movement of the 1960s were ambiguous. New enemies requiring novel oppositional moves take the place of the asylum. Foucault warns that "everything is dangerous,' including the very "communities of action" that arose to fight yesterday's enemy.[65]

Political Genealogy II

The second form of political genealogy mentioned by Foucault represents his most ambitious hopes for the potential rewards of genealogical research. The key text here is not, as with the other forms of genealogy discussed above,

"Nietzsche, Genealogy, History" but rather Foucault's "Two Lectures." As a result of the kind of local and particular criticisms of institutions and practices in which Foucault and others have engaged, we are now witnesses to an "*insurrection of subjugated knowledges.*"[66] In this insurrection, two kinds of knowledge have emerged. The first kind includes knowledge that reveals the existence of previously concealed historical material. These "historical contents allow us to rediscover the ruptural effects of conflict and struggle that the order imposed by functionalist or systematising thought is designed to mask. Subjugated knowledges are thus those blocs of historical knowledge which were present but disguised within the body of functionalist and systematising theory and which criticism . . . has been able to reveal."[67] An example of this would be Foucault's own work in *Madness and Civilization,* discussed above.

The second category of subjugated knowledge must be understood as "something which is in a sense altogether different" from the first, "namely, a whole set of knowledges that have been disqualified as inadequate to their task or insufficiently elaborated: naive knowledges, located low down on the hierarchy, beneath the required level of cognition or scientificity. I also believe that it is through the re-emergence of these low-ranking knowledges, these unqualified, even directly disqualified knowledges . . . that criticism performs its work."[68] Examples of these "unqualified, even directly disqualified knowledges" provided by Foucault are "that of the psychiatric patient, of the ill person, of the nurse, of the doctor — parallel and marginal as they are to the knowledge of medicine — that of the delinquent, etc."[69] Unlike the first grouping of subjugated knowledges, this second category is undeveloped and inexpressible in smooth, continuous discourse. An example might be "the outbreaks of hysteria in psychiatric hospitals during the second half of the nineteenth century [which] were really a mechanism in reverse, a counterblow against the very exercise of psychiatry: psychiatrists were brought face to face with the hysterical body of their patients. . . , without their having either sought this or even known how it came about."[70] First, then, we have blocks of historical knowledge that are "mature" — they are "buried knowledges of erudition."[71] Second are "naive," regional, undeveloped knowledges, which stand lower on the totem pole of cognition. Both kinds give us a historical knowledge of struggles: "In the specialized areas of erudition as in the disqualified, popular knowledge there lay the memory of hostile encounters which even up to this day have been confined to the margins of knowledge."[72]

Foucault especially highlights the value of the second category of disqualified knowledge. What the genealogical project "really does," he notes, "is to entertain the claims to attention of local, discontinuous, disqualified, illegitimate knowledges against the claims of a unitary body of theory which would filter, hierarchize and order them in the name of some true knowledge and some arbitrary idea of what constitutes a science and its objects."[73] The goals here are not so different from those discussed in the section on historical genealogy: to undermine and destabilize those historical objects that are uncritically accepted. What is ambitious and different about this side of genealogy is the status Foucault gives to the liberated fragments of knowledge unearthed by genealogy.

These fragments—especially those in the second category—are "liberated" in two senses. First, the genealogist frees them from the subjection imposed by unitary discourses—here the historian does the liberating. But they are also uniquely free of association from unitary discourses—and it is in this way that they are liberating *for us*. It is because these fragments have remained fragments, ignored and untouched by unifying global theories, spared from "the attempt to think in terms of a totality," that they are "capable of opposition and of struggle against the coercion of a theoretical, unitary, formal and scientific discourse."[74] Erudite kinds of knowledge that have been subjugated also play a role in this, but they are at least internally consistent and have a place somewhat higher up on the cognitive hierarchy. The critical force of erudite knowledge results from its exclusion from today's power-knowledge circuit and the knowledge of conflicts that the exposure of this exclusion awakens. The more popular, less formal, and local knowledges that Foucault discusses represent a kind of "differential knowledge incapable of unanimity . . . which owes its force only to the harshness with which it is opposed by everything surrounding it."[75] Foucault believes, in other words, that in the course of genealogical research he has discovered (in the second category of subjugated knowledge) forms of knowledge that are not integrated into any power-knowledge circuit. Their potential to disrupt the dynamic between power and knowledge in the disciplinary age is what attracts Foucault to them.

But no sooner is the promise of these naïve knowledges revealed than a problem arises: "Is the relation of forces today still such as to allow these disinterred knowledges some kind of autonomous life? Can they be isolated by these means from every subjugating relationship? . . . And, after all, is it not perhaps the case that these fragments of genealogies are no sooner brought to life . . . than they run the risk of . . . recolonization?"[76] Today's unitary discourses are not so rigid as to be unable to work these fragments into their own account. An obvious defense would be to work the bits of knowledge into an oppositional strategy and discourse before the ruling discourses can get to them. But Foucault — at least in "Two Lectures" — rejects this move: "And if we want to protect these only lately liberated fragments are we not in danger of ourselves constructing, with our own hands, that unitary discourse to which we are invited, perhaps to lure us into a trap, by those who say to us: 'All that is fine, but where are you heading? What kind of unity are you after?' "[77]

On at least one level, however, the goal of producing these previously discredited knowledges is not to *protect* them but rather "to establish a historical knowledge of struggles and to make use of this knowledge tactically today."[78] If that is the case, certain conditions exist for the entry of these local fragments of knowledge into the fray. As we have already seen Foucault argue in another context: "No 'local center,' no 'pattern of transformation' could function if, through a series of sequences, it did not eventually enter into an overall strategy. And inversely, no strategy could achieve comprehensive effects if it did not gain support from precise and tenuous relations serving . . . as its prop or anchor point."[79] Strategies designed to oppose modern configurations of knowledge-power need the support of liberated fragments; liberated fragments will remain ineffectual as long as they remain isolated from broader strategies.

It is true that once these disqualified bits enter into a strategy of resistance they lose their status as bits and are no longer opposed by everything that surrounds them. Foucault's attachment to these particles of knowledge appears to involve their isolation from any cycle of truth and power. They do not claim to represent a form of truth and so act as monads of knowledge unassociated with forms of power — admittedly a striking discovery in the era of disciplines and power-knowledge. But this does not free them from the requirement that to be useful they must play their role in the strategies of opposition, which will, perhaps unfortunately, denude them of this unique characteristic.

I can imagine only two scenarios for these disinterred fragments. In the worst-case scenario, they are co-opted by the dominant discourse. No sooner are these pieces put into circulation than some power-knowledge circuit embraces them as its own. An opportunity for opposition is lost, while the forms of hegemony operating at the present time are allowed to grow stronger through acquired diversity. In the better-case scenario, oppositional strategies integrate them into their own discourse. This is a good scenario, but a dangerous one. To take an example cited by Foucault, antipsychiatry succeeds in routing asylums, but in the process of formulating a successful strategy, it becomes something of a discipline, and the previously liberated knowledges are integrated into it. But perhaps all this proves is that "we always have something to do," something to oppose with our "hyper- and pessimistic activism." We can liberate as many fragments as we like, but we will always have this "ethico-political choice to make every day"—namely, "to determine which is the main danger."[80]

It seems to me, then, that Foucault recognizes that subjugated knowledges —specifically of the "popular" and local variety—have this unique character of being isolated from every dominating relationship. As such they constitute a radical challenge to unitary discourse. But—and this is what Foucault appears to regret—this unique character must be sacrificed if effective strategies of opposition are to be devised. Once integrated into a strategy, once they help form a previously nonexistent "we," they are no longer outside the confines of power-knowledge and may indeed become elements in a future "main danger."

But the difficulty does not cease with the loss of bits of autonomous fragments. It turns out that the effort to conduct local researches that do not start out from a pre-given "we" is constantly threatened by genealogies' own products. We live in a period of the increased "efficacy of dispersed and discontinuous offensives." But the "amazing efficacy of discontinuous, particular and local criticism" is threatened (as discussed above) by "global, *totalitarian theories.*"[81] As the products of genealogy are taken up, used, and integrated into global forms of resistance, they turn on their origins and threaten local criticism with yet another invitation to "think in terms of a totality."[82] Every new "we," it turns out, both creates the need for and threatens the formation of another new one.

In this chapter, I have tried to show the different kinds and applications of the tool fashioned by Foucault for critical uses in the era of power-knowledge: genealogy. The task of genealogy is to "separate out, from the contingency that has made us what we are, the possibility of no longer being, doing, or thinking what we are, do, or think. . . . It seeks to give new impetus, as far and as wide as possible, to the undefined work of freedom."[83] Foucault dismisses universal and comprehensive accounts of Western societies as simplistic and misleading. In their place, he offers a picture of a plurality of powers that come together in a provisional and sometimes accidental manner. But what kind of "freedom" grows out of a criticism of this sort of power? I answer this question in the next two chapters.

V   The "Plebeian Aspect"

The Myth of the Revolution

In Foucault's account, the exercise of power involves three simultaneous operations. First, a domain of knowledge is constituted concerning a bigger or smaller slice of the world. Foucault's focus has been the human sciences, where knowledge concerning madness, delinquents, perversion, and so forth is developed. This knowledge is neither final nor cumulative. In new circumstances, new forms of knowledge will develop, and within one set of circumstances, various interpretations of the same phenomenon will compete for acceptance. Second, on the basis of this knowledge a set of rules is established, which has to do not only with what will or will not count as knowledge but also with the material conditions, the actual disposition of the objects of that knowledge — which, in the case of the human sciences, means categories or groups of individuals. In this way, the knowledge of a Tuke or Pinel concerning what constitutes madness and what distinguishes it from other forms of antisocial behavior becomes literally institutionalized.[1] Third, this knowledge and the rules that regulate both it and its objects establish a field of activity within which individuals recognize themselves as subjects of a certain kind—as wife, patient who is mentally ill, student, husband, psychiatrist, professor.[2] Put this way, it is perhaps not so difficult to appreciate Foucault's complaint, mentioned in chapter 1, concerning his reputation as the philosopher who said that power and knowledge are the same thing. Obviously, the power a psychiatrist has to commit someone to an asylum or a course of treatment is not the same thing as the knowledge that provides the basis for that decision. At the same time, the relationship between the knowledge possessed and the power exercised is fundamental.

These three "moments" through which power becomes effective—knowledge, rules, subjectivity—correspond to oppositional possibilities. The knowledge that constitutes a domain of power can be questioned with respect to its historical development. In chapter 4 we reviewed this possibility in detail. The rules that govern the formation and elaboration of a sphere of knowledge can in turn be reversed and "revalued." And the forms of subjectivity that an objectifying knowledge endeavors to construct as vehicles of power can be hijacked and turned in directions not originally intended.[3]

But none of these oppositional possibilities can be pursued without at the same time freeing critical thought from its own triangle of knowledge, discipline, and subjectivity, known as "the Revolution." Here we are not to understand this term in a narrow sense. There is an emancipatory vision at the heart of much of Western social theory.[4] At a high level of abstraction, liberals cannot be said to be enemies of revolutionary politics, which is true not only because today's liberal was yesterday's revolutionary but also because of the close link between the competing visions of human nature that were to be realized through political action. Human emancipation and a Revolution that can be broadly understood in terms of a focus on political action have been so closely associated that it is very difficult to separate them. Questioning the Revolution and its ability to provide the hoped-for emancipation results in a fractured field of political analysis. The ruling paradigm is, as it were, overturned. The resulting hostility directed toward Foucault arises in large part, perhaps, from the threat represented by the attempt to separate these conjoined twins—only one can survive. On the other hand, unless the operation is performed, both will die.[5]

Developments in Europe since Foucault's death serve only to underscore the importance of Foucault's project and the declining relevance of the political model that has informed much of the political analysis of the twentieth century. It has now been some time since the socialist regimes of the East inspired hopes for an alternative to Western forms of social organization. Foucault was certainly around long enough to reject that experiment and to express his support of the dissident movements active there.[6] There is no denying, however, that a profound change in the social and intellectual landscape occurred with the revolutions in East Germany, Czechoslovakia, Romania, and later within the Soviet Union itself. From the point of view of the West, these revolutions did not embody an ideal so much as formally call a halt to all such attempts. In this context, Foucault's discussion of Kant's *The Contest of the Faculties* is instructive.[7] The important thing about the French Revolution, Kant maintained, was not the success, failure, or even desirability of that specific event but rather "the *passion* or *enthusiasm* with which men embrace the cause of goodness" as a result of it.[8] It was the effect of the Revolution on its spectators that provided proof for Kant of the "moral tendency of the human race."[9] What is important, as Foucault explains, "is the way in which the Revolution provided a spectacle, the way in which it was welcomed all around by spectators who did not take part in it, but who observed it, attended it, and, for better or for worse, were carried away by it. . . . What is important in the Revolution is not the Revolution itself, but what takes place in the heads of those who do not make it or, in any case, who are not its principal actors."[10]

By this criterion, the revolutions of 1989 cannot be said to conform to the 1789 model. As revolutions go, these were ideal: swarming masses of people swamping one police state after another with the overwhelming power of their moral demands. Violence was kept to an absolute minimum. At the same time, the changes in regime were fundamental and irreversible. But if we follow Kant's procedure of checking the response of the revolution's spectators to determine its moral effects, we see no corresponding "passion" for change or progress, despite all the enthusiastic applause. Undeniably noble principles fueled the outbursts, and genuine revolutions certainly took place, and yet the "sympathy" felt for the dramatic, popular outbursts did not "almost border on enthusiasm" in the religious sense that Kant uses that term. We were not involved — our lives and social worlds were not implicated — in the events of 1989.

One way to think of our relation to the 1989 revolutions in the socialist bloc countries is provided by a comparison with Marx's complaint about the relatively backward state of German politics in the early 1840s. The political and social life of Germany, for Marx, was pre-historic, *"beneath the level of history"*: "If one were to begin with the status quo in Germany, even in the most appropriate way, i.e., negatively, the result would still be an *anachronism*. Even the negation of our political present is already a dusty fact in the historical lumber room of modern nations. I may negate powdered wigs, but I am still left with unpowdered wigs. If I negate the German situation of 1843 I have, according to French chronology, hardly reached the year 1789, and still less the vital center of the present day."[11] The physical destruction of Marx's Germany in 1843 and Erich Honecker's in 1989 was, for all that, still a task. It is just that in both cases "the spirit of this state of affairs has already been refuted."[12] When Marx wrote the words just quoted he was still a "young Hegelian," and the reference to *Geist* (spirit) should be understood in that philosophical context: There was no positive sense of Geist to be affirmed through the destruction of German reality. Rather, the historically "current" developments were to be found across the Rhine in France or perhaps across the channel in England. Important as they are, events in the East also lack the sense of Geist appropriate to our peculiar modern setting. We can negate Nicolae Ceauşescu or Enver Hoxha without, according to Western chronology, having reached the "legitimation crisis" first identified by Habermas in the early 1970s.[13]

The revolutions of the East were revolutions with a lowercase *r*. For all their interconnectedness and simultaneity, they were plural in character, irreducible to one another rather than so many manifestations of a guiding spirit. They were, to leave the Hegelian language behind and return to (a reversal of) Kant, much more important for their participants than for their onlookers and sympathizers.

The revolutions in the East have resulted in a kind of ironic disappointment. For all their drama, they signal the end to attempts in the twentieth century to realize the ends of human emancipation through the reorganization of social life. The consequences for this, for both observers and participants, have barely begun to make themselves felt. Where emancipation means revolution and revolution means the transformation of society in line with certain normative ideals of human freedom, it is difficult to avoid feeling a certain directionless tug when Ceauşescu and Honecker are treated as such elemental forces in human history that they are allowed to pack human liberation in along with their collected works as they exit from the world's stage.

The reaction of both observers and participants to the revolutions of the East signal a turning point in modern political thought. With the demise of the "Revolution," both as a viable goal and as a millennial promise, two conclusions are possible. We can continue to affirm the connection between liberation as goal and "Revolution" as event. In that case it will be difficult to avoid concluding that the former must go down with the latter. Or we can detach the goal from the discredited means used to achieve it. This latter expedient will no doubt be unsuccessful without a major effort to contemplate what is involved in the task of liberation in the first place. One of Foucault's primary goals is to achieve both a reconceptualization of human freedom and a successful separation from the means used to achieve it until now. This is what stands behind his opposition to "solutions," his unwillingness to "accept the word *alternative*," and his description of his own position as one that leads "not to apathy but to a hyper- and pessimistic activism."[14]

"Alternatives" and "solutions" are usually associated with a revolutionary transcendence of the social world or with projects of reform that seek to improve existing structures incrementally. If revolution is discounted, either a conciliatory reformism or—if the latter is viewed as a dead end—a defeatist pessimism becomes the prevailing social attitude. Foucault wants to deny these intellectual alternatives their supposed absolute character—or at least this is one way he can be read. He wants to develop a postrevolutionary ethos that does not degenerate into apathy or, implicitly, into an accommodationist reformism. Events since his death in 1984 make this effort even more interesting and relevant than it was during his lifetime.

Yet it seems that many of the more sensitive treatments of Foucault find it necessary to elaborate a recognizably normative position of some kind for him that will also act as the basis for a more positive vision of the kind of polity he would prefer. But this interpretive move not only is designed to improve on unsatisfactory readings of Foucault but also serves to satisfy the authors' own desire to work out an oppositional ethos that takes into account the primary theoretical insights of postmodern thought in general. William Connolly, one of the most innovative readers of Foucault and Nietzsche, argues that the "central idea" of this positive vision is to "modify liberal theory and democratic practice until they incorporate a greater degree of 'agonistic respect' into relations between incomplete, contending, and interdependent identities. Liberal presentations of tolerance and diversity are welcome, as far as they go. But they typically do not reach far enough into the contingent, constructed, and relational character of social relations, most particularly into the ways personal and collective identities are constructed through the definition of difference."[15] Judith Butler takes a similar view. What we need—in the face of the constructed character of gender identities—is a set of "coalitional strategies that neither presuppose nor fix their constitutive subjects in their place."[16] Such strategies would respond to the need for "another normative point of departure for feminist theory that does not require the reconstruction . . . of a female subject who fails to represent, much less emancipate, the array of embodied beings culturally positioned as women."[17] Just such an alternative normative perspective, according to Butler, can be found in an "antifoundationalist approach to coalitional politics" that takes the "transformation or expansion of existing identity concepts as a normative goal."[18]

Perhaps an insight into Foucault's own approach to politics can be achieved through a comparison with these other readings on postmodern politics. What both Connolly and Butler appear to do is to take the Nietzschean/Foucauldian insight that both violence and selection are involved in the construction of subjectivity and on this basis dismiss constructed subjectivity as an appropriate basis for oppositional political action. Connolly argues that there is an "evil" present in the form of "undeserved suffering imposed by practices protecting the reassurance (the goodness, purity, autonomy, normality) of hegemonic identities."[19] Somewhat similarly, Butler argues in *Gender Trouble* that "the political construction of the subject proceeds with certain legitimating and exclusionary aims."[20] A little later she asks: "Is the construction of the category of women as a coherent and stable subject an unwitting regulation and reification of gender relations? And is not such a reification precisely contrary to feminist aims?"[21]

With references to the possibility of a "positive vision" of society based on "agonistic respect," Butler and Connolly are making a very important claim. They are saying it is possible to derive a normative political theory from the revelation that cultural artifacts and even kinds of human beings are produced by constraint, through exclusion of "otherness," and various other coercive and undemocratic-sounding activities. Usually postmodernism has been associated with the claim that norm-based moralities are expressions of value designed to legitimize and endorse particular wills to power. Butler and Connolly want to revise that conclusion. As the genealogies of Nietzsche, Foucault, and others have suggested, if forms of subjectivity, along with other kinds of cultural artifacts, are "manufactured," then it follows that something has been left out, put to the side, suppressed. What has been left aside, what has been repressed, has been manifestly subjected to the coercive and repressive action of a particular exercise of *power*. This is exactly what Connolly is objecting to, I take it, when he argues that an "undeserved suffering" (hence unjust, hence objectionable on normative grounds) has been "imposed by practices protecting . . . hegemonic identities."

I would like to suggest that two errors are made here. First, it seems that these two authors mistake *specific* genealogical studies produced by Foucault, which trace the concrete ways in which particular power fields construct subjectivity, for a *general* criticism of all exercises of power in the construction of subjectivity. But such a generalization will not work—not in Foucault's terms and probably not in anybody else's terms either. That Foucault didn't think exercises of power (complete with "undeserved suffering," "hegemony," "regulation," and "reification") aimed at fabricating determinate psychic dispositions were a priori objectionable—and thus inadmissible on *normative* grounds—can be seen in his often admiring description of just such practices in the last two volumes of the sexuality series. What Connolly describes as "evil"—an interesting choice of words given the author's stated desire to escape the "Augustinian imperative"—Foucault treats in a much more ambiguous manner. This ambiguity is present even in *Discipline and Punish:* a "discipline" that teaches one how to write cannot be reasonably opposed just because shaping and constraining is occurring in the context of a hierarchical power relation. The question for both Foucault and Nietzsche for assessing cultural artifacts has never been, Was power used here? For them, such a question is precritical, and so is an attempt to elaborate a critical position based on it. The risk Butler and Connolly run in trying to locate a normative ground for political action in the suppression of "difference" is a retreat to the view that "power" is objectionable whenever there is repression or shaping of any kind. The key insight of Foucault's career, however, was precisely that power was more "productive" (of psychic states, kinds of knowledge, populations, and so on) than repressive.

The second, more political problem with a politics of "difference," one that provides hints as to why Foucault might not have endorsed it (and why theorists using Foucault as a resource for such a view are mistaken), has to do with its lack of discriminatory power. A coalitional politics of difference could not possibly live up to its own billing: we might want to reject some identity formations (skinheads), while positively valuing others, such as the drag queens discussed by Butler.[22] In other words, the "politics of difference" shares the same difficulties with other normative and vaguely humanist notions: it is too ambiguous, does not tell you enough about the political context of one's decisions or alliances and, taken seriously, might lead one to endorse things that one (reasonably) does not want to endorse.[23]

The Enlightenment Program

In the 1982 essay "The Subject and Power," Foucault engaged in one of his many reflections on the significance of Kant's essay "What Is Enlightenment?"[24] Certainly, Foucault wishes to transform Kant's reflections on Enlightenment rather than simply reproduce them. Still, there are elements of Kant's argument that impressed him for their relevance to modern conditions. Kant describes Enlightenment as the effort to exit from a state of "self-imposed immaturity."[25] For instance, instead of letting the pastor tell us how to read the Bible, we should be striving to understand it on our own. Rather than being satisfied with learning to obey the drill sergeant's shouted commands, we should retain our freedom of thought and limit the sphere in which duty and obedience hold sway.[26] To successfully leave this state of self-imposed immaturity, Kant cites a condition: "For Enlightenment . . . all that is needed is *freedom.*" But this freedom is the one thing that the clergy, officials, and rulers deny to those under their control. There are, in fact, "restrictions on freedom everywhere."[27]

The task of removing these restrictions, broadly or narrowly conceived, has been the central problem of an old tradition in political theory. The problem can be stated this way: What conditions must be met for individuals and the societies they live in to be truly free? Freedom as understood by a wide variety of thinkers in the Enlightenment referred to a full and unimpeded use of reason to order one's own life, the life of society, and humanity's relationship to nature. At the same time, two versions of the tradition associating reason with freedom moved in different directions. First, there is the view that individuals are inherently capable of exercising autonomy and using their own reason but that this capacity is frustrated by certain conditions. The solution is to provide individuals with a number of essential protections and rights and remove all obstacles to the development of individual autonomy, allowing the natural qualities of individuals to blossom. This, of course, is the optimistic-liberal version of the Enlightenment project.[28] Certainly, broad social conditions — guarantees of personal freedoms, for instance — must be achieved before the individual can be said to have an opportunity to become autonomous. Revolutions may even be required so as to reach these conditions. But in the end the emphasis of the liberal program is the individual and his or her development.

The second version of the tradition associating freedom with autonomy and the use of reason developed as a response to the inadequacies of the first version. Here the view is that society creates the individuals of which it is composed. If a certain kind of free individual is desired, with particular capacities as well as certain disinclinations, attention must be paid to what kind of society will produce that individual. The liberal approach seeks to free the individual from archaic and unjust institutions that thwart the expression of an already existing, essentially rational core. Critical theory, on the other hand, points to the continued irrational effects of a system that allows the dominant elements of the economy and social life to develop in an arbitrary fashion. In this context, the freedom of the individual is put at risk by a contingent environment. As a result, the liberal notion of freedom is criticized as being too anarchic to be associated in any meaningful way with rationality.[29]

To a lesser extent with liberalism—and in a more pronounced way with critical theory—how society is constructed is ranked above other elements as the primary concern in securing freedom. The same goal, however, is approached from different directions. Liberals want to remove obstacles to freedom, whereas critical theorists want to build a society that will make a rational existence possible. Both liberal theory and critical theory are ultimately concerned with the fate of the individual. It is just that the best—indeed, the only—way to secure conditions for individual flourishing is in a reordering of the social setting. With liberalism, this rebuilding stops at the point where a number of essential rights have been won for individuals and groups, along with the elimination of social conditions and institutions that contradict or indirectly frustrate the actualization of those rights. Critical theorists argue that this solution is fundamentally inadequate. What is required is a society that will positively reinforce, through its institutions as well as its culture and habits, the existence of the rational individual. We can see, then, how Kant's comment about the need for freedom so as to practice enlightenment is inflated to the point where society and its organization assumes primary importance over the individual.

Foucault wants to criticize critical theory and liberalism as inadequate for pursuing enlightenment. Both emphasize society-wide solutions, an approach Foucault believes has reached a dead end. At the same time, Foucault wants to propose a new understanding and emphasis for the term "Enlightenment."

Critical theory, as we have seen, can be perceived as an extension of liberal theory. Simply by complaining that liberalism fails to deliver on its promises, critical theorists implicitly admit that the two traditions have common ends. The emphasis here will be on critical theory and some of the difficulties Foucault finds with its precepts and practices. It will be clear as we proceed that the same difficulties are there to be found with liberal theory.[30]

Critical theorists tend to describe individuals as creatures of the totality within which they function. Marx, the first and best critical theorist, argues that although there is no timeless or universal human essence, that does not mean—as a hasty reading might suggest—that the "human essence" does not exist. Rather, what must be understood is that this "human essence" is "no abstraction inherent in each individual. In its reality it is the ensemble of social relations."[31] It exists, but historically, not absolutely. The character of this essence can be discovered in the way humans produce their own existence. "By producing their means of subsistence men are indirectly producing their actual material life." As Marx states, "This mode of production must not be considered simply as being the reproduction of the physical existence of the individuals. Rather it is a definite form of political activity of these individuals, a definite form of expressing their life, a definite *mode of life* on their part. As individuals express their life, so they are. What they are, therefore, coincides with their production, both with *what* they produce and with *how* they produce."[32] Thus Marx's declaration of independence from the idealism of the young Hegelians is not associated with a contemptuous dismissal of the whole idea of human essence. Rather, Marx argues that the sum of productive forces, along with the social forms of intercourse, "which every individual and generation finds in existence as something given, is the real basis of what philosophers have conceived as 'substance' and 'essence of man.' "[33]

What can it mean to say that the human essence is real but at the same time relative to the social forms of a historical period? Is that not a misuse of the term "essence?" Why not simply give up that word and speak instead of humans as products of their social circumstances and then go on to specify how those circumstances can be transformed?

In fact, there are real benefits involved in retaining a commitment to a true human nature, however historicized. Marx's complaint about Ludwig Feuerbach and by extension the whole Hegelian school had to do with their attempts to criticize the social world around them from the standpoint of an already existing and abstract human essence. But since this essence enjoyed no concrete embodiment in the world, it remained without content, existing as a merely "internal, dumb generality." There was no practical link between this kind of essence and the world for which it was supposed to act as a model. In addition, nothing in this kind of criticism explained the source or active agent of the transition from this world to one that realized the human essence. By historicizing this essence—while pointedly refusing to abandon the whole idea—Marx put himself in a position of being able to refer to the concrete historical developments giving rise to this "ensemble of social relations" with its concomitant human essence as well as those conditions capable of producing a new ensemble and a different, presumably better essence. Far from attempting to abandon the human essence as a foolish illusion, Marx was involved in an energetic—one is tempted to say "desperate"—effort to save it from its fate as a "dumb generality" in the hands of the young Hegelians.

Marx used an increasingly empirical and scientific vocabulary and method to ground the work for a new and more appropriate human essence in something other than wishful thinking. The world that we live in now and the kind of human essence produced in it are not merely a cognitive error on the part of society's inhabitants about which critical theory will then go on to enlighten us. The human essence does not hover over this state of affairs in an abstract, undetermined way, acting as a vague critical principle. It is, on the contrary, directly produced, a thing of this world, leading a "profane" existence. It follows for Marx that if we want to change this essence, we must transform its real basis, namely, the social, cultural, and economic totality in which it is produced. Just because our essence is composed of the ensemble of social relations, only a complete transfiguration of that ensemble can change our essence. Only when that is accomplished will a real opportunity present itself to lead the rational, autonomous existence for which we somehow seem to have been meant. Obviously, Marx confronts a problem regarding the status of this true or more appropriate human essence that will be realized in a postcapitalist society. What is the source of this new, final, and true human essence in an account that grounds its persuasive power in a historicization of the latter? This and other questions are easy to imagine, but the pursuit of them, interesting as they are, is not our task here. What is important to notice about Marxist theory for our purposes is that the freedom or serfdom of the individual is tied to, and must wait on, the fundamental reorganization of society.

It is easy to see how this linking of the human essence to the social totality carries with it some risks—however useful it might have been for Marx in his polemics with the young Hegelians. One enters into an all-or-nothing mode. Marx tried to bring together a sober, empirical account of the determining elements of the social world with a belief that the emancipation of humanity was just around the next epochal corner. Surely there are unavoidable strains associated with such a joining. The fit between revolutionary enthusiasm and scientific rigor is never going to be very tight, which accounts for the peculiar fact that the "same" doctrine can produce a deterministic Karl Kautsky and a voluntaristic Georg Lukács.[34]

We can see the opposite effects of treating the social world as a totality in the work of Max Weber. Weber believed the relentless advance of a bureaucratic rationality associated with instrumental reason was irreversible and threatened to undermine the conditions of individual freedom. He too believed that the social world—especially in its modern setting—was best understood as a totality (not his term) that was increasingly characterized by a bureaucratic ethos.[35] A very disappointing kind of human essence was being propagated more and more extensively in wider areas of social life, and like Marx, Weber had very little to do with the idea that some purer or more primal human being only needed to be extracted from the accumulated mistakes and accidents of history. What Weber lacked, and what the Marxists did not lack, was a belief in the possibility that some kind of epochal shift—brought on by revolution or some other internally generated systemic collapse—would manage to clear the way for a new structure of human existence. Indeed, he believed that the primary alternative to capitalist society of his day—socialism—would only increase the threats to individual freedom by accelerating the range and power of bureaucratic rationalization.[36]

The Frankfurt School provides an interesting illustration of both sides of this all-or-nothing stance associated with viewing the social world as a totality. In the 1930s, during its more "unorthodox" phase, prospects for redirecting the social whole led to a sense of optimism. By the late 1940s and 1950s, however, this optimism had turned into a pessimism based on the belief that the current totality could not be transformed.[37]

For Foucault, the alternating resigned and optimistic stances inspired by the point of view of the totality leads to equally unsatisfactory ways of relating to the present. The optimistic mode results in a millennialism that looks to the world being transformed—either "soon" or "very soon." The present does not matter except as an entry point to the new world.[38] With resignation, all that can be found in the present is a repetition or intensification of the already dominant social forms.[39] Both attitudes are forced on us—in turn, as it were—by regarding the world we live in as a totality. Either some epochal transformation comes along to redefine the totality—and depending on our estimate of the chances for this, we are more or less optimistic—or that hope is discounted and, assuming a negative assessment of the world around us, a resigned pessimism holds sway. Foucault wishes to question the assumptions standing behind this holistic view of modern societies. As we saw in chapters 1 and 3, he goes to a great deal of trouble to present a picture of power that is not unitary but fractured and makeshift in its unity. From Foucault's perspective, critical theory as usually practiced results in a picture of society that is much too organized, neat, and seamless. It is simply not the case, according to Foucault, that all the most important institutions—cultural, economic, and social—are subordinated either to the needs of a dominant class (Marx) or an inescapable developmental imperative (Weber). Critical theory's accounts of unified, purposive, and nearly conspiratorial "totalistic" societies oversimplify the construction of power formations in society, which results in an oppositional ethos that swings between the extremes of a millenarianist expectancy and conservative resignation. One way of seeing Foucault's work is as an attempt to save critical thought from these repetitive and inefficacious themes. His goal is to stake out a position somewhere between the diametric responses associated with the revolving door of revolutionary optimism and pessimism. This mood is captured in a 1983 comment:

> The solemnity with which everyone . . . engages in philosophical discourse . . . strikes me as a flaw. I can say so all the more firmly since it is something I have done myself. . . . I think we should have the modesty to say to ourselves that, on the one hand, the time we live in is not *the* unique or fundamental or irruptive point in history where everything is completed and begun again. We must also have the modesty to say, on the other hand, that — even without this solemnity — the time we live in is very interesting, it needs to be analyzed and broken down, and that we would do well to ask ourselves, "What is the nature of our present?" [40]

This last question is best answered, as we saw in chapter 3, with a complex local and ascending analysis of the construction of societies. Such an approach frees critical thought from the extreme requirement of a root and branch transformation of society. In chapter 4 I looked at this same effect from a methodological standpoint. This plural and strategic perspective on society is consequential for our view of the possibility of change. Because not everything is run from a central headquarters, because local circuits of power-knowledge have their own rationality, their own means and ends, local struggles do not have to wait for revolutions in the broader structure in order to be meaningful, actual agents of change. The fact that the whole system is not changed does not mean, as it does with a long tradition in political theory, that none of the parts can change. At the same time, the results of local struggles, actions, or movements — whatever we want to call them — can have significant effects precisely because broader structures are built up on the basis of these local centers.

One meaning of enlightenment for Foucault is the intervention — both socially and individually — on the part of the subjects of a particular domain of power and knowledge into that domain's operations so as to question and transform it. Critical thought itself is not exempted from the matrix of knowledge, rules, and subjectivity that constitutes the more familiar domains of madness, delinquency, and so on. If one of the primary features of enlightenment is the *Ausgang* — "exiting" from the dominance of an authority that has become "almost second nature" in order to become self-reliant and mature [41] —

then "enlightenment" for practitioners of critical thought means discovering an exit point in the power-knowledge network that operates under the sign of "the revolution."

From Revolution to Revolt

Foucault's dismissal of revolution as a workable critical paradigm has to do, first of all, with an acknowledgment of the disappointments it has produced: "I belong to a generation of people that has seen most of the utopias framed in the nineteenth century and at the beginning of the twentieth century collapse one after another, and that has also seen the perverse and sometimes disastrous effects that could follow from projects which were the most generous in their intentions."[42] Foucault wishes to look past "the revolution" as a constitutive political principle: "If politics has existed since the nineteenth century," he comments, "it is because the revolution took place. . . . Politics always takes a stand on the revolution." If it turns out the revolution is not desirable, politics cannot remain the same. It would then, as Foucault puts it, "be necessary to invent . . . something else as a substitute for it. We are perhaps experiencing the end of politics. For politics is a field that was opened up by the existence of the revolution, and if the question of the revolution can no longer be posed. . . , then politics is in danger of disappearing."[43]

Four years after he made the above comments (during a 1977 interview), Foucault expanded his discussion of the revolution in a brief essay on the occasion of the Iranian revolution.[44] The first question Foucault asks is whether we should condemn the Iranian revolution that overthrew the Shah in light of the government by mullahs that followed. Foucault's answer is no, but this response requires him to explain the continued meaning and significance of revolutionary action once it is separated from the revolutionary goal.

Before addressing that vexing question, however, Foucault first attempts to explain—very schematically and briefly, to be sure—how the revolution came to be seen as the vessel of so many meanings and values. The individual, class, group, or nation that revolts, Foucault says, always stands outside the normal course of human events. The revolt irrupts into history and disturbs it from the outside. This very quality, however, gives revolt a quasi- or even straightforwardly religious character, allowing it to speak of another world that should transcend or replace this one.[45] But where does this impulse come from? To what can the desire to understand revolts in terms of "the revolution" be traced? This question can be easily expanded. It is not only revolt that is seen in this light. Incremental progress, too, is often interpreted in relation to a closer approximation to a conception of human nature.[46] The short answer is that this perspective is a long-standing element of the Western tradition. As stated by R. N. Berki, in an insightful commentary on the origins of Marxism: "The notion of a perfect, ideal world, distant from and defined in sharp contrast to 'actual existence' but one which serves as the yardstick of our comprehension of actual existence . . . supplies the motive force and justification of political action. This of course is not confined to 'revolutionary' political action." The wide applicability and use made of the transcendent vision is what prompts Berki to suggest that "revolutionary Marxism was 'traditional' precisely in being revolutionary." [47]

By understanding revolts as signs of this transcendent world, Foucault argues, we achieve a generally successful reading of revolts back into history. They became the vehicles that took us into the beyond, or at least the next step on the way to it, and in this way revolutions were given a comprehensible role in the economy of history. This taming of revolts makes them rational once again, effecting a "repatriation" of them.[48] We are given a standard for assessing, perhaps even "disqualifying" revolutionary action. This is precisely the approach to revolt that Foucault criticizes in the Iranian case. Our assessment of the revolt that overthrew the Shah should not be influenced by the kind of regime that succeeded it. Just such an appraisal is required if we insist on reading revolts as discrete manifestations of "the revolution." The point is that in the late twentieth century, "the revolution" and the politics that swirl around it can no longer act—if they ever did—as reliable evaluative bases from which to measure the value of revolts. To continue to apply revolutionary criteria to revolts in a postrevolutionary era is to condemn revolts to extinction, or at least meaninglessness. The question Why revolt? so often used as a challenge to Foucault's politics, turns suddenly about to confront his critics.

There is, Foucault says, an irreducible element to revolt that threatens all despotisms—"today's as . . . for yesterday's," the Shah's as well as that of the mullahs.[49] The question whether it is "useless to revolt" is usually informed by a background assumption: the revolt—or, to speak more generally, political action—will be meaningful and successful only if the position of humanity is advanced in the attempt, if heaven is brought a little closer to earth. Of course, this is no absolute requirement. There can be wrong turns, U-turns, and partial successes. But the standard for political action remains the same. But, for Foucault, as we shall see, the consequences of revolts are not a good place to look for their justification.

Turning, in the same piece, to examples closer to his own concerns, Foucault points to the criminal and what he calls the "madman." Revolt does not make the first "innocent" or the second "sane." It is not that every revolt stands for and helps to produce some higher conception of humanity. The desire to make heroes of those who revolt—Palestinians, Vietnamese, the proletariat, young people, women, and so on—is directly connected to the assumption that some higher truth not achieved or understood by those who stand outside the revolt is contained within. Foucault abandons this tradition in Western thought. Instead of asking, Is there or is there not a reason to revolt? Foucault turns to the empirical observation that "there are revolts and that is a fact": "One does not have to maintain that these confused voices sound better than the others and express the ultimate truth. For there to be a sense in listening to them and in searching for what they want to say, it is sufficient that they exist and that they have against them so much which is set up to silence them."[50] It is not the consequences of revolutions that should be examined in assessing their value. An interesting reversal is at work here: Foucault is often accused of providing no normative criteria for evaluating political action.[51] But if Foucault can be seen as struggling to address the normative dimension of revolt, those who insist on the link between ethical values, revolt, and its consequences can be said to face the reverse dilemma: Do we really wish to condemn the Iranian revolution against the Shah because the country ended up in the hands of the mullahs? Are we willing to return a verdict of "not useful" against all the revolts in the East if ethnic strife, civil war, economic downturns, and social disruptions of all kinds are the result? Is that where the true significance of such revolts can be found? Assuming the answer, again, to be no, we are entitled to go on to ask how Foucault assesses the value of revolts and, by extension, the kind of oppositional activity that leads up to them.

In his brief piece on the Iranian revolution, Foucault asserts that all liberties, all the rights that we cherish and hope to protect, have their final anchor in revolt.[52] Notice the inversion: instead of revolt being referred to normative goals for its justification, it is rights, liberties, and norms themselves that— for Foucault—have their foundation in revolt. What is immediately striking about this passage, of course, is Foucault's claim that rights have an anchor of any kind. This will come as a surprise to many of his critics, who assume that Foucault's move away from normative criteria deprives critical activity of any imaginable basis. It is true, however, that natural rights—and with them all other essentialist accounts of human nature—cannot act as such an anchor. Such accounts are simply too diffuse, by themselves, to act as an effective bar to the encroachments of power. The themes of humanism are "always tied to value judgments" which "have obviously varied greatly in their content, as well as in the values they have preserved. . . . From this, we must not conclude that everything that has ever been linked with humanism is to be rejected, but that the humanistic thematic is itself too supple, too diverse, too inconsistent to act as an axis for reflection."[53] The "great themes" of humanism, natural rights, and so on, Foucault concludes, "can be used to any end whatever."[54] Revolts, on the other hand, have this in their favor: to make headway they must tailor themselves to the specific circumstances in which they occur. In addition, revolts both draw on and underline the limits power in fact cannot exceed if it is to continue to be productive. Of course, it is true that revolts, both large and small, have never — down to today — stopped referring to those "great themes" in explaining their goals both to those who participate in them and to those who look on. But then, as Foucault himself says in the quotation above, "not . . . everything that has ever been linked with humanism is to be rejected." As Marx was perhaps the first to point out, those engaged in revolt feel compelled to justify their acts relative to the paradigm of revolution.[55] That is, each revolt is expected to specify what new and truer expression of the human essence is being forged in its fires. But this compulsion to thematize revolts into universal descriptions of humanity is not what is genuinely interesting or useful about revolts for Foucault. What is really going on — and what then is unfortunately obscured by the incessant process of thematization — is the precise, locally specific, and historically relative mapping out of the topography of power: "What makes . . . resistance and revolts . . . a central phenomenon in the history of societies is that they manifest in a massive and universalizing form, at the level of the whole social body, the locking together of power relations with relations of strategy and the results proceeding from their interaction."[56]

The "Plebeian Aspect"

The kind of oppositional ethos Foucault prefers is indicated, among other places, in "Power and Strategies." There Foucault talks about the incredible but repeated instances of opposition that crop up in the Soviet Gulag. Instead of asking which vision of a better world stands behind these acts of resistance, Foucault argues we must open our eyes to "what enables people there, on the spot, to resist the Gulag, what makes it intolerable for them, and what can give the people of the anti-Gulag the courage to stand up and die in order to be able to utter a word or a poem. . . . What is it that sustains them, what gives them their energy, what is the force at work in their resistance, what makes them stand and fight? . . . The leverage against the Gulag is not in our heads, but in their bodies, their energy, what they say, think and do."[57] A name is given to the "leverage" mentioned above: the "plebs." The latter should not be seen, however, as a determinate sociological entity. Rather, there is "something in" classes, groups, and individuals that "escapes relations of power." No "plebs," then, but a "plebeian aspect" that exists "everywhere, in a diversity of forms, extensions, energies, irreducibilities."[58]

Obviously, the above comments are very vague and must be made specific to be useful. At most, they provide us with the beginnings of a vocabulary. They do not yet take us very far in understanding the source of this "plebeian aspect," nor is it yet clear how the activity of the "plebeian aspect" provides the anchors for rights and protections that Foucault mentions in his piece on the Iranian revolution.

One possible reading of Foucault's use of "plebs" would refer to a Nietzschean argument about the nature of knowledge and the kinds of realities and truths that humans build up around themselves. Nietzsche believed that all knowledge was a selective process that of necessity ignored vast areas of the world around it in order to come up with a picture of the world that was both useful and manageable.[59] No amount of knowledge could be comprehensive—indeed, it was the nature of knowledge to be anything but comprehensive. Social arrangements also should not be seen as expressing some fundamental truth about human nature. Instead, they were attempts to manipulate society's interaction with its environment (and between its members) in ways that optimized chances for survival and growth. In this way, too, societies never dominated, controlled, or created all the impulses, desires, and needs of their members, though they were certainly capable of generating and manipulating some.[60]

With this Nietzschean approach, we have part of our answer about the source of the plebs' existence. One of Foucault's central claims about the functioning of power is that it is creative rather than simply repressive. It is not so much that an essential human nature is covered over by social constraints whose removal will set us free. Rather, power produces the kinds of individuals that make up society, that fill its roles and carry out its functions.[61] This argument is frequently taken to imply a strict determinism and with it a pessimistic assessment of the chances for social change. If we are the sort of individuals that the disciplines Foucault describes make of us, how can resistance be imagined? The need for an oppositional lever of some kind is what has driven critical theorists down a twisting road in search of some group of interests, located somewhere in or outside the current social structure that can oppose the existing dominant social forms. This search has been motivated by the assumption that if some better, truer — more human — human essence cannot be discovered somewhere now or in the future, then the job of critique becomes impossible. And, indeed, some critical theorists, most notably Adorno, did come to the conclusion that the prospects for resistance were slight.[62] Critical thought was reduced in his eyes to commenting on the latest downward turn in the negative dialectic.

Too often, commentators on Foucault see him as reproducing the same note of pessimism found in Adorno. A good recent example of a generally sympathetic treatment of Foucault that has difficulty freeing itself of the notion that to talk of constructed individuals is to talk of *determined* individuals can be found in Honi Fern Haber's *Beyond Postmodern Politics*. Though she claims she wants to come to Foucault's "defense" against those who criticize him for failing to provide normative criteria for oppositional politics,[63] she nonetheless reproduces the very error on which Foucault's critics rely for their persuasive power: "Foucault often writes as if power constitutes the very individuals upon whom it operates. . . . But if, as this thesis implies, individuals are *wholly* constituted by the power/knowledge regime Foucault describes, how can discipline be resisted in the first place?"[64] The criticism which Haber repeats here — and on which she expands in subsequent pages — is simply not the problem Haber and others make it out to be. The rest of this section on "the plebs" is designed to explain why. But of Haber's recital of this old refrain, we could ask the following: What is the logical connection between the idea that individuals are "wholly" constituted and the idea that resistance is impossible? The author writes as if the link between these two statements is logically self-evident, whereas it needs to be closely examined and rigorously specified. Second, it seems a mistake to think of Foucault as writing about *the* power-knowledge regime. For as long as Foucault's readers see him as describing a closed universe of a single kind of power à la the Frankfurt School, for that long will he be completely misunderstood. Examples of this kind of reading can be cited without end and stretch from the beginning of Foucault's critical reception to the present.[65]

A Nietzschean reading of the construction of social reality would seem, however, to escape the dilemma of critical theory introduced by the Frankfurt School and wrongly ascribed to Foucault by so many of his readers. In Nietzsche's view, individuals are produced by determinate social relationships.[66] But this production is always going to involve a process of selection. Not everything about an individual will be "created" by the social powers that affect her or him. No art is comprehensive enough for that. In fact, in a sense the word "creation" is the wrong one. The individual in Nietzsche's account is not so much created as formed into a productive and usable shape out of a multiplicity of drives, tensions, instincts, and capacities. In this shaping, some elements of the individual are left to the side, assigned a subordinate role, or otherwise left out of account. Thus, while the individual has certainly been made in some sense, it does not follow that she or he is now essentially and irretrievably the creature of dominant powers. There can be a number of reasons for this, but sticking to the Nietzschean argument here, we could say that a great deal that has not been noticed by society is left over once society has finished shaping the individual to its needs.[67] Individuals are made but never determined "all the way down" such that only a massive shock of the kind provided by revolutions will offer the opportunity for change. As Foucault puts it, "something like the subject" exists but in "forms which are far from being completed." Measuring his distance from Husserlian phenomenology, he denies that the subject precedes the world and acts as the condition for the possibility of experience. Quite the reverse: "It is experience . . . which results in a subject, or rather, in subjects. I will call subjectivization the procedure by which one obtains the constitution of a subject, or more precisely, of a subjectivity which is of course only one of the given possibilities of organization of self-consciousness."[68] To summarize, if the process of what we call "subjectivization" is provisional, never completed, resulting in a plural and shifting psychic structure, it follows that individuals can be constituted without, however, being determined. Opposition does not have to wait on recastings of the entire social structure to be effective.

Secondary commentators on Foucault have nonetheless had a great deal of difficulty freeing themselves from the supposed requirement that oppositional activity make reference to a normative ideal as realized in a distinct kind of polity before it can be taken seriously. More frequently, this takes the form of calls for a "politics of difference" that, when boiled down, turns out to be little more than a retreat to more familiar notions of democratic pluralism and justice, along with a series of concessions to critics of postmodernism generally and Foucault in particular. A good example of this retreat to normativity can be found in an essay by Jane Flax that discusses the relation between justice and "difference."[69] There Flax argues that "a post-modernist–feminist approach to the problem of domination would entail a search for ways to free the play of differences. The post-modernist engagement in and preference for play, fragmentation, and differentiation have a quite serious, even normative, purpose." Flax understands this normative purpose as a "clearing of spaces in which many disorderly or local forms of life could flourish,"[70] which results in four principles for constructing and maintaining a just polity: (1) a "reconciliation of diversities into a restored but new unity. . . . Claims to justice may be made on the basis of preserving the play of differences"; (2) a "reciprocity" that "connotes a continuous though imprecise defined sharing of authority and mutuality of decision"; (3) a form of "recognition" that both "acknowledges the legitimacy of the other" while also "identifying with the other"; and (4) a form of "judgment" that "involves the capacity to see things from the point of view of another."[71] But what is such a vision of justice but the basic liberal, pluralist version we all learned about in a first-year political philosophy course, spiced up with a heavy salting of deconstructive rhetoric? And doesn't commitment to such abstract normative criteria carry with it the same risks to which postmodernists and feminists have been alerting us for decades? For instance, would theorists of "difference politics" support the inclusion of, say, a contingent of pro-life lesbians and gays at a gay pride or women's rights march in the name of "preserving the play of differences"? At the Gay and Lesbian Pride fest in Boston (held in June 1995), participants thought otherwise and tried to pull down the anti-abortion banner of the "Pro-Life Alliance of Gays and Lesbians." A leader of this pro-life alliance knew how to play the "difference" card in response, saying: "The crowd's jeers and obstruction of free speech rights, and our right to be part of the festival, were an action of intolerance and hatred. The mob made a mockery of the reason we gathered today — to celebrate the diversity of the gay community and to ensure the legal rights of each individual."[72]

A second point that might help explain Foucault's vague comments about the "plebs" is the reversibility of power relations and the discourses that accompany them. We saw an example of this earlier when discussing the "reversibility" of discourses.[73] The term "homosexual," for example, is introduced not as a value-neutral label but is accompanied by a range of scientific studies and conclusions that have as their purpose an objectification and pathologization of homosexual practices. This definition is then taken on by those it was supposed to condemn and to a certain extent is celebrated.[74] The negative valuation of important elements of the description of homosexuals is simply reversed. Foucault discusses many similar examples. That is, the possibility exists of reversing the meaning and role of subjective states themselves. Fou-

cault cites the example of the pathologization of women in the eighteenth century, which centered on the claim that women were "nothing but their sex,"
which in turn was "fragile, almost always sick and always inducing illness."
The response of some feminists was to beat the sexologists at their own game:
"Are we sex by nature? Well then, let us be so but in its singularity, in its irreducible specificity. Let us draw the consequences and reinvent our own type
of existence, political, economic, cultural."[75]

   This point about the reversibility of discourse must be tied to the first point
above derived from Nietzsche. Subjective states can be reversed—"revalued"
might be a better term—only if there exists some point from which such
states are experienced as somehow debilitating or limiting. The Nietzschean
argument about the restricted capacity of societies to shape individuals fully
provides such a vantage point. Another way of making the same point is to
note the plurality of subjective forms present in each individual. Not only are
individuals called on to play a variety of roles—student, worker, executive,
and so on—in modern societies, but different (if related) subjectivities are, in
addition, constructed to fulfill those roles effectively. As a result, it is possible
for experience in one realm of subjective life to reflect critically on events and
valuations in another. "The subject," he writes, "is not a substance."

> It is a *form* and this form is not above all or always identical to itself. You
> do not have towards yourself the same kind of relationships when you
> constitute yourself as a political subject who goes and votes or speaks up
> in a meeting, and when you try to fulfill your desires in a sexual rela-
> tionship. There are no doubt some relationships and some interferences
> between these different kinds of subject but we are not in the presence of
> the same kind of subject. In each case, we play, we establish with one's
> self some different form of relationship.[76]

One kind of "interference" possible to imagine between one subjective sphere
and another is a critical one. If in one arena I am (at least putatively) regarded
as an important and equal participant in a cooperative enterprise (as a citizen
or in a religious organization), a contrary constitution in another sphere (as
employee in a corporation, as a married woman) will perhaps lead to a critical comparison. Thus, Foucault gives us two (related) reasons that allow us to
imagine the possibility of effective, meaningful resistance to dominant social
patterns even while affirming that subjective states are constituted: first, it is
impossible to shape the full range of possible human capacities according to
a single use or even set of uses, and second, the subject is actually a plurality

of subjective forms, each adapted to specific spheres, while interacting with one another as well. Notice the difference here from Marx's argument in his *Theses on Feuerbach* and *The German Ideology:* in those works and in most of the major ones that follow, individuals are constituted. Up to that point Marx, Nietzsche, and Foucault would agree. But unlike the latter two, Marx maintained that individuals were wholly constituted by activity in a single sphere: that of work, or labor.[77] Here Foucault and Nietzsche diverge from Marx. The interesting consequence of this difference is that the first two thinkers present a more optimistic estimate of the objective possibilities for resisting or otherwise questioning subjective forms along with the practices and institutions that work to form them. This is true even though one misreading of Foucault (aided, at times, by Foucault himself) takes his argument about the constitution of the subject as a bar to both the possibility and the desirability of oppositional activity.

Important as the above points are, however, they express the case for the possibility of resistance from a standpoint outside, as it were, a determinate power relationship. Foucault actually makes a more subtle argument about the existence of freedom inside a power relationship. The first two points above describe power as insufficiently comprehensive to determine and control all existing or possible constructions of human subjects, institutions, customs, and so on. In what follows, Foucault's argument will be that a similar kind of space is produced in the very process of defining a power relationship. The "plebeian aspect" that we are in the process of specifying, then, will have as one of its most important sites the dynamics produced by power relationships themselves.

In "The Subject and Power" Foucault argues that on a conceptual level "power" relationships must be sharply distinguished from relationships of "violence." With violence, the body is directly touched, whether it is maimed, incarcerated, or killed. Exercises of power, by contrast, are designed to influence the *actions*—rather than the *bodies*—of the persons they are addressed to. Seen this way, a power relationship requires "two elements which are indispensable if it is really to be a power relationship: that 'the other' (the one over whom power is exercised) be thoroughly recognized and maintained to the very end as a person who acts; and that, faced with a relationship of power, a whole field of responses, reactions, results, and possible inventions may open up."[78] One "conducts" power relations in the same sense that one conducts an orchestra. Foucault also uses the term "government" as "the way in which the conduct of other individuals might be directed."

It is in this context that Foucault introduces the notion of freedom: "Power is exercised only over free subjects and only insofar as they are free. By this we mean individual or collective subjects who are faced with a field of possibilities in which several ways of behaving, several reactions and diverse comportments may be realized."[79] The freedom involved, however, is not, as in a broadly Kantian scheme, inherent in the individual human beings who make up the power relationship. The absolute precondition for the erection of political structures, modes of conflict resolution, income distribution policy, and so on of a Kantian political scheme is the view of humans as essentially free. Human beings are rational; they have reasons for the actions they take and the agreements they enter into. This capacity for rationality is what distinguishes humans from the rest of the universe, which for its part is determined by laws of nature that are blindly followed.[80] Kant's ethics demands that individuals enter into political societies so they can express their free nature through the formulation of and obedience to rationally derived laws.

Foucault's use of the term "freedom" is far removed from this: "Rather than speaking of an essential freedom, it would be better to speak of an 'agonism' — of a relationship which is at the same time reciprocal incitation and struggle."[81] In a sense, however, a kind of essential freedom—though not Kant's—is implied in Foucault's account: it is power relationships themselves that require freedom. They can operate "only over free subjects." Freedom is "essential" to their operation.[82]

What is the basis of this kind of freedom, however? Why do power relationships require freedom in which to operate? And, because it has a different basis from the more familiar version associated with Kant, what characterizes this kind of freedom?

A part of the answer has to do with the very complex nature of the human material involved in a power relationship, especially in modern conditions. In this context, we should recall Foucault's discussion of "reason of state" in "Politics and Reason." At the origins of the modern state, the discovery was made that the resources of the state were enhanced by providing "a little extra life" to the population within its borders. Since that time the link between increased individual capacities and the development and intensification of power relations has grown stronger, not weaker.[83] The result is that no successful power relationship is able to develop that does not treat individuals in some real sense as ends in themselves. As Foucault puts it, one indispensable element of a power relationship is that " 'the other' (the one over whom power is exercised) be thoroughly recognized and maintained to the end as a person who acts." This, it seems, is a peculiarly modern function of power relationships. For his part, however, it appears that Foucault believes this to be a more widely distributed feature of power.

However it is placed on a historical time line, the freedom produced by power relationships itself has no universal features. This is because, very simply, power relations themselves are not universal but also specific to the context in which they operate. This differentiation of power relations is what "makes all the more politically necessary the analysis of power relations in a given society, their historical formation, the source of their strength or fragility, the conditions which are necessary to transform some or to abolish others. . . . Bringing into question . . . power relations and the "agonism" between power relations and the intransitivity of freedom is a permanent political task inherent in all social existence." [84] Neither the character of power relations nor the substance of freedom specific to them is permanent.

There is, then, no universal element present in every revolt, regardless of the issue or form the revolt itself takes. Freedom cannot be defined absent the material conditions in which it is exercised. Freedom is not a set of rights that can be exhaustively specified. Rather, freedom is the actual set of choices that a determinate social setting provides — and cannot help but provide — for the participating actors. In addition, it is not true, for Foucault, that the options available are so static or one-sided that the dominant pole of a power relationship benefits regardless of the choices actors make. Regimes that attempt to create such closed systems use two strategies: they either suppress those elements of life (art, political activity) dangerous to their ends or seek to imbue these spheres with the logic and purposes of the regime itself. The twentieth century shows us examples of both, and neither can be said to have had no successes. But nothing can eliminate "the possibility of that moment when life will no longer barter itself, when the powers can no longer do anything, and when, before the gallows and the machine guns, men revolt." [85]

The possibility of revolt is connected to one of the two senses of strategy discussed by Foucault at the end of "The Subject and Power." In a stable power relationship, one is able to act on the (somewhat predictable) actions of others. Thus, the male knows that the adoption of a certain attitude will produce a certain behavior in the female, the teacher knows that a certain level of professional status will result in certain responses by colleagues and students, the factory owner is able to rely on the wage relation to provide a steady supply of labor, and so on. Even within this relatively stable power relation, however, the individual acted on still retains his or her independence. Clearly, however, the freedom utilized in a particular setting is relative to that setting. For instance, Foucault gives the example of a plan by factory owners to encourage savings among workers. By promoting this as a value, the owners hope to tie their workers down to one job, reducing absenteeism and job hopping. The workers learn their lesson—only "too well"—and go on to organize a strike fund with their savings.[86]

Power relations that are productive and efficient cannot be based on permanent physical coercion. The individuals involved must truly decide to enter into the game described by a particular power relation. Once on the playing field, participants do not lose their capacity for reasoned choice or refusal, which always exists at least as a potential. "There is no relationship," Foucault says, "without the means of escape or possible flight."[87] One reason for the unconditioned character of this claim is every power relationship's need for willing players. Certain conditions must be met if "those who are acted upon" are to continue their willing and thus productive participation. There is a kind of freedom inherent, then, in the power relationship itself, and with this freedom exists the possibility of subverting or modifying the power relationship.

In our efforts to specify the content of Foucault's comments about the "plebeian element" active in revolts and opposition to power, we have identified two aspects. First, the epistemological argument drawn from Nietzsche asserts that although individuals and social structures are without a doubt historically produced by determinate systems of power, the idea of construction is not to be understood in an exhaustive sense. Rather, individuals are selectively fashioned in order to produce human material conducive to a particular social and political arrangement. Other elements—though not "truer" or more "human" ones—are suppressed by or subordinated to the currently dominant power relationship. Though not emphasized, these other drives, instincts, and tensions do not disappear and can provide a basis for resisting a particular power formation. "Individuals" are indeed "produced." But they are not created wholly and exclusively in terms of the power relations they inhabit.

In addition, the valuations associated with power relations are always reversible. There is always the possibility of challenging the significance or function of a particular classification or construction of subjectivity. The plurality of power relations in society and their interaction, mutual encouragement, but also their interference with one another inevitably produce a plurality of perspectives from which comparative assessments can be made. The very fact that the resulting subjectivity for individuals is plural rather than unified acts as a partial guarantee that a specific power relation (and there is never just one) will never succeed in wholly capturing and completely determining the individual.

Second, Foucault's notion of the "plebs" can be further clarified by reference to the need for freedom if a power relation is to produce the kind of useful behavior needed to make it profitable and efficient. Systems of power that rely on coercion for their operation make poor use of the human material at their disposal.

There is something incomplete, however, about our elucidation of the "plebeian aspect" up until now. With both points above, the impression is likely to form that the only kind of freedom Foucault recognized comes from the existence of two kinds of space: that left unaccounted for by a particular constitution of an individual, and that required for the operation of a power relation. These are indeed crucial elements, but in a number of places Foucault talks about the need to move beyond currently dominant power relations to something new. This might sound like a return to the theme of revolutionary transcendence, but in fact the transcendence Foucault has in mind has little to do with the term as it is usually understood.

One key concept that pops up a number of times in Foucault's writings is "imagination." "We have to imagine and build up what we could be," he says in one place, in opposition to subjectivity as now understood.[88] Similarly, he points to the need to "imagine new schemas of politicization."[89] The very "attitude of modernity" is tied to a "desperate eagerness" to "imagine" the world other than it is.[90] At the deepest level, Foucault's objection to totalizing, essentialist themes such as natural rights and humanism is that they restrict the potentially freer play of human thought and action.[91]

The possibility of imagining these new freedoms must be accounted for. It does not appear that the two elements of the "plebeian aspect" discussed up to now do so. The fact that power relations are "actions upon actions," requiring the willing cooperation of those on both sides of the relation, points to a freedom that is internal to and expressed through the existing power relationship. True, Foucault speaks of the necessity of exit points in a power relationship. These exit points, however, exist as possible countermoves within a strategic situation rather than as actual doors leading to a position outside it. Similarly, the realization that the construction of individuals and social environments is never total, never results in a closed system, although it points to the possibility of "counterconstructions," does not tell us much about how they would be realized.

A different approach to the "plebeian aspect" is signaled in Foucault's introduction to Georges Canguilhem's *The Normal and the Pathological*.[92] There he asserts that humans live of necessity in a "conceptually structured environment." The usual charge against "concepts" made by "life" philosophers of the early twentieth century is that their abstract character inevitably distorted our comprehension of the objects they purported to describe.[93] But for Foucault the fact that an individual structures the surrounding environment with the use of concepts "does not prove that he has been diverted from life by some oversight or that a historical drama has separated him from it; but only that he lives in a certain way. . . . Forming concepts is one way of living, not of killing life; it is one way of living in complete mobility and not immobilizing life."[94]

Once a social world is constructed, however, cognitive activity does not simply come to an end. The production of concepts introduces innovations into this environment, ones that have the potential to introduce mutations.[95] In the life sciences, concepts introduce the possibility of error: "At life's most basic level, the play of code and decoding leaves room for chance, which, before being disease, deficit or monstrosity, is something like a perturbation in the information system, something like a "mistake." In the extreme, life is what is capable of error."[96] This point is not limited to the life sciences, however: "If we admit that the concept is the answer that life itself gives to this chance, it must be that error is at the root of what makes human thought and history. The opposition of true and false, the values we attribute to both, the effects of power that different societies . . . link to this division—even all this is perhaps only the latest response to this possibility of error, which is intrinsic to life."[97]

The concept, which both responds to and initiates the possibility of error, is that around which true-false distinctions are deployed. Error and chance make possible new configurations of the true-false distinction. Different conceptions of what it means to be human as well as different ideas of what power relations are legitimate can result from this "possibility of error, which is intrinsic to life." It is this potential for mistakes that is not fully accounted for in a description of freedom restricted to the historically specific dynamics of interlocked strategies associated with power relations.

Whereas Nietzsche, as Foucault says, believed that "truth was the most profound lie," Canguilhem sees truth as "the most recent error."[98] If there is a kind of freedom here, it obviously has even less to do with some final form of human liberation than it does with the more restricted, locally specific kinds of freedom that Foucault discusses in "The Subject and Power." Instead of reading revolts as revolutions—or, for that matter, as hopeless and impossible gestures—Foucault can be understood as arguing that they should be seen as "errors" in the sense described above. It does seem, then, that Foucault is introducing a sense of freedom that in a way transcends the current alignment of forces so as to create something new.

We already know that normative truths about human nature are criticized by Foucault as simultaneously vague and overly restrictive in their depiction of human freedom—and criticized also for producing some of the worst disasters in human history. But as we can see from the above linking of error, concepts, truth, and the possibility of transformation, some idea of truth must indeed be retained. If concepts and the true-false distinctions tied to them are a way of living life rather than a means to smother it, if truth is not the biggest lie but only the most recent mutation, what objection can there be to a commitment to truth? Put this way, Foucault has no objection. His goal is not to destroy truth but to explore the history and contingencies that make it up in order to determine the possibilities for surpassing the restrictions it currently imposes.[99]

From one side, error is at the root of human thought in the sense that it is what produces new concepts to replace old ones. From the other, thought—in the sense Foucault wishes to use the term—is a means of freeing ourselves from ossified concepts and moving onto new territory. Thought both produces concepts and makes it possible to criticize them. Seen from this second perspective, "thought . . . is what allows one to step back from [a] way of acting or reacting, to present it to oneself as an object of thought and question it as to its meaning, its conditions, and its goals. *Thought is freedom in relation to what one does*, the motion by which one detaches oneself from it, establishing it as an object, and reflects on it as a problem."[100] The word "thought," here, does not refer to philosophical reflection.[101] Rather, Foucault argued that the way we conceive of the world and our relation to it is central to our makeup. By excavating and questioning the way we view the world, new possibilities for introducing "error" into our lives are opened up. This is accomplished by using a form of criticism that neither strives for nor is based on some foundational ethic or set of norms. The kind of critique Foucault pursues "will not seek to identify the universal structures of all knowledge or of all possible moral action, but will seek to treat the instances of discourse that articulate what we think, say, and do as so many historical events."[102] These events can be reflected on and the constitutions of ourselves resulting from them considered, rejected, or even affirmed.

This sort of freedom does indeed appear to differ from the kind of relational freedom that Foucault discusses in "The Subject and Power." There, the existence of freedom is very much relative to the specific power relation in which individuals participate and the possibilities opened up by them. That appears to be an overly restrictive reading of Foucault's understanding of freedom. Standing behind power relations and the freedoms that Foucault asserts are associated with them is the thought that makes them possible. If that thought changes, the power relation and the kind of freedom associated with it change as well.

None of this is meant to justify a slide into voluntarism. Foucault admits that individuals and the types of practices, habits, and so on in which they engage are not "independent from the concrete determinations of social existence."[103] That is, individuals and groups are without a doubt born into and molded to interact with a historically singular mode of social existence. The interesting thing for Foucault, however, is that these universal structures (as he calls them) in which the individual is located do not directly determine the actions of individuals in society: "Singular forms of experience may perfectly well harbor universal structures; they may well not be independent from the concrete determinations of social existence. However, *neither those determinations nor those structures can allow for experience . . . except through thought.*"[104]

All kinds of practices, Foucault argues, are "inhabited" by thought — are mediated by it. That is why a history of thought, in Foucault's sense, would include not only the great philosophers but also the practitioners of various disciplines, administrators, social reformers — indeed, potentially all those who work to link a way of understanding a problem to the institutions and practices of society.[105] The "work of thought on itself" is possible because thought plays this mediating role between the universal structures in which an individual finds herself or himself and the customs, practices, and habits that the individual is called on to execute in the context of those structures.

We have identified three elements of the "plebeian aspect," which can be thought of as Foucault's replacement for the revolutionary paradigm that has structured political thought throughout most of this century. We will remember that for Foucault "there is certainly no such thing as 'the' plebs; rather there is, as it were, a certain plebeian quality or aspect. There is plebs in bodies, in souls, in individuals, in the proletariat, in the bourgeoisie, but everywhere in a diversity of forms and extensions, of energies and irreducibilities. This measure of plebs is not so much what stands outside relations of power as their limit, their underside, their counterstroke, that which responds to every advance of power by a move of disengagement."[106]

Each of the three "forms" that characterize the plebs can be thought of as "irreducibilities." First, of selective and plural constitution Foucault states: "The individual is not to be conceived as a sort of elementary nucleus. . . .

In fact, it is . . . one of the prime effects of power that certain bodies, certain gestures, certain discourses, certain desires, come to be identified and constituted as individuals."[107] Read from a determinist angle, such a description of the individual seems to call into question the possibility of oppositional activity. Interpreted from the Nietzschean side, however, the absolute nature of the constitution of individuals drains away. Individuals are always selectively constituted from a plurality of drives. One of the proofs of this is that constitution is never a single act but instead one that goes on all the time, in a plurality of spheres, with no one sphere being primary. There is no complete constitution of any individual. In addition, no individual is ever marked by just one kind of constitution.

Second, the formulation of individuals as ends, not means, familiar from its association with Kantian ethics, can be applied to Foucault's description of the minimum prerequisites of a modern power relationship. Only with Foucault it is not a maxim resulting from an appreciation of human nature but a necessary element in the construction of an efficient power relationship. The treatment of individuals as ends comes not from ethical but from strategic considerations of efficacy. Two conclusions follow: the principle of choice and the possibility of refusal are elements of the irreducible presence of freedom in a power relationship, and to this is joined the indefinite fate of all tactics and maneuvers, as we saw with the example of the workers using the employers' savings scheme to establish a strike fund. The attempt to influence, control, and render predictable the (voluntary) actions of others requires that the objects of one's action can choose among a variety of responses, drawing on resources from both within and without the power relationship. In addition, the "playing field" and its rules as established by a certain power relationship, along with the maneuvers executed on it, provide players with sometimes unintended resources and opportunities for counterattacks.

Finally, at the same time, the role of thought helps to explain the existence of freedom within power relationships while also suggesting the possibility of moving beyond them to something new. In "The Subject and Power," Foucault discusses the characteristic feature of modern power relationships as a "set of actions upon other actions."[108] Seen this way, "power is less a confrontation between two adversaries . . . than a question of government," where this last term is understood as the guidance and coordination of human material.[109] Coercion and its violence, along with consent and its voluntarism, are not at the core of the art of government — rather, they act as resources for the latter. The best way to control the range and choice of options open to participants in a power relationship is to turn some of its key prerequisites into accepted and, finally, unquestioned ways of thinking. This end may be achieved with the help of violence and may require a notion of consent to make it legitimate. But neither violence nor consent is at the heart of what makes a structure of power acceptable. The necessary mediation of thought does not, however, force us to conclude that critical activity confronts a dead end. Such a pessimistic conclusion is warranted only if we insist on seeing ourselves behind the bars of a totality—itself a kind of thought whose effects on our habits and assumptions can be questioned. Foucault believes that "criticism . . . does not mark out impassable boundaries or describe closed systems; it does bring to light transformable singularities. These transformations could not take place except by means of a working of thought upon itself." [110]

Modes of thought produce practices, gestures, and habits. "There is no experience which is not a way of thinking." [111] It follows that for one set of actions to have its impact on another set, thought is the irreducible transmitting medium: "There is always a little thought even in the most stupid institutions; there is always thought even in silent habits." [112] The consequence Foucault derives from this is very much at odds with a pessimistic assessment of the possibilities of social action. Indeed, moving beyond today's power structures to something new is not only possible but inevitable. This something new is not seen, however, in terms of a transcendence of a profane reality. The source of real change is not revolt in service to an ideal: rather, it is the inevitability of error. No structure of power, as we saw above, is able to produce or maintain itself except by shaping the human material that makes it up in a certain way. The power relation, that is, is imbued through and through with "thought"— ways of perceiving oneself and one's relation with others. It is the fact that power relations must be channeled through this medium of thought that introduces the possibility of "errors of transcription," to use a genetic metaphor. It is impossible to conscript the activity of thought once and for all to the interests of one side of a power relationship—it would stop being "thought" in that case. This leads Foucault to characterize thought as irreducible. Its use in establishing and maintaining power relationships is simultaneously necessary and hazardous. There is no guarantee, for instance, that today's silently accepted habit will not become tomorrow's unaccepted invasion of the human personality: "Criticism is a matter of flushing out . . . thought and trying to change it: to show that things are not as self-evident as one believed, to see that which is accepted as self-evident will no longer be accepted as such. Practicing criticism is a matter of making facile gestures difficult. . . . As soon as one can no longer think things as one formerly thought them, transformation becomes both very urgent, very difficult, and quite possible." [113]

We can see how this third plebeian aspect plays a fundamental role in the previous two. The criticism of old ways of thinking—as embodied in practices—often ends up pointing to those elements of ourselves that have been left behind or suppressed in the familiar structures of experience (the first plebeian aspect). At the same time, one of the most important "exit points" of any active power relationship (the second plebeian aspect) is going to be the possibility that individuals or groups will perceive their role from a perspective incompatible with the continued functioning of the power relationship.

Three irreducibilities, then, make up Foucault's "plebeian aspect": (1) we can be constituted only selectively, with other constitutions always possible; (2) modern power does not work with slaves; in constructing a playing field where actions work on actions, choice, countermoves, and oppositional strategies are always going to be possible; and (3) thought is the irreplaceable conduit of power; as a consequence, old constructions can be changed or discarded and new ones created. It is this last possibility that Foucault explores in his treatment of "technologies of the self," to which we now turn.

Varieties of Morality

In the introduction to *The Use of Pleasure*, Foucault explained his decision to interrupt the course of study begun with *The History of Sexuality*. The focus of the latter was on a criticism of the "repressive hypothesis," which conceived of sexuality as a constant factor that was repressed and deformed by various power formations. Let our essential sexuality bloom without hypocritical constraints, repression theorists maintained, and human liberation, in this and perhaps other fields as well, would result.[114] Foucault's contrasting view is captured by the "power-knowledge" phrase: Sexuality (like the individual) was created by power, not repressed by it. If we ask ourselves critically how we have been hurt by power, we should look not for the answer in those essential features of ourselves that have been crushed by it but for whatever features have been created by it—which we now think of as essential parts of ourselves.

The difficulty associated with such a self-assessment—How do I gain access to and criticize what power has quite literally made of me?—leads Foucault to a significant reworking of his material. He admits that the "rejection of [the repressive] hypothesis was not sufficient by itself."[115] What that rejection and the associated alternative of power-knowledge as an interpretive framework failed to account for was "the forms within which individuals are able, are obliged, to recognize themselves as subjects of this sexuality."[116]

In other words, what was missing was the element of self-referentiality that

would make it possible for the individual to establish a certain distance between herself or himself and that part of the self—however essential it might
be—constituted by power. A theoretical shift was now required "in order to
analyze what is termed 'the subject.' "[117] It would be wrong, however, to assert
that earlier modes of analysis failed to address the question of the subject. The
shift in question is not from ignoring the subject to confronting it but from
an account that focuses on external forces impinging on the individual to one
that also takes fuller account of the individual as a crucial relay point in the
workings of power. It is not enough for a knowledge of madness to develop,
combined with rules for its development and implementation of its findings in
a social setting. In addition, categories of individuals must come to see themselves as mad in the appropriate way. But in learning how to be governed or
how to govern themselves in accordance with a certain construction of subjectivity, individuals can also learn how not to be governed. Opened up, then, as
both a possible area of investigation and a field of human liberty are "those intentional and voluntary actions by which men not only set themselves rules of
conduct but also seek to transform themselves, to change themselves in their
singular being."[118]

With the appearance of a subject capable of contributing something to its
own constitution, Foucault seeks to retain a nonfoundationalist understanding of subjectivity while he sketches his understanding of the ambiguous term
"morality." Three senses of morality are discussed in *The Use of Pleasure:*

(1) "Morality" can refer to a set of codes or proscriptions that is propagated throughout society.[119] Though Foucault makes it clear that moral
codes can be more or less explicit than this, a simple example would be
the Ten Commandments.

(2) Morality can refer to the behavior that members of society adopt
with regard to the proscriptions—obeying or rejecting them, for example.[120]

(3) Next, Foucault discusses the various ways in which one can carry
out the dictates of a morality. As an example, he points to the demand
that marital partners practice strict conjugal fidelity: "There will be many
ways   to practice that austerity, many ways to 'be faithful,' " from ob-
servance of certain external obligations to a struggle with and mastery
over desire itself.[121]

According to Foucault, the bare existence of a moral code of some kind
leaves open a broad array of possible relations that ethical subjects will establish with themselves. This is what Foucault calls the "determination of the ethi-

cal substance."[122] Before an individual carries out a prescription, he "delimits that part of himself that will form the object of his moral practice."[123] Individuals might focus on the passions that interfere with the operation of their reason or on establishing hierarchical or reciprocal relations of some kind with others. To take an example, acts of adultery might be barred to us, but to enforce that law, individuals might work to subdue their passions or submit themselves to the guidance of a teacher. Depending on the path chosen, a different kind of morality is exercised and a different focal point for subjectivity is identified.

Another element in the task of forming oneself as an ethical subject is the "mode of subjection" practiced, with which the individual "defines his position relative to the precept he will follow."[124] We might subject ourselves to a rule as a result of our membership in a group or as part of a tradition we affirm — many other possibilities could be listed. A third consideration is the kind of activity chosen to put the (amorphous or explicit) code into effect. The goal of sexual austerity can be achieved through complete renunciation, through the study and application of a set of precepts, or "through a decipherment as painstaking, continuous, and detailed as possible, of the movements of desire in all its hidden forms, including the most obscure."[125]

What is the status of this self-referential subject that appears so suddenly in Foucault's work? As some critics have pointed out, it appears that with *The Use of Pleasure* Foucault returns to more traditional accounts of subjectivity.[126] But the Foucault of the early 1980s is best understood as finally embracing a more recognizably Nietzschean approach to the subject. As we saw above in the case of morality, different kinds of subjectivity with very diverse structures and procedures are produced by varying applications of a moral code. In addition to the multiple possible subjective forms within a specific area of life, such as morality, Foucault believes dissimilar subjective forms are at work in diverse fields of activity. A certain kind of freedom is supported by the plurality of subjective forms. We are not free because we ultimately possess ourselves but because no one, finally and irreversibly, possesses us. As Foucault notes, each of us is not so much a unitary individual as a collection of subindividuals who in turn are propelled by distinct drives and motivations.[127] The various relations of dominance and submission among these subindividuals are never once and for all finalized. This very instability and the possibility for change that it provides is, for Foucault, the locus of freedom for each individual.[128]

It goes without saying that the broader social and cultural setting in which an individual finds himself or herself will be a limiting factor for the forms of subjectivity that can be pursued. As Foucault shows in his discussion of morality in the introduction to *The Use of Pleasure,* although the moral act is often performed for its own sake, "it also aims beyond [itself], to the establishing of a moral conduct that commits an individual, not only to other actions always in conformity with values and rules, but to a certain mode of being, a mode of being characteristic of the ethical subject."[129] Foucault summarizes his description of the elements contributing to the formation of a specific subjectivity in the area of morality as follows:

> All moral action involves a relationship with the reality in which it is carried out and a relation to the code to which it refers; but also implies a certain relationship with the self. . . . There is no specific moral action that does not refer to a unified moral conduct; no moral conduct that does not call for the forming of oneself as an ethical subject; and no forming of the ethical subject without "modes of subjectivation" and an "ascetics" or "practices of the self" that support them. Moral action is indissociable from these forms of self-activity, and they do not differ any less from one morality to another than do the systems of values, rules, and interdictions.[130]

Thus, the subject is conceived as the product of a number of practices, both individual and social. And not only is the subject a product of these practices, but—especially in the modern setting—more than one form of subjectivity is created to deal with the diverse fields of activity in which individuals find themselves called on to act. The individual in Foucault's account is still caught up in "power relations," no doubt, but since she or he participates in forming some and potentially modifies the effect of others through interaction with them, the structuralist ethos is left behind. Both social and individual contexts are identified as arenas for the creation of practices, individuals, and truths. In other words, a space for freedom has been cleared.

Foucault's general comments on the dual character of morality—both socially and individually produced—are elaborated on in a concrete social setting both in *The Use of Pleasure* and *The Care of the Self*. Moral behavior is determined against the background of the Greek polis in *The Use of Pleasure*. The focus here will be on *The Care of the Self*, however, because it deals with a historical period that, Foucault felt, shares with our present some issues concerning the relation of the individual to a sometimes alienating social context—specifically, the deteriorating Roman Empire of the second century.

> Beginning with Christianity we have . . . an appropriation of morality by the theory of the subject. But a moral experience essentially centered on the subject no longer seems satisfactory to me today. Because of this, cer-

tain questions pose themselves to us in the same terms as they were posed in antiquity. The search for styles of existence as different from each other as possible seems to me to be one of the points on which particular groups in the past may have inaugurated searches we are engaged in today.[131]

The Roman Empire and its urban societies are an interesting choice for Foucault. As Foucault notes, some commentators point to the emergence of an individualism in the first and second centuries that is said to accord more importance to the private lives people led, with a concomitant alienation from the political realm. The rise of ethical concerns associated with figures such as Seneca and Marcus Aurelius is then said to grow in the soil of a fractured political existence. Summarizing this account, Foucault cites the view that as individuals were "less firmly attached to the cities, more isolated from one another, and more reliant on themselves, they sought in philosophy rules of conduct that were more personal. Not everything," Foucault admits, "is false in a schema of this sort,"[132] but as his own account unfolds, it becomes clear that Foucault believes that not much of it is true, either. What Foucault intends to show is that the ancient empires were far from being a dress rehearsal for modern alienation and atomism. Foucault never used history as a mirror that would tell us what we are through our reflection in a distant time. As always, the discussion of the Roman Empire will show us the contingent and unnecessary character of what we are by demonstrating, in this case, how a situation that is in some respects similar to our own produced problems and patterns of interaction vastly different from our own.[133]

The first problem that Foucault identifies with the account of imperial ethics as a retreat from politics and social life is an intellectual one. The term "individualism," Foucault argues, is not used in a sufficiently subtle manner. In fact, "entirely different realities are lumped together" in the use of this term.[134] The bourgeois countries of the West during the nineteenth century are examples of "societies in which private life is highly valued, in which it is carefully protected and organized, in which it forms the center of reference for behaviors and one of the principles of their valuation." Ironically, however, this kind of individualism is relatively weak, as the "relations of oneself to oneself are largely undeveloped."[135] Foucault does not expand on the supposed weakness of this kind of individualism, but his remarks suggest that an individualism conceived almost exclusively in terms of the protections that safeguard it tends to bypass—or presupposes the answer to—the more fundamental question of the value and purpose of the subjectivity to be protected. Only if subjectivity is confronted as a shaped product of diverse forces—with the possibility of re-formation that this implies—will a "relation of oneself to oneself" become possible.

Foucault mentions two other brands of individualism. First there is the domestic realm of family life, where patrimonial interests dominate. But more important for our interests—and certainly more centrally thematic for *The Care of the Self* as a whole—is the third type of individualism, which has to do with "the intensity of the relations to self, that is, of the forms in which one is called upon to take oneself as an object of knowledge and a field of action, so as to transform, correct, and purify oneself, and find salvation."[136]

The problem with the functioning of disciplinary power is that individuals are subjected to forms of power that are extremely difficult to identify and almost impossible to resist. What Foucault sees as valuable about technologies of the self is the possibility that an individual might be produced who is more aware of the possible effects of disciplinary procedures and so stands in a better position to resist them.

Foucault lists a group of practices and exercises developed by Greek and especially Roman thinkers of the first two centuries, through which their practitioners sought to "convert to themselves."[137] This last phrase refers simply to the need individuals felt during this period to focus on themselves, not to allow external commitments and responsibilities to infringe on the task of self-care. The practices and exercises involved the use of journals to establish a correspondence with oneself—a time for meditation set aside to recall and contemplate guiding principles or useful aphorisms. Letters to and discussions with others on these themes, whether with friends or teachers, are also mentioned. Seneca is shown going through a strict examination of his day's activity in order to assess progress—for instance, in the overcoming of bad habits.[138] Foucault works hard to distinguish the motivation behind such self-examination from the later use of broadly similar techniques on the part of Christianity. He points to the Roman Stoic Epictetus as providing "the highest philosophical development" of the theme of self-care.[139] In this practice, mental representations must be examined with the same care as is a suspect coin. And the standard by which this currency is to be judged will be "the famous Stoic canon that marks the division between that which does not depend on us and that which does." A similar Christian concern with representations, on the other hand, centered the inquiry on what came from God and what came from the devil, which in turn required an increasingly advanced and subtle hermeneutic. But for the Roman Stoic, "to keep constant watch over one's representations, or to verify their marks the way one authenticates a currency, is not to inquire (as will be done later in Christianity) concerning the deep origin of the idea that presents itself; it is not to try to decipher a meaning hidden beneath the visible representation; it is to assess the relationship between oneself and that which is represented, so as to accept in the relation to the self only that which can depend on the subject's free and rational choice."[140] The Roman Stoic appears to possess a knowledge of self, of the quality of his relation to himself that would allow him to "resist power," if we take power to mean external forms of coercion and domination, modes of subjectivity imported from the outside. That is precisely the beauty and relevance Foucault discovers in the Stoic care of the self in comparison with the normalizing mode of subjectification characteristic of the disciplines and "biopower."

What Foucault very much wished to avoid in his work on power and individualization in the 1970s was any concession to the idea that subjectivity, however conceived, was prior to the social and institutional arrangements individuals found themselves in. Whether dressed in liberal or phenomenological garb, such views were simply bankrupt to Foucault. The rejection of these views led him, as I have already argued, to adopt a broadly "constructed" approach with regard to the constitution of individuals. The irony dogging this effort throughout the 1970s, however, was that the individuals created by power as unable to generate forces of their own that are "resistant," as Foucault says, to power. This difficulty is what leads Foucault to admit, at the beginning of the 1980s, that "when I was studying asylums, prisons, and so on, I insisted maybe too much on the techniques of domination."[141] The problem with such an approach to subjectivity, as Foucault goes on to say, is that a purely external account of the relationship between power and individuals falls into the error of understanding power in terms of violence and coercion,[142] an error that Foucault warned us about frequently but which he admits he fell into himself during the 1970s.[143]

In *The Care of the Self* Foucault points out that it is possible to conceive of other forms of discipline — self-disciplines, as it were — and that these provide examples of the functioning of power, examples that do not show coercion over oneself or others. In addition, they have the merit of acting as potentially defensive barriers to the "techniques of domination" associated with the disciplines that Foucault surveyed in *Discipline and Punish*.

Interestingly, however, these self-disciplines advocated by the Roman Stoics often appear similar to the superficially liberal "juridical model of possession": "One 'belongs to himself,' one is 'his own master.' . . ; one is answerable to oneself, one is *sui juris;* one exercises over oneself an authority that nothing limits or threatens, one holds the *potestas sui.*[144] The difference with the liberal account of the person is that this self-ownership is not achieved formally and abstractly but substantively, as one who takes oneself as an object to be developed and cultivated: self-ownership or self-possession is not a presupposition but rather the consequence of a lifelong practice. The parallel between what the Stoics advocated in the first and second centuries and what Foucault recommends for his contemporaries is strongest at this point. In the interview published as "On the Genealogy of Ethics," Foucault is asked about the kind of ethics it would be desirable to fashion in the modern context. In response, Foucault complains that art is reserved for objects but should be extended to individuals,[145] just as Nietzsche recommends in section 290 of *The Gay Science.* Precisely this self-aestheticization was achieved by the Roman Stoics: "The experience of self that forms itself in this possession . . . is the experience of a pleasure that one takes in oneself. The individual who has finally succeeded in gaining access to himself is, for himself, an object of pleasure."[146]

Foucault anticipates two related objections to this vision of an emphasis on self—or "conversion to self," as he calls it. The heightened importance accorded personal ethics in the Roman world is said by some to result from "a weakening of the political and social framework within which the lives of individuals unfold. Being less firmly attached to the cities, more isolated from one another, and more reliant on themselves, they sought in philosophy rules of conduct that were more personal."[147] And indeed, taken by itself, Foucault's account of the care of the self leaves itself open to the objection that while it might make for more fulfilled individuals, perhaps themselves more resistant to disciplinary encroachments, it makes no provision for the social interaction among individuals.[148] As Foucault himself has pointed out in "The Subject and Power," the "trick" at the heart of Western societies, whose springs and sleight of hand must be exposed and understood, is the "combination in the same political structures of individualization techniques, and of totalization procedures."[149] One way to understand this combination would be as follows: On the one hand, through dividing practices some individuals are selected out as "cases"—the sick, mad, delinquents, sexual perverts, and so on. Persons so identified are the true "individuals" of our society in Foucault's view.[150] They are the ones who are picked out, exhaustively analyzed, about whom thorough histories are written, and so on. Out of this series of exclusionary practices, into which so much effort is invested in determining what makes one mentally ill or deviant, a concomitant picture of health or normality takes shape that is then applied to society as a whole through state institutions as well as by other power centers. Thus, an ethic that focuses exclusively on the care of the self would seem to disarm itself in the face of this two-pronged offensive. As individuals, we might be able to make "cases" out of ourselves and truly develop our own individuality, but this would have little or no effect on the continued efficacy of the "demonic" societal apparatus as a whole.[151] A few of us might be able to develop a discipline-resistant ownership of self, but such ownership would come at the cost of social isolation from the public sphere. Foucault cannot help but be aware that such a reading of his views would provide critics with additional proof of Foucault's "conservatism" and "quietism."[152]

Foucault's first response is to deny that the care of the self in the period of the Roman Empire and Hellenic monarchies was in fact accompanied by social withdrawal: "It needs to be emphasized, on the contrary, that local political activity was not stifled by the establishment and strengthening of those great overarching structures. City life, with its institutional rules, its interests at stake, its struggles, did not disappear as a result of the widening of the contest in which it was inscribed." Foucault goes on to suggest that the reading of this period of history as a "universe become too vast" was a feeling anachronistically imposed on the Greco-Roman world.[153] The picture of a unitary imperial power was, in fact, just as false as the story of a Stoic inward-turning retreat from it: "Rather than imagining a reduction or cessation of political activities through the effects of a centralized imperialism, one should think in terms of the organization of a complex space. . . . It was a space in which the centers of power were multiple; in which the activities, the tensions, the conflicts were numerous; . . . and in which the equilibria were obtained through a variety of transactions."[154] In this complex space, local powers and their political life were not so much crushed as utilized for the collection of taxes, the staffing of armies, and so forth, which in turn politicized the municipalities.[155]

It was in this context that the ethic of the care of the self flourished. It was exercised not to achieve solitude, Foucault argues, but to define and control the conditions under which one could enter political life. This control also implies, of course, the possibility of refraining from participation. But abstention was neither dictated nor the logical outcome of the care of the self.[156]

In addition to considering historical questions about the relation of the Stoics to the imperial world, Foucault addresses the contemporary bias standing behind the assumption that the cultivation of self is in contradiction to participation in social life and involvement with others. Two sources of this bias are identified. First, a focus on the care of self is often viewed as immoral, "as a means of escape from all possible rules."[157] The Christian tradition in particular, according to Foucault, preached self-renunciation, the very opposite of self-care, as the path to self-knowledge. A secular tradition associated with Kant also "respects external law as the basis for morality": "our morality . . . insists that the self is that which one can reject."[158] Second, "philosophy from Descartes to Husserl" has identified the thinking subject, abstractly conceived, as the foundation for knowledge.[159] These two continuing trends in the modern world, one moral and the other philosophical, have made it very difficult for us to conceive of the care of the self as playing anything other than a suspect moral and epistemological role. Foucault concludes that in the modern world, "there has been an inversion between the hierarchy of the two principles of antiquity, 'Take care of yourself' and 'Know thyself.' In Greco-Roman culture knowledge of oneself appeared as the consequence of taking care of yourself. In the modern world, knowledge of oneself constitutes the fundamental principle."[160]

Foucault's answer, especially to the first objection, is contained in *The Care of the Self*. Now, Foucault was adamant that his histories were not to be seen as providing examples of behavior for us to copy today. "There is," he writes, "no exemplary value in a period which is not our period." One of the things history can do, however, is show us how something that exists arose as "a historical event, one which was not at all necessary, not linked to human nature, or to any anthropological necessity."[161] It is not that we should live like the Stoics of the first and second centuries but that, contrary to what our expectations might be, they provide instances of an ethic of care of the self which leads to profound self-knowledge and which improves and deepens social relations. Foucault places special emphasis on this point: the practices of the self-employed in the Greco-Roman world "constituted, not an exercise in solitude, but a true social practice,"[162] which contributed to "an intensification of social relations."[163] Easiest to identify are the schools and communities that grew up to promote such practices. More informal, and perhaps more consequential, was the interaction between friends, where one would ask for advice and the other would gladly give it, with these roles being understood as interchangeable.[164] More generally, however, Foucault identifies the devotion to self during the period under review as part of a response to a crisis of subjectivity. The "agonistic game" of establishing one's superiority over others that was characteristic of Foucault's description of the self in the Greek city-states, as outlined in *The Use of Pleasure*, now "had to be integrated into a far more extensive and complex field of power relations" typical of empire if the individual were to succeed in forming himself "as the ethical subject of his actions . . . which could enable him to submit to rules and give purpose to his existence."[165] The motivations of the movement around care of the self were themselves social and were designed to make participation in a more complex social and political sphere possible (if one so chose) while ensuring that one's own autonomy and freedom were affirmed.

It is difficult to avoid reading Foucault's discussion of Stoic ethics, along with the context in which it was practiced, as anything other than a thinly veiled commentary on our present. Surely one of Foucault's prime objectives is to respond to those who insist that no morality or ethical action is possible absent universal, abstract, timeless, and normative guidelines about the essence of human behavior. In *The Care of the Self* Foucault does suggest an alternative moral (if not normative) framework: the care of the self. Disciplinary power is to be resisted because it impedes one's ability to form oneself as a subject of one's own activities. It was in this sense that Foucault turned to Kant's little essay "*Was ist Aufklärung?*" Near the end of his essay also titled "What Is Enlightenment?" Foucault complains, in a manner similar to Kant, that we are not yet "mature."[166] For Kant this meant that we did not use the reason present in all of us to order our lives and societies but instead relied on external authorities such as priests and royalty. For Foucault our immaturity consists in our inability to shape our own subjectivities in the face of the silent and invisible work of the disciplines. Indeed, the assumption that subjectivity is a universal birthright bars the insight that the attainment of subjectivity is a task at all and effectively gives free rein to those forces that would shape it in one way or another.

No legal or institutional constraints dictated the practice of the care of the self, which included the exercise of a rigorous ethics, in the empires at the beginning of the first millennium A.D. Nor was such activity the outcome of a view of humanity's position in the universe relative to God.[167] As I have tried to outline above, Foucault put a noticeable emphasis on the social—as opposed to the solitary—context in which the care of the self was exercised. This social setting involved, as already mentioned, the circulation of roles, as individuals at different times sought and gave advice. The resulting mutual interaction led to a "round of exchanges with the other and a system of reciprocal obligations."[168] Foucault is also insistent in pointing out that the cultivation of the self was often seen as an important prerequisite for participation in political life rather than an escape from an immoral or alienating order.

Since at least part of the aim of self-cultivation centered on the conditions under which one could perform socially, without losing oneself in the increasingly complex political scene associated with empire, it turned out that "the intensification of concern for the self" went "hand in hand with a valorization of the other." This is because, according to Foucault, "the dominion of oneself over oneself is increasingly manifested in the practices of obligations with regard to others."[169] The mutually obligatory mode of self-cultivation is particularly evident in the case of marriage, where "the relationship one establishes with oneself and the rapport one forms with the other," far from contradicting each other, are instead mutually reinforcing. "The art of conjugality is an integral part of the cultivation of the self."[170]

Foucault is attempting to show us recognizably moral stances that have a source other than the subject with rights or a universal morality. His point is that it is "not always the same part of ourselves, or of our behavior, which is relevant for ethical judgment."[171] There was, for instance, certainly a tendency in Stoic ethics, which Foucault himself mentions, for the duties we perform and the obligations we owe to be conceived in terms of the human being's status as a rational being.[172] But many of the same practices and obligations were equally enforced in the context of an aesthetics of existence, where the relationship with self was the dominant factor, to which other sorts of activities were secondary, if indispensable. Human beings can be conceived as rational agents or as individuals uniquely equipped to practice self-care and be able, under both rubrics, to develop personal and social ethics.[173]

Foucault's Enlightenment

As we have discussed, the plebeian aspect is Foucault's replacement for the revolutionary paradigm of the twentieth century. That paradigm was criticized for its depiction of society as a totality that only a revolution could transform. But as we saw as well, the plebeian aspect also includes the possibility of significant transformations from one power context to another.

How do technologies of the self fit into this account? In "Politics and Reason," Foucault refers to modern societies as "demonic." In "The Subject and Power," he uses a less dramatic formulation, referring to the "political 'double bind' which is the simultaneous individualization and totalization of modern power structures."[174] In response, he calls for "new forms of subjectivity," and it is easy to see the link between this and the discussion of technologies of the self in *The Care of the Self* and elsewhere.

The political relevance of "technologies of the self" is at times obscured, however, by Foucault's argument linking them to an aesthetics of existence.

"In our society," Foucault argues in one place, "art has become something which is related only to objects and not to individuals, or to life. . . . But couldn't everyone's life become a work of art? Why should the lamp or the house be an art object, but not our life?"[175] The whole tone and content of at least *The Use of Pleasure* and perhaps portions of *The Care of the Self* have contributed to the impression that Foucault was enamored of Greek and Roman practices of the self. Adding to the confusion, however, is Foucault's own denial that he viewed Greek practices of the self as a viable alternative to modern forms of subjectivity.[176] In the critical literature it is often assumed that Foucault was promoting a nonpolitical kind of ethical self-cultivation in his final books and interviews.[177] This is then used to dismiss the late work as narcissistic, as representing a turn away from political concerns, and in any event a reversal of Foucault's previous views on subjectivity as an artifact of external powers. What remains unexplored by these critics, however, is the more politically oriented purpose behind Foucault's discussion of the technologies of the self.[178]

To examine this side of the matter, it would be well to consider an earlier form of the argument about the role of the individual in political activity. In "Truth and Power" and elsewhere, Foucault opposes the role of the "specific" to the "universal" intellectual.[179] This comparison does not involve the kind of aesthetic considerations that appear in later writings and so provides a good introduction to the political applicability of technologies of the self.

As Foucault presents it, the "universal" intellectual is typified by Enlightenment thinkers such as Voltaire who act as "the bearer[s] of values and significations in which all can recognize themselves."[180] Either as spokespersons for some revolutionary agent (the proletariat, the third world, and so on) or as such agents themselves, universal intellectuals speak of the world as it should be as opposed to its actual, profane existence. In this way, the universal intellectual is connected to the idea of totality discussed earlier, acting as the "consciousness/conscience of us all": "Just as the proletariat, by the necessity of its historical situation, is the bearer of the universal (but its immediate, unreflected bearer, barely conscious of itself as such), so the intellectual, through his moral, theoretical and political choice, aspires to be the bearer of this universality in its conscious, elaborated form."[181] In contrast to the intellectual who announces the "just-and-true-for-all,"[182] Foucault describes the emergence of the "specific intellectual," especially since World War II, though its origins can be traced back further. The psychiatrist, the technician, the social worker, the scientist—all figures that, ironically, Foucault elsewhere indicts for their complicity in a "society of normalization" — are here presented as potential agents of an alternative oppositional activity.[183] What separates these "local" intellectuals from their "universal" counterparts is the former's connection to restricted areas of concern because of their specific expertise. Foucault proposes:

> Within these different forms of activity, I believe it is quite possible . . . to do one's job as a psychiatrist, lawyer, engineer, or technician, and, on the other hand, to carry out in that specific area work that may properly be called intellectual, an essentially critical work. When I say "critical," I don't mean a demolition job, one of rejection or refusal, but a work of examination that consists of suspending as far as possible the system of values to which one refers when . . . assessing it. In other words: what am I doing at the moment I'm doing it? At the present time . . . doctors, lawyers, judges carry out a critical examination, a critical questioning of their own jobs that is an essential element in intellectual life.[184]

The example presented by Foucault is the atomic scientist J. Robert Oppenheimer, whose unmatched professional qualifications resulted in a singular capacity to speak out on nuclear issues. But as Foucault recognized, Oppenheimer in fact represented a unique linkage of the universal and specific intellectual. It was his "direct and localized relation to scientific knowledge and institutions that enabled him to speak with authority." But as "the nuclear threat affected the whole human race and the fate of the world, his discourse could at the same time be the discourse of the universal. Under the rubric of this protest, which concerned the entire world, the atomic expert brought into play his specific position in the order of knowledge. And for the first time, I think, the intellectual was hounded by political powers, no longer on account of the general discourse which he conducted, but because of the knowledge at his disposal: it was at this level that he constituted a political threat." [185]

Oppenheimer and others like him provide a special case of the connection between a universal discourse about the fate of humanity and a specific one related to precise technical knowledge. The knowledge of most specific intellectuals will not have such immediately broad implications. It remains local, applicable only to a restricted sphere. Just this kind of knowledge, however, is at the heart of the productive capacity of "biopower" or "power-knowledge." Knowledge of psychic states, of population trends, internal family dynamics, time management, "personnel relations," and dozens of other fields are the stuff out of which the "power" in "power-knowledge" is constructed.

In considering the oppositional potential of the specific intellectual, it is important to keep in mind two points made earlier. First, discourses are tactical elements in strategies, which, as Foucault says, are not once and for all in the service of one or the other side of a power relation. Rather, they circulate, often performing different roles—or the same role—in different strategies. Thus it should not come as too much of a surprise that disciplines attacked by Foucault in some places for their collaborative relationship to modern power are in other places pointed to as possible sites of resistance. Second, "no power," as Nietzsche says, "could maintain itself if its advocates were nothing but hypocrites."[186] The effectiveness of the strategic game Foucault has labeled "biopower" depends on the genuine independence of its individualizing and totalizing aspects. Of course, exceptions exist, but few specific intellectuals in the West see themselves as—nor are they in fact—functionaries of the state. However strategically effective this combination of independence and overall coordination might be—and clearly Foucault believes it has been tremendously resourceful—it makes possible in addition the existence of local sites of resistance.

In the "ascending" analysis of power promoted by Foucault, the truly productive site for the creation and application of the disciplines is the local setting of the clinic, prison, school, or hospital ward. In this context, it does seem to make sense for oppositional interests to focus on these more narrowly defined areas. But while arguing for the importance of redirecting oppositional activity to more local spheres, Foucault is also aware of the criticisms directed against confining oppositional activity to a restricted range. In one place, Foucault summarizes his critics' complaints as follows: " 'Beware: however ideally radical your intentions may be, your action is so localized and your objectives so isolated that at this particular spot the adversary will be able to handle the situation, to yield if necessary without in any way compromising his global position; even better, this will allow him to locate the sites of necessary transformation; and so you will have been recuperated.' "[187] This essentially Leninist argument makes room for the "local" struggle in one of only two ways: if it is able to symbolize adequately the general contradiction of society as a whole; or when it can act as the "weak link," allowing the whole chain of capitalist exploitation (or whatever) to be broken. But this argument, Foucault contends, is convincing only if one accepts the assumption on which it is based—namely, that societies are characterized by one essential contradiction around which everything else unfolds and against which everything must be measured. Drop that assumption, and the antilocal prejudice goes with it. As Foucault says,

"When I speak of power relations, of the forms of rationality which can rule and regulate them, I am not referring to Power—with a capital P—dominating and imposing its rationality upon the totality of the social body. In fact, there are power relations. They are multiple; they have different forms."[188]

Foucault is certainly right to jettison the Leninist argument about the weak link: a thesis, as Foucault comments, "which is barely on a level with the preliminary training given to a sublieutenant in the reserves."[189] We may also grant Foucault's argument that current power formations are a stew of will and chance rather than a tightly integrated, top-down structure. These considerations, however, may only reduce the difficulties faced by those engaged in local oppositions without eliminating them. Consciously planned or not, the strategies into which local circuits of power-knowledge fit are consequential for the individuals who inhabit them—this much Foucault does not dispute. In "Truth and Power" Foucault addresses this predicament: "The specific intellectual encounters certain obstacles and faces certain dangers. The danger of remaining at the level of conjunctural struggles, pressing demands restricted to particular sectors. The risk of letting himself be manipulated by the political parties or trade union apparatuses which control these local struggles. Above all, the risk of being unable to develop these struggles for lack of a global strategy or outside support; the risk too of not being followed, or only by very limited groups."[190]

Specific intellectuals, in other words, need an Oppenheimer effect: some way that their local struggles can participate in a broader assault on the circumstances that provide the environment for the disciplines in which they are active. Foucault suggests that the work of specific intellectuals can have such a cumulative effect by posing a challenge to the general "regime of truth" that governs the production of truthful and hence socially acceptable statements and acts.[191]

The "generality" to which local action can be related should not, however, be understood as a reintroduction of the totality through the back door. It is, instead, restricted to "the level of the Western societies from which we derive." Issues of "sickness and health . . . crime and the law; the . . . role of sexual relations, and so on" contribute to a "historically unique" set of questions that recur in a variety of forms.[192] Understanding the background sources of these forms can both inform the conduct of local struggles and provide a basis for coalitions and wider self-understandings.

Foucault admits, then, that local action can and should make reference to the broader circumstances in which it occurs. But as we have seen in Foucault's treatment of the specific intellectual, the emphasis is on the value of local, site-specific oppositional activity. Foucault gives three reasons for preferring a local over a global approach to change. First, it is in the local arena that new forms of power are invented, applied, and revised. "Power's condition of possibility . . . must not be sought in the primary existence of a central point."[193] In this context, "one must," as Foucault puts it, "conduct an *ascending* analysis of power, starting . . . from its infinitesimal mechanisms, which each have their own history, . . . their own techniques and tactics, and then see how these mechanisms of power have been—and continue to be—invested, colonized, . . . transformed, . . . extended, etc., by ever more general mechanisms."[194] Larger interests "engage with . . . technologies that are at once both relatively autonomous of power and act as its infinitesimal elements." This is, for Foucault, the fundamental feature of the construction of power in the modern era. If, then, "power is everywhere; not because it embraces everything, but because it comes from everywhere,"[195] a straightforward consequence is that the multiple local, relatively autonomous sites contributing to "power's condition of possibility" are plausible targets for effective resistance.

Second, the plurality of power refers not only to the existence of diverse centers of power but also to the variety of forces, technologies, and different kinds of knowledge that are pulled together to make up larger systems. A picture of power as a fractured entity, very much subject to change because it is so fragile, turns out to be Foucault's final assessment of power. In the previous paragraph, local resistance is preferred because locally produced knowledge and techniques are the building blocks of larger constructs. Here the consideration is that power formations, once constructed, are patched together from blocks that retain their autonomy and thus their hard edges. The fit among the different parts is always far from exact. This inexact fit has to do with the resistance that components of a strategy will offer to full incorporation. It is, in addition, not always in the interests of the broader power structure that all elements of a strategy be subsumed under one "rationality." This fractured depiction of power once again points to a preference for local forms of resistance.

Finally, we must, Foucault says, "turn away from all projects that claim to be global or radical." The reasoning behind this conclusion is based on the primary events of the twentieth century—fascism and its horrors and the failed revolutions in the East: "In fact we know from experience that the claim to escape from the system of contemporary reality so as to produce the overall programs of another society, of another way of thinking, another culture, another vision of the world, has led only to the return of the most dangerous traditions."[196] In the name of resolving a more fundamental contradiction, global and revolutionary projects for change miss the true sources of modern power, often reinstituting them under another banner. A small example would be Lenin's respect for the Taylor system of time management that forced workers in factories to economize their movements so as to keep up with an ever faster assembly line. Soon after taking power, Lenin called the Taylor system "a combination of the refined brutality of bourgeois exploitation and . . . [one] of the greatest scientific achievements in the field of analyzing mechanical motions during work." He called for the "study and teaching of the Taylor system" so as to "adapt it to our own ends."[197] Thus, the value of the goal acts as a legitimating cover for the reinscription of oppressive practices.

Foucault did not believe he was advocating an unfortunate but unavoidable retreat from "real" solutions into an inefficacious localism. Rather, as we just saw, he disdains projects of transformation of "society" for *their* impotence. He was convinced that local actions were the best way to introduce changes into the larger structures of power: "I prefer the very specific transformations that have proved to be possible in the last twenty years in a certain number of areas that concern our ways of being and thinking, relations to authority, between the sexes, . . . I prefer even these partial transformations . . . to the programs for a new man that the worst political systems have repeated throughout the twentieth century."[198] The fact that actions are local does not mean that they are forever disconnected from one another in their effects. There is room for cross-fertilization as well as alliances. What does have to be given up, however, is the "hope of ever acceding to a point of view that could give us access to any complete and definitive knowledge of what may constitute our historical limits."[199] In other words, there is no version of the "totality" in Foucault's understanding of Western societies.

The "specific intellectual" is one figure Foucault proposed would fit into a new emphasis on "local" struggles. This too is the context for the functioning of those "technologies of the self" that were discussed earlier. By beginning with the specific intellectual, we have temporarily avoided that part of Foucault's argument that emphasizes the values of artistic self-creation. It is now possible, however, to bring the aesthetic dimension of Foucault's approach to the self back in, placing it firmly in the context of the discussion of biopower and the unique importance that local sites of activity and struggle have within it. Once this is done, the connections among a number of terms and phrases that swirl about in Foucault's writings in uncertain relation to one another are exposed to view. At the same time, it will be possible to respond to the concern that an aesthetic approach to the self escalates the tendency toward social retreat and atomism.

As we saw earlier, Foucault wonders why our lives cannot be works of art when mundane objects like lamps or houses can. This seems to be an ill-advised comparison. The result could be the mistaken impression that what Foucault is really after is a society where individuals, no longer subject to the dictates of external agencies, pastoral or disciplinary, are allowed room to grow and blossom. What would the conditions for such a blossoming be? As Foucault has rejected global schemes for remaking society, the natural conse-quence appears to be a society in which some individuals develop an aesthetic relation to themselves while paying very little attention to the broader social context in which they and others must work. Society would be asked only to tolerate the array of unique individual types that would result. Now, this vision of society tolerating a spectrum of individual types may or may not be pleas-ing. It may even be plausibly inferred from some of Foucault's comments. It is not, however, his ultimate political view.

In "What Is Enlightenment," Foucault presents a much more carefully worked out discussion of the kind of "art" he wants to promote for the indi-vidual than we can extract from the lamp analogy. The kind of artwork dis-cussed in this essay is no arbitrary or whimsical expression of personal pref-erences but is deeply caught up with the world in which it is embedded. The artist Foucault praises is not attempting to escape a tedious or hopeless reality but seeks instead to transfigure it. At the same time, this transfiguration "does not entail an annulling of reality, but a difficult interplay between the truth of what is real and the exercise of freedom. . . . For the attitude of modernity, the high value of the present is indissociable from a desperate eagerness to imag-ine it . . . otherwise than it is, and to transform it not by destroying it but by grasping it in what it is."[200] Thus, an artistic relation to the contemporary world entails grasping the dynamics of the social world in which one lives. At the same time, this artistic attitude is expressed in terms of the relation one has with oneself: "To be modern is not to accept oneself as one is in the flux of passing moments; it is to take oneself as object of a complex and difficult elaboration. . . . Modernity does not 'liberate man in his own being'; it com-pels him to face the task of producing himself."[201]

The relation to the social world in which the individual works and the re-lation to oneself can be thought of, respectively, as the sphere of the specific intellectual and the care of the self. The two practices refer to different levels of our experience of the world, but it is not hard to see how they call out to each other: to understand their position in the social world, specific intellectuals will need to come to grips with what the world has made of them on the subjective level. Those practicing self-care will find the social world they inhabit to be an unavoidable element in their own constitution.

It does seem, though, that Foucault ranks self-care over the work of the specific intellectual. Not everyone is capable of being a specific intellectual in the sense this term is described by Foucault. Not all of us occupy those middle and upper positions in government and business that give the specific intellectual a role in the transmission of "knowledge-power." We are, however, specific *individuals*, with each of us a unique intersection point of a variety of forces and disciplines, only some of which are implanted by the outside world. It follows that technologies of the self can be seen as an extension of the possibilities of the specific intellectual to a broader context. By entering into the activity of shaping our own subjectivity, each of us can potentially thwart, challenge, or at least question the ways in which we have been made. And let us again emphasize the political impact of such a project: in a society that relies on the unrecognized permeability of subjective states, the spread of technologies of the self will result in so many newly resistant points. Art enters into such practices not as self-absorption but as a consequence of the intricate ways in which we have been constituted. To understand ourselves, to participate in our own self-creation, is to take into our hands an elaborate artifact of modern culture that requires skill to manipulate. It is the lack of that skill—and more, the lack of a perceived need for acquiring it—that leads Foucault to assert that there is still something "premature" or "premodern" in our comprehension of ourselves and our world.[202]

"Technologies of the self" can be thought of as an extension of the critical potential of the specific intellectual to a broader arena. In his essay "What Is Enlightenment?" Kant argued that for the practice of enlightenment, all that was needed was freedom.[203] One sense in which this was meant was as opportunity. That is, we needed to be given sufficient room, free from intruding authorities, to think for ourselves. In a long tradition of critical theory, this opportunity could come only in the context of a thorough transfiguration of society.

Foucault, as argued extensively here, denies that the totality has this kind of dominance and internal unity. In the place of power with a capital *P*, we are shown a picture of society built up from a plurality of forces. This pluralistic image of society radically alters our relation to broader social forms. Specifically, it provides part of the freedom that Kant argued was necessary for

enlightenment. At the same time, individuals are depicted as (selectively) constituted subjects. Despite the deterministic tone of this claim, it too is part of
the conditions needed for practicing enlightenment in Foucault's sense. Never
approaching a "final" constitution, always caught up in a number of competing forces, finally protected by the "irreducible" medium of thought, the
subject always contains within it the possibility of self-constitution. Of course,
for as long as the forces that are fashioning the subjective states of individuals are external ones, individuals will very much be a product of those forces.
The first step of enlightenment is to come to grips with the powers that too
often are the unacknowledged masters of our selves. Allowing other forces to
shape us, with no intervention on our part, leaves us immature. The "care of
the self" that Foucault introduces in his late work has to do with exiting that
state of immaturity and participating in the world of self-construction. This
can involve not only establishing "relations with the self" but also relations
with others so as to pursue common goals.

In discussing enlightenment, then, Foucault wishes to effect a kind of reversal in the discourse that is usually associated with that term. He wants to reject the assumption that to engage in the art of enlightenment, the individual
must wait on the fulfillment of inflated, implausible, and, in all probability,
disastrous restructurings of the totality. Power-knowledges at their base are
local phenomena—however much broader structures are built up with their
support. At the same time, power-knowledge is productive of the subjective
states and dispositions so crucial to our own orientation to these structures.
With the strategic consideration that power is not monolithic or total, Foucault introduces technologies of the self and the specific intellectual as tactical
possibilities for changing the way in which we think about ourselves and relate
to the world around us.

V I   Politics, Norms, and the Self

Long before the destruction of the Berlin Wall, Foucault sensed the impasse confronting oppositional activity in the West. And what is this impasse but the inability to *think* opposition? "Thought," however, not only refers to carefully arranged arguments or compelling alternative schemes but can also be understood as a material, almost bodily disposition. In fact, we sense this deeper layer of thought in others all the time. Some say or even reflect very little and yet manifest patterns of thought that have settled deep in their bodies; others who are perfectly willing to articulate their views show that their most important constitutive thoughts are beyond rational dialogue. "Thought," for Foucault, is "something . . . essential in human life and in human relations. . . . It is something that is often hidden, but which always animates everyday behavior."[1] What thought, what truth animates today's oppositional stance?

The Politics of Our Selves and the Role of Rights

For a long time Marxism was able to provide a narrative that animated critical behavior. It allowed one to situate opposition in terms of a promise of human liberation that could be guaranteed through its association with a scientific—thus irrefutable—knowledge. As such stories have lost their aesthetic appeal, it has become more and more difficult to think that way. Foucault's suggestion is that we shift the situs of our valuation away from the new world that criticism is supposed to achieve and toward the activity of critical thought itself. As we saw in the introduction to this book, criticism should be treated as an end in itself, as a virtue. And virtues must be cultivated.

Shall we do away with narratives? Or do we need some story to help us think, critically or otherwise? In "What Is Critique?" Foucault tells us that with a little more daring, he would have titled his talk "What Is Enlightenment?" [2] Perhaps the enlightened attitude to criticism is one that allows it to do its own job without forcing it into the role of means to some greater end. In that case, does the aesthetic element of politics drop out? More likely, it plays a transformed role.

If criticism is a virtue that promotes "reflective indocility," politics is the arena in which various kinds of governance intersect with more or less docile, more or less resistant objects of governance.[3] In an important sense, politics is an art. This is an old claim, but when Foucault makes it his critics claim to hear something odd and perverse. But politics is an art for the same reason that the term "art" applies to the endeavors with which it is usually associated. In politics, a plurality of elements that are more or less resistant to change and responsive to pressures according to this or that measure of permeability and flexibility must be configured by a human will. Unlike the sculptor, the politician confronts an environment that is unstable and a material that may not only resist being formed but also has access—potentially—to arts of refusal.

The theme of the care of the self should be thought of in this context. It has three ingredients. First, as discussed in a previous chapter, care of the self means examining the various things that present themselves for admission to the soul or mind of the individual.[4] Second, the individual must see to his or her own constitution by consciously deciding on the character and direction of existence to the extent that such is under the individual's control. Third, the individual should be skilled at penetrating and assessing the artistic designs of others who are operating in the same sphere of action. The individual will not be able to "take care" of herself or himself without an ability to censor what comes from the outside, to fashion herself or himself according to selected criteria, and to develop an aesthetic sense that allows for the appreciation and evaluation of the projects of others.

Not surprisingly, Foucault's proposals for oppositional activity read less whimsically when we keep in mind his descriptions of the political world and the characteristic operations of power that take place in it. As presented in detail here, Foucault argues that the distinctive nature of modern power is its capacity to produce dispositions and habits. Disciplines call forth traits in individuals; arts of governance shape the behavior of populations. It is in this setting that the theme of the care of the self can play its role.

Take, for instance, the third leg of the self-care theme: penetrating the artistic designs of others. The key to such an evaluation is to determine the "connections between mechanisms of coercion" that confront the individual and the "contents of knowledge" that act as their support.[5] Knowledge combined with power results in a specific real-world entity (the Panopticon, the housewife, monomania, and the like) designed to install docility, productivity, a predilection to confess, and so on. Once revealed, how can the individual relate to such techniques of power? The discourse of legitimacy does not apply to them, but a developed capacity to discern the particular dynamic of a power-knowledge circuit might allow one to develop the reflective indocility that Foucault talks about.[6]

The politics of the self should not be dismissed as narcissistic flight from "real" politics precisely because politics as it actually functions depends on various constitutions of the individual. For Foucault, what we refer to as the subject is the result of a "combination of processes" and forms "which are far from being completed." A long philosophic tradition beginning with Descartes argued that the subject is the condition for the possibility of experience. On the contrary, for Foucault: "It is experience which is the rationalization of a process, itself provisional, which results in a subject, or rather, in subjects. I . . . call subjectivization the procedure by which one obtains the constitution of a subject, or more precisely, of a subjectivity which is of course only one of the given possibilities of a self-consciousness."[7] "Empirical" individuals are in reality an ensemble of subindividuals of various descriptions.[8] Some of these are installed from the outside by constructs of power-knowledge. Once installed, however, such implantations never remain wholly foreign agents. They must compromise and cooperate with other subindividuals to be effective. This means that a newly political attitude toward ourselves should replace the solitary—and hence unproblematic—picture of subjectivity that has dominated Western thought until recently.

Only when we comprehend the forces that make us up as individuals will we be able to respond to the overflow of activities aimed at governing the individual. The first step is to reject the assumption that individuals are unitary—that what we appear to observe empirically about individuals is also true psychically. But this step can be taken only if there is an alternative to the familiar subject-centered conception of a unitary psychic experience. The need for this alternative is what makes the Greeks so interesting for Foucault. For the Greeks, "there is no subject," he notes, "[w]hich does not mean that the Greeks did not strive to define the conditions in which an experience could take place—an experience not of the subject but of the individual, to the extent that the individual wants to constitute itself as its own master. What was missing in classical antiquity was the problematization of the constitution of the self as subject."[9] The view of the self as a subject was, according to Foucault, the accomplishment of Christianity: "But a moral experience essentially centered on the subject no longer seems satisfactory to me today. Because of this, certain questions pose themselves to us in the same terms as they were posed in antiquity. The search for styles of existence as different from each other as possible seems to me to be one of the points on which particular groups in the past may have inaugurated searches we are engaged in today."[10] It is, for Foucault, an absurd prejudice to describe the care of the self as narcissistic and "nonpolitical." On the contrary, the creation and governance of individuals is at the heart of the operation of modern power. In his researches on the self, Foucault was not retreating from social life and political concerns—let us minimally admit that such was not his purpose—but exploring historical constructs that would suggest new ways to engage modern power.

What prevents the recognition and manipulation of this proliferation of subselves is a generally liberal political account of individuals and the notion of rights that is tied to them. Understanding Foucault's position on individuality and rights will take us a long way toward an understanding of the political role of "self-care" and "technologies of the self."

According to classic liberal thinkers from Hobbes to Rawls, individuals possess themselves in an unproblematic and unreflective manner and are the irreducible units of political analysis. No aesthetic or activity of any kind is required to achieve this self-possession, which may precede social formations (family, tribe, city, nation), as with Hobbes. Or, in a more sophisticated version, the individual will come into being only in the context of these social groupings, as with Adam Smith and Adam Ferguson.

In general, though, a Foucauldian criticism of liberalism would focus in part on the latter's weak psychological underpinnings. Part of the reason why liberalism ignores the constructed character of individuals may lie in the accidental fact that liberal thought developed at a time when human psychology was itself undeveloped. And when Freud and others began to develop their insights, these were presented in an avowedly nonpolitical form. Whatever the reason, it should be clear by now that Foucault sharply disputes the liberal dismissal of the politics of the self. For Foucault, marginalizing the individual, either by describing him or her as unproblematically univocal or by granting the psychological an important but strictly nonpolitical status, is both a mistake and part of a strategy that allows the disciplines to function unexamined.

What of the rights of individuals that liberalism guarantees? From a liberal perspective, what Foucault misses are the normative descriptions of the individual that protect it from invasive powers. Standing behind most liberal proposals for the organization of society are descriptions of human beings as bearers of certain rights.[11] Societies protect these rights, or the former are described as illegitimate. The duties that society and government can reserve to themselves are in fact traceable to the individual rights that society was designed to protect.

Perhaps a dialogue could be imagined between a liberalism enlightened by Foucault's criticisms and a Foucault interested in liberalism's protective guarantees for individuals. Such a dialogue might come to the following conclusions: Certainly, Foucault would agree, what are commonly thought of as liberal guarantees are important and valuable. This is true even if the depiction of the individual provided by liberal thought is undeveloped or simply wrong. To engage in the activity of self-care, to practice technologies of the self, individuals—however described—are still going to need the reservations of personal space and the guarantee of public rights that liberalism uniquely (in our history, at least) provides. Liberal thinkers can, for their part, concede that the bare assertion and even protection of a range of basic rights does not exhaust the work of freedom. It could even be admitted that there is a straightforward political dimension to the construction of the individual which is consequential for the functioning of broader arrangements.

For Foucault, however, such a dialogue ends up conceding too much ground to liberalism. Liberalism, for Foucault, fails to capture and indeed obscures the dynamic that propels human freedom. The primary confusion that liberalism introduces in understanding human social arrangements, as I argued in chapter 1, is its focus on consent as the privileged site of political and social legitimacy. But for Foucault a theory that traces rights back to the consent of individuals and societies has its efficacy undermined by forms of power that work below the level of such surface phenomena.

We should not conclude, however, that Foucault contemptuously dismisses rights. Instead, it seems he sees a "bad fit" between a discourse on rights and the operations of disciplinary power. The former looks to a highly visible, centralized power whose goals and means are agreed to beforehand. But power of the latter type is dispersed and operates in a realm that is not, by its nature, consensual. Rights do not provide a defense against disciplinary power. What if, however, individuals and whole societies believed that rights provided an adequate defense against all the most important kinds of power in society? In that case there would be—from an oppositional standpoint—a bad fit between the functioning of an important kind of power and the means available for opposing it. Rights are not inherently bad. It is just that at the particular historical juncture Foucault discusses, they produce a false sense of security, allowing a powerful force to go undetected and unopposed.

In modern Western societies, rights have the potential to play a dangerous—because it is disarming—role. What attitude does Foucault adopt toward them? There are several possibilities.

(1) Rights are somehow inherently bad. This option, however, we have already disposed of.
(2) Rights are bad because they help to solidify the status quo.
(3) Rights are only part of the story of human freedom:
   (a) they may be the most important part, but for too long we have ignored other important kinds of relations with others, or
   (b) they are not as important as is usually thought.
(4) Rights are not bad, good, or partly good, but irrelevant.

With the exception of the first possibility, Foucault has expressed some version of each of the above views at one time or another.[12] This is not because he is theoretically inconsistent but because rights played distinct roles in the context in which they were discussed.

We should remember, too, that Foucault does not intend to play the role of the universal intellectual who will tell us what kinds of rights we should want or if we should want any at all.[13] He does not feel the need to say everything. He is not trying to produce a Foucault handbook on all we will ever need to know about freedom. That said, however, Foucault's deepest criticism of rights focuses on two points. First is their conservative character: They tend to formalize and legitimate yesterday's battle lines at the expense of the search for new frontiers. (More will be said about this later in the context of the modern women's movement.) But rights often fail to protect even yesterday's hard-won freedoms when new battles are under way. Supposedly fundamental rights are either too general to be effective as guarantees, as a history of the right of free speech makes clear,[14] or too specific to retain their relevance, as is the case with the Third Amendment right to refuse quartering of soldiers in peacetime. Second, rights are usually presented as covering the whole ground of human freedom. Foucault believes that they often represent only a thin strip of human experience.

They should not for that reason be abandoned. When Foucault does speak up in defense of rights, however, it is never in terms of some foundational view of the human personality. Thus, in 1977, when the French government sought to extradite the lawyer for a German terrorist group, Foucault spoke of "the right to a lawyer who speaks for you, with you, who allows you to be heard and to preserve your life, your identity, and the force of your refusal. . . . This right is not a legal abstraction or a dreamer's ideal; this right is part of our historical reality and must not be erased from it."[15]

Adapting Rights to the Modern Setting

As Foucault himself admits, the liberal discourse on rights does dominate oppositional strategies.[16] A series of errors and creative adjustments are made with regard to rights to make them fit modern conditions more adequately.

We Are Free No Matter What

Everyone agrees that possession of an enumerated and restricted list of rights and guarantees constitutes freedom. Once this status is achieved, the work of human freedom is done. Freedom means freedom of speech, religion, association, and so on. Some democratic tenets are also included: one person, one vote. Juridical protections are also attached: no one shall be convicted of treason without the testimony of two eyewitnesses.[17] If these freedoms and protections exist, then I am free, or I live in a free society. This is true even if these rights and protections lack effective value for my life as I actually live it.

Foucault would dispute the connection between a set of basic rights and freedom. As mentioned in the last section, rights discourse does not cover sufficient ground to claim the whole territory of human freedom for itself. For instance, many women in the late 1950s and 1960s found themselves in psychologically and financially dependent relationships with men. Every one of the rights usually thought of as basic was possessed by these women at the time, and yet they had a very hard time describing themselves as "free."[18]

Expansive Rights

An attempt is made to expand the list of basic civil rights (freedom of association, religion, and so on) to include the latest balance of forces in a particular political battle. We tend to distort the vocabulary of rights to fit the latest episode in the political struggle. Not just a right to free speech, then, but a right to an abortion; a right to life; a right to a clean environment, a job, neighborhood control; and so forth. For Foucault, this exclusive focus on "rights" as the only intelligible way to map opposition in modern society is one which is understandable but which he hopes to work past. Systems of power—disciplines—that have nothing to do with rights but instead function through the creation and normalization of individuals are responded to with a reformulated and ultimately unworkable discourse of right. As Foucault puts it:

> What we have seen has been a very real process of struggle; life as a political object was in a sense taken at face value and turned back against the system that was bent on controlling it. It was life more than the law that became the issue of political struggles, even if the latter were formulated through affirmations concerning rights. The "right" to life, to one's body, to health, to happiness, to the satisfaction of needs, . . . this "right"— which the classical juridical system was utterly incapable of comprehending—was the political response to all these new procedures of power which did not derive, either, from the traditional right of sovereignty.[19]

The move to oppose non-rights-based systems of power with a transfigured, even distorted discourse of rights is neither surprising for Foucault nor something to be regretted: "We must make allowance for the complex and unstable process whereby discourse can be both an instrument . . . of power, but also a hindrance, a stumbling-block, a point of resistance and a starting point for an opposing strategy. Discourse transmits and produces power, it reinforces it, but also undermines and exposes it, renders it fragile, and makes it possible to thwart it."[20]

But from the fact that individuals and groups are able to tailor the discourse of rights to fit a strategic situation far removed from the context of sovereignty, it does not follow that there is no point in developing more appropriate tools and analyses. If "rights" are supposed to be permanent descriptions of the attributes and necessary buffers that human beings require, then our own history can tell us, without Foucault's help, that rights are not truly what is being sought as we shift from the "right" to an abortion to the "right" to a clean environment. From the other side, those older, supposedly more basic rights, such as the right to free speech and so on, will fail to describe our status as free human beings to the extent that they lie dormant, unexercised, and irrelevant to the actual power relations we find ourselves in.

In the period leading up to the collapse of the regimes in the East, when these freedoms were needed and even used despite being forbidden by the authorities, "freedom of speech" and so on did play a role in expressing the freedom of individuals in those contexts. This is true even though these "rights" were not recognized—that is, even though they were not rights! On the other hand, the right to free speech in the West has a tendency to retreat from its critical function as few find it applicable in determinate power-knowledge contexts.

What kinds of rights, in the end, should we want? Or do we perhaps want to dispense with the term "rights?" We might then reformulate our question as follows: What kinds of protections; what kinds of arrangements, agreements, and reservations of personal space; and what kinds of expressive activities are to be preferred and worked for? It seems that for Foucault it would be a mistake to give a definitive answer to such questions, which would be like wanting to know ahead of time what kind of tactics will be appropriate for the conduct of a particular battle. We will not know what we will need in a particular context until we are in it, and to the extent that a restricted list of rights limits our resourcefulness, creativity, and options, the existence of such a list is ambiguous in its effects. In the second stage, Foucault would point out that groups and individuals will actually create an activity or protected area and establish its presence in the face of determined opposition. Neither consensus nor universalistic formulas will be employed; instead, a creative act will shift the alignment of forces and open up a space of freedom that was not there before.

Beyond Rights: The Triangle of Self, Truth, and Freedom

Foucault provides us with a case study of the "creationist" approach to freedom in a study of the ancient practice of "parrhesia."[21] This term easily translates from the Greek as "free speech" and so provides for an instructive comparison with the modern conception of rights.

Truth and Risk

Parrhesia is a very specific kind of "free speaking" in a distinctive social set-ting. For instance, expressing a view at a meeting might be an act of free speech, but it is not free speech in the parrhesian sense. Parrhesia takes place when someone in authority is confronted with an unpleasant or even danger-ous truth and where the safety of the individual who speaks or writes is not assured. Thus, Foucault defines parrhesia as a kind of "truth-speaking" that puts the speaker at risk.[22] The danger associated with the act of parrhesia dis-tinguishes this kind of truth-speaking from a variety of other kinds. In a peda-gogical setting, for instance, truthful information can be transmitted. Simi-larly, someone with high social status can fulfill an official function through a speech act ("the motion is denied") and in the process say something true.[23] In both cases, however, the truth that is spoken will not put the speaker at risk.

An example of parrhesian discourse provided by Foucault is the confron-tation between Plato and the Greek tyrant Dionysius the Younger.[24] In the middle of a conversation, Plato begins to discuss what the just man is and the connection between this and happiness, reviewing in the process some of the themes in *The Republic* about supposedly all-powerful tyrants being in fact the unhappiest of men. The truly just man, Plato maintains, will be happy whatever his material circumstances as a consequence of the inner harmony of his soul. Dionysius immediately sees Plato's words about tyrants, justice, and happiness as a direct attack on him and orders Plato sold into slavery — a con-dition that "will not do Plato any harm," Dionysius jokes, "because as a just man, he will still be happy as a slave." [25]

Clearly a difference exists between Plato's speech in front of an actual tyrant and the same comments made to Glaucon and Adeimantus in *The Repub-lic*.[26] Because Plato put himself at risk, because he "spoke freely" in front of a power — whether a tyrant, as here, or in front of an assembly, as with Soc-rates — that had the power to banish, enslave, or execute, his comments took on a parrhesiastic quality. We could think of parrhesia, then, not merely as "free speech" but as "frank speech in the face of indeterminate danger." The danger in question could include the threat of death. But this ultimate risk does not have to be present. An official might refuse to bend to the whims of the crowd and risk loss of livelihood or even banishment. "However many forms parrhesia takes, the act of speaking the truth pulls the one who has spo-ken it towards costly consequences," which nevertheless cannot be determined beforehand.[27] The tyrant might kill you, the mob might banish you — or the first may raise you up to a high state position and the second applaud you for daring to speak a necessary truth. In any event, the parrhesian act is played out in a conflictual context.

Truth and Self

The parrhesiastic act opens up a space of freedom and truth that was not there before. Foucault calls it a kind of "eruptive truth-speaking" in which a breach is caused.[28] But what is eruptive here refers not only to the relation between the speaker and the listener but also to the relation that the parrhesiast establishes with herself. On this level, however, the meaning of the word "truth" shifts fundamentally: now we are talking about the truth of the being of the individual. The parrhesiastic act implicitly asks and answers the following question: What kind of individual would place herself in significant danger through the utterance of a truthful statement? Apparently, such an individual has managed to construct a relation between self and truth such that not only the particular utterance ("Dionysius is a tyrant") is perceived as true but also the very being of the person is looked on as "true." In the latter sense, the term "truth" is closer to the idea of independence and even authenticity: the individual has constructed her own truth-self bond that stands outside the dominant one. Since the treatment of Dionysius by his courtiers and others as something other than a tyrant is based on a lie, the relation that those surrounding him have with themselves is similarly suspect.

Indeed, the power of the statement "Dionysius is a tyrant" does not come from its correspondence with reality. Obviously, everyone knows that Dionysius is a tyrant. Plato and Dion do not create that truth. On some level even Dionysius knows it. The question of the "level" on which one is allowed to operate turns out to be important, however.

Plato asserts the truth that is unspoken. Despite his unquestionable status as a tyrant, Dionysius creates around himself a field of truth and power, one of the rules of which is that he not be described or denounced as one. His courtiers, along with others who come into contact with him, enter into this game. The game has its rewards and even its own opportunities for movement, for tactics—in other words, its own space of freedom. By bringing out into the open the silent lie on which this game rests, Plato disrupts the playing field with a free act. Rules that governed the interaction of Dionysius with those around him are suddenly put out of operation. But this could be done only by someone whose relation with himself is formed by another set of rules, another bond between self and truth different from the one that operates among Dionysius and his courtiers. The result is a triangle of self-truth-freedom. The parrhesiast believes in the truth of what has been said and puts herself "on the line" — and not only physically — for the truth in a way that displays her freedom.[29] The very being of the speaker manifests itself as an unbreakable union of self-truth-freedom and is inserted into a contrary and even dangerous setting.[30] The "playing field" of the latter is disrupted, and this too makes new moves — new freedoms — possible.

The Timing of Freedom

We should compare the distinctive self-truth-freedom triangle described by Foucault to the more familiar formulations in critical and liberal theory. For critical theory, freedom exists as a potential in human beings to be realized through a radical transformation of society at some point in the future. Once this freedom is achieved, the truth of what human beings are will finally achieve expression. For liberal theory freedom is associated with an essentially rational, self-directing, and independent core that is already present in every human. Again, gaining access to this rational core reveals the truth of what it is to be human. Though they disagree about "timing" — critical theory pointing to the future, liberal theory to the present — both standpoints agree that the freedom characterizing human beings is essential to them. Since the freedom and truth of human beings is of a foundational nature, its properties are communicable and hence subject to rational dialogue and potential objects of consensus.

With parrhesia, Foucault describes a kind of truth-self-freedom triangle that differs from the critical-liberal account in crucial respects. We should notice, however, that Foucault does not dispense with the values "freedom" and "truth." Instead, he recasts them. Neither is discovered as part of our rational core or at the end of a history that is somehow necessary. Instead, these values are created, on larger and smaller scales. This is why, for instance, Foucault speaks of parrhesia as an eruptive truth-speaking (*eruptives Wahrsprechen*).

There is a great deal of interesting material in Foucault's discussion of parrhesia, not all of which, unfortunately, can be discussed here. As with all Foucault's historical studies, it is important to remember that he is not recommending, much less insisting, that we all become parrhesiasts. For our purposes, Foucault's discussion of parrhesia makes two points.

First, the parrhesiast is not someone who discovers himself, either in the form of the "hidden secrets" of Freud's psychoanalysis or as a rational being as with Kant. Rather, he "invents himself" and confronts the task of "producing himself." [31] This task—however different the means, resources, and contexts—is one that modern individuals face as well. We may not become parrhesiasts—that specific game of truth, self, and freedom belongs to another day. But that we must create ourselves out of the diversity of forces around and in us—or be created by others through default—is, for Foucault, a constant.

Second, this self-creation has a political dimension. Depending on the kind of individual you are, you will interact with the forces you come across in various ways. The parrhesiast forms a triangle of truth, self, and freedom that manifests itself in a distinctive manner. Parrhesia is not a right that others recognize or that society endorses. This is why the translation of this term as "freedom of speech" is misleading. In our modern context, "freedom of speech" is something that is not just socially but also institutionally recognized and guaranteed. But the right to talk in this specific Greco-Roman context is not one that is provided for all. Most are not up to it—even most of those identified with the nobility. It is not something that can be accorded to all who consent to broad structures of social life. To speak in the manner of the parrhesiast is to establish, confirm, and manifest a mode of being. The state of being of the individual, the correlation of that being with a truth that refers to both the makeup of the person and the actual statement made, along with the concomitant freedom of the person who speaks and the "free" status of the statement—free of personal interest, free of rhetorical tricks—all come together to create a right to speak that did not exist before and will not exist again until the next "eruption of truth" associated with parrhesia. Unlike rights as we usually think of them, however, this right is not shared with others.

For the reason just mentioned, the kind of "right" associated with parrhesia must be put in quotation marks, so accustomed are we to using that term in a purely institutional context. We could move closer to a more appropriate sense of the word "right" in the parrhesian sense if we were to think of the kind of right we tend to assign to those—and only those—who have gone through a certain experience. Veterans of a war have a "right" to speak about the conduct of war in a way that others do not, because it is hard to avoid acknowledging the truth of what they say, a truth that is more than simply "objectively" or "evidentially" true. Instead, it is a truth that is manifested through the being of the individual. War speaks to us through them.

For Foucault, there is no question of dispensing with institutional rights that now exist. Efforts to restrict or eliminate constitutionally guaranteed rights would be opposed by Foucault just as much as by anybody else. But there is a difference between refusing to allow one set of social powers to remove promised liberties and positively asserting that the bare possession of these rights makes one a free individual. (As an indicator of Foucault's view of this matter, we could cite Foucault's assertion that "perhaps one must not be for consensuality, but one must be against nonconsensuality."[32]) Nor does the protection of these rights commit one to the view that such and such a list is "basic" and reflects a fundamental human nature. This is precisely Foucault's own criticism of humanism: "What I am afraid of about humanism is that it presents a certain form of ethics as a universal model for any kind of freedom. I think there are more secrets, more possible freedoms, and more inventions in our future than we can imagine in humanism as it is dogmatically represented on every side of the political rainbow."[33]

Rights and the Women's Movement[34]

The rights we have are not to be tossed aside, but neither are they to be thought of as "essential." In a particular setting, we will have to use political judgment to help us invent that set of responses, acts, and freedoms that will destabilize, reconfigure, or even affirm the situation in which we happen to find ourselves. We can think here of Machiavelli's complaint, in his *Discourses,* that individuals fail to change their nature to fit new circumstances and end up being destroyed.[35] Seen from this angle, the transformative side of the "care of the self" should assure us of its political value.

Foucault rejects both the following options: (1) the individual is a self-contained psychic unit independent of external controls — someone holding this position could, of course, admit the influence of external factors but would nevertheless maintain that the central dynamics of a person's being are to be found within; and (2) individuals are products of the social world they inhabit. Again, from this side the importance of the particularities that might mark this or that individual need not be denied, but the social nature of individual formation is regarded as dominant. Foucault rejects both these positions and has been accused of holding each in turn. One interviewer, referring to movements for self-realization in the United States, asks Foucault if his focus on the self is in any way comparable. "In France too," Foucault comments, "there is a movement of the same type and of the same intensity."

> I think of subjectivity in another way. I think that subjectivity and identity and individuality have been a great political problem since the '6os. I think there is a danger in thinking of identity and subjectivity as quite

deep and quite natural and not determined by political and social factors. The psychological subjectivity that the psychoanalysts deal with — we have to be liberated from this kind of subjectivity. We are prisoners of certain conceptions about ourselves and our behavior. We have to liberate our own subjectivity, our own relation to ourselves.[36]

The individual is neither independent of nor wholly defined by social powers but a focal point, a level on which a plurality of forces interact, struggle, compromise, and end up producing temporary alignments that mark the individual for a period of time. The battles and alliances producing these alignments can be surveyed to construct a "genealogy of the modern subject as a historical and cultural reality." The reality in question is not, however, static. The subject can change as alignments shift, "which is of course politically important."[37] Politically important, because if the individual is not once and for all created as a unitary monad, if the individual is plastic and can be shaped, then the productive and creative force that the individual represents will be contended for.

In the early development of the women's movement we see an excellent example of the social and political importance of just such a shift. At a certain point, a significant minority of American women began to describe and experience their existence as unbearably oppressive. This redescription and rejection of a woman's role in American society was accomplished — initially, at least — despite the opposition not only of those thought to benefit from the subjugation of women — namely, men — but also by those professionally charged, as it were, with the task of describing and interpreting our experiences for us — psychiatrists, family counselors, social workers, and so on.[38] The relation of some version of "self-care" here to the birth and growth of a social movement is clear. Dissatisfaction with a life as mother and caretaker (of others) can be described as a rational response to oppression or as a manifestation of an underlying mental illness, which can be treated with therapy or perhaps controlled with drugs. These two very different paths (revolt versus Valium), marked out by competing conceptions of the self, help explain why Foucault refers to the shifts in subjectivity as self-evidently political.[39]

More than any other movement in modern times, the women's movement took up the question of the disposition of forces internal to the individual as unavoidably central to effective action in a broader social context. But we should not be led into a false dichotomy between "theory" and "practice." Women did not first prepare themselves in consciousness-raising groups to effect change once outside. The consciousness-raising groups and other self-transforming practices that groups and individuals applied to themselves were the sites of change.[40] It was in recognition of this already-achieved transformation in the subjective disposition of women that other social forms adjusted themselves. Men found themselves in relationships with suddenly different partners who were unwilling—really unable—to play the old games. Psychiatrists found their terms and criteria for defining mental health changed "from below" by patients, while official political bodies confronted a magically altered political map. (Even the Republican Party endorsed the Equal Rights Amendment for a time.) Husbands, employers, and others found themselves in a position relative to women analogous to that experienced by Dionysius in his confrontation with Plato. (I leave to the side the obvious differences.) That is, the women were appealing to a certain set of experiences which they claimed were not accessible to others but which should define and structure any discussion of women's status. The result is a debate or discussion that is inherently asymmetrical.[41] Just as with the war veteran, the truth involved is not of an evidentiary but an experiential kind. By their engagement in certain practices, by transformation of their past into a new kind of experience, a new truth about women that was "eruptive" rather than dialogic was manifested in the being—Foucault might say the bodies—of women.[42] Here we note that the constitution of an experience out of a past that results in a realigned subjective structure is a move that Foucault, using very different materials, shares with the women's movement.[43]

The women's movement is illustrative of another theme in Foucault, though this time negatively. As with most movements of social and personal change, participants in the women's movement tended to describe the new matrix of power relations—the new triangle of self-truth-freedom—as representing the last (rather than the most recent) word on what human nature is. In her pioneering work *The Feminine Mystique,* Betty Friedan spoke of how women could not "grow to their full human capacity" as housewives.[44] A central theme of *The Feminine Mystique* was that personal satisfaction was simply impossible behind the invisible bars of a suburb, mass-producing peanut butter sandwiches for neighborhood children and greeting one's husband on his return from the "World" with a drink and dinner, just like ordinary people.

The first step of the move away from this life, according to Friedan, is rejectionist: the American woman "must unequivocally say 'no' to the housewife image."[45] This "no," however, requires a real-world expression to become effective. Friedan argues vigorously that women should get out of the house and pursue professional careers.[46] Women would become truly human when they finally occupied their rightful place in the world of finance, government, business, law, and so forth.

For many years Friedan's account was praised as well as condemned as "bourgeois feminism." In fact, it and the movement it helped advance brought down far more barriers and emancipated many more lives than other "radically radical" efforts. Much of the program outlined in *The Feminine Mystique* was realized—a fate that is, however, double-edged for any reformer. Through the 1970s, women entered the workplace and professions in record numbers, a development aided by economic factors as well as cultural and political ones. This shift did indeed eliminate barriers, recast attitudes, and in general change the position of women throughout the country—though it is possible to overstate the extent of the transformation. In addition, some very negative consequences made themselves felt. Instead of being forced into motherhood and an immature dependence on a worldly husband, women found themselves postponing childbirth until well into their thirties so as to nurture fledgling careers. An overload of family and neighborhood concerns was replaced by an overload of professional commitments. Enter Betty Friedan's *Second Stage*, where "feminist mystique" replaces "feminine mystique": "Our failure," Friedan concedes, "was our blind spot about the family."[47] Friedan's was the principal work by a significant group of veteran participants in the women's liberation movement to reject much of what that movement had come to stand for.[48] It turns out that staying at home to rear children can be an expression of human nature, too. In the case of Carol Gilligan, author of *In a Different Voice*, the "care" (of others) that is a typical role for some women is not so much an expression of human nature as of women's own unique nature.[49] The culture industry duly signed on with yet another rendition of women's nature with *Baby Boom*, supplanting *Diary of a Mad Housewife*, *Coming Home*, and other efforts such as the film version of *A Doll's House*.

One, two, three—many human natures are ascribed to women, then. But the very multiplicity of "the human essence," which shifts and changes direction at a pace that rivals the fashion cycle, might suggest to us that this and the humanism tied to it are critical principles that either do not fit modern conditions or are the product of a very old error.[50]

A moment parallel to the switch in perspectives that Friedan underwent from *The Feminine Mystique* to *Second Stage* is discussed in an interview with Foucault. *Madness and Civilization* exerted an important influence on the antipsychiatry movement of the 1960s and 1970s. One of the objects of this movement was the large institutions that housed people with mental illness.

Once again, as the result of a mix of political, economic, and theoretical factors, these large institutions were closed down and patients were relocated in halfway houses or fled to the streets, which did not end all problems, however. Indeed, it created some new ones—inadequate supervision, a rise in homelessness, drug abuse among former patients, and so on. Refering to a book by Robert Castel that documents the miserable condition of former patients, a development that Castel traces to the antipsychiatry movement, Foucault states: "I agree completely with what Castel says, but that does not mean, as some people suppose, that the mental hospitals were better than anti-psychiatry; that does not mean that we were not right to criticize those mental institutions. I think it was good to do that, because *they* were the danger. And now it is quite clear that the danger has changed. For instance, in Italy they have closed all the mental hospitals and there are more free clinics, and so on—and they have new problems."[51]

The Demand for Criteria

We are now in a position, I believe, to answer some of the criticisms leveled at Foucault by critics such as Habermas. Foucault, it is said, is part of a large and regrettably influential—though certainly merely fashionable—band of Continental relativists. Nancy Fraser puts the complaint about Foucault very succinctly: "What Foucault needs and needs desperately, are normative criteria for distinguishing acceptable from unacceptable forms of power."[52] Does Foucault feel this desperate need? If not, why not?

First we should be clear about what we are asking. What are "normative criteria"? "Criteria" means "standards of evaluation." With the topic under discussion, such standards are public. Everyone has access to them, so that the act of evaluation and the conclusions reached can be repeated by similarly competent observers. "According to these criteria, the patient is brain-dead" is a statement that more than one person, competent to confirm that the situation of the individual matches the criteria, could make. Transposed to our discussion, the sentence would run as follows: "According to these criteria, this individual's rights have been transgressed."

What about the adjective "normative"? It might appear that this word has no referent significantly different from "criteria." Norms are standards. To say "normative criteria" might be like saying "standardish" or "standardlike" standards. But there is a bit more to the word "normative" as Fraser uses it than this. What is distinctive about normative criteria is that they refer to invariant ethical qualities associated with the human character. A norm in Fraser's sense, then, is an ethical term that to a greater or lesser extent describes some essential quality in humans that must be defended, respected, or expressed in institutional and interpersonal contexts.

Perhaps an element of Foucault's response to Fraser is already evident to the reader. In Foucault's world, norms do not protect already existing individuals with fully developed personalities from the encroachments of power. On the contrary, norms are a tool of power that plays a significant role in shaping human beings.

But when we talk about criteria in Fraser's sense, are we talking about norms in Foucault's sense? Fraser and others might be happy to endorse criticisms of disciplinary normalizations precisely on the grounds of the ethical criteria that Foucault appears to dismiss. Foucault would reply that norms in the disciplinary setting help create or reconfigure individuals. We saw this in chapter 2, where the normal human child is one who becomes the specified individual type in an established time frame.[53]

Norms in the ethical sense are clearly bound up with, indeed subordinate to, the actual creation of the individual. The reason for this should be obvious: standing behind any ethical ought—on which are built rights, protections, and so on—is a stable description of what a human being is. This is the thorn that norms are repeatedly caught on: to be universal themselves, they require a stable and universal human subjectivity. All discussion of rights, then, must make reference to this background premise: What is the nature of human subjectivity? And even, Do human beings have "a subjectivity"? Is that the best way to describe the psychic phenomena that occur under the cover of the empirical individual?

Once we answer these—very big—questions, we can go on to determine what the relation is between persons, freedom, and rights. Three considerations dominate Foucault's approach to these matters. First, a plurality of psychic forms make up what we see as the empirical individual at any point in his or her life. The relation of forces among these forms are subject to change—by the introduction of new forces, a shift in the balance of power among existing forces, or as the result of other events. Second, individuals are not stable. A list of rights—especially if these are thought to constitute human freedom—will not be able to "keep up" with the evolving individual and so will act as a conservative drag on further development. And, finally, human freedom is not a thing we unambiguously possess via the rights assigned to us. Freedom—given the description of human personality that Foucault offers—can only be

creative. As personality structures change, activities and the rights that protect them also change.[54]

Foucault's view that "there are more secrets, more possible freedoms, and
more inventions in our future than we can imagine" refers back to his view
of what human beings are and what freedom for them means.[55] This relation
between rights and freedom is addressed directly in a 1982 *Christopher Street*
interview:

> That in the name of respect for individual rights someone is allowed to
> do as he wants, great! But if what we want to do is to create a new way of
> life, then the question of individual rights is not pertinent. In effect, we
> live in a legal, social, and institutional world where the only relations pos-
> sible are extremely few, extremely simplified, and extremely poor. There
> is, of course, the fundamental relation of marriage, and the relations of
> family, but how many other relations should exist, should be able to find
> their codes not in institutions but in possible supports, which is not at all
> the case![56]

For Foucault, then, it follows that if the creation of individuals is foundational for the ethical norms we may establish, then the creation of individuals—how that happens to us, how we do it with or to ourselves—takes primacy
over the ethical norms. What was acceptable yesterday may not be acceptable
today: "Humanism may not be universal but may be quite relative to a certain
situation. . . . For instance, if you asked eighty years ago if feminine virtue was
part of universal humanism, everyone would have answered yes."[57] Including,
we can assume, most women. We should, of course, dispense with the absurd
and condescending idea that all who precede us were trying to become like us,
or really were like us but were not allowed to say so, or if they did say so were
not listened to, and all the other tricks designed to assure us that we live at
history's summit. At a certain point the position of women in this country became intolerable. At the same time an opportunity presented itself (the 1960s)
to alter that position. Once that change was under way, as women transformed
themselves along with the power relations that made up their lives, new norms
and new criteria emerged. Women were now different. What it meant to deal
with this new thing as a human being changed.

What women in the 1950s and early 1960s "desperately needed," to borrow
Fraser's term, was not a stable and reliable set of old norms but new modes
of being that would produce new norms. Indeed, if these new styles of being
had not been created—and, along with them, new norms—it would have been

impossible to know in what way the old power relations from which women were emerging were "intolerable" or "inhuman." For Foucault, it is difficult for humans to understand and interact effectively with the worlds they create as long as they have a "fixed view of it." Individuals must move onto "undefined territory" and "move things in relation to one another to make them useful."[58] Effective liberation movements do not discover the core of the human personality: they make possible the "destruction of what we are . . . [and] the creation of something entirely different."[59] Instead of finding out "what we really are," we discover what we have been in the process of moving away from it to become something else. There is, then, this simultaneously transformative and comparative element in Foucault's vision of how we live in the world that keeps him away from universal norms as the appropriate critical vehicle.

If the creation of new individuals produces new norms, the conclusion that follows for Foucault is not that no such things as norms exist but that there are too many of them on which to base a universal ethics: "What we call humanism has been used by Marxists, liberals, Nazis, Catholics."[60] Two thoughts follow: First, universal ethics are too vague and general to stand as an effective bar to actions we find repugnant. As a consequence, individuals and groups with very concrete, time- and place-bound norms arising out of material power relations have no trouble at all dressing up their unique perspective as the last word in human nature: "there is a very tenuous 'analytic' link between a philosophic conception and the concrete political attitude of someone who is appealing to it; the 'best' theories do not constitute a very effective protection against disastrous political choices; certain great themes such as 'humanism' can be used to any end whatever."[61] The second point is alluded to in the quotation above. Confronted by a plurality of normative standpoints, both within and without herself or himself, the individual must engage in an act of political choice. But again this is no mere nod of assent to a vague yet heartwarming morality. A more "demanding attitude" is necessary: "At every moment, step by step, one must confront what one is thinking and saying with what one is doing, with what one is. . . . The key to the personal-poetic attitude of a philosopher is not to be sought in his ideas, as if it could be deduced from them, but rather in his philosophy-as-life, in his philosophical life, his ethos."[62] In this description of the philosopher, we are reminded of the parrhesiast's triangle of self-truth-freedom and of the technologies of the self that weld such triangles.

In one place, Foucault tells us that he "believes in the freedom of people. To the same situation, people react in very different ways."[63] This freedom, however, draws on how individuals are made. Once again, this construction can be dominated by unacknowledged forces, in which case one's freedom is co-opted by external forces for external ends. Or the individual can check the influence of outside factors and participate in the act of self-formation. Such activity will not ensure politically correct choices. For Foucault, such things do not exist. It will allow the individual to make "enlightened" political choices, where by "enlightened" he means able to intervene in and participate in determining the construction of one's subjectivity. Nothing more can be promised.

Such an intervention will be political on two levels. At the individual level, as individuals are made up of shifting coalitions of forces, a "politics of ourselves" will be needed to occupy and direct ourselves. At the societal level, as illustrated by the women's movement, how we manage, confront, and seek to redefine ourselves is immensely consequential for the way we interact with broader social structures.

But in the process of intervening in oneself, in all the discussions about self-care, technologies of the self, knowledge-power, and so on, is there no underlying ethic? Does Foucault really provide us with no philosophic justification for the work that he does and seems to recommend for others? In fact, Foucault does quite explicitly redefine the task of philosophy for the world in which we live, as he understands it. In one interview, Foucault is asked about what motivated the change in direction from the first volume of *The History of Sexuality* series, which addressed nineteenth-century "biopolitics," to the second, which was concerned with Greek technologies of the self in the fourth century B.C.: "I changed my mind. When a piece of work is not also an attempt to change what one thinks and even what one is, it is not very amusing. I did begin to write two books in accordance with my original plan, but I soon got very bored."[64]

I have already briefly discussed Foucault's notion of the "book experience"[65] and the importance of changes in the way something is experienced in Foucault's work. Despite the personal and rather casual way in which Foucault presents this same issue above, the effort to "change what one thinks and even what one is" is at the heart of Foucault's understanding of what philosophy is. We might compare this new role for philosophy with the old one Foucault rejects, which we have already met earlier in this work: "There was the great period of contemporary philosophy, that of Sartre and Merleau-Ponty, in which a philosophical text . . . finally had to tell you what life, death, and sexuality were, if God existed or not, what liberty consisted of, what one had to do in political life, how to behave in regard to others, and so forth."[66]

Philosophy cannot shoulder that burden any longer, if indeed it ever could. But philosophy has not thereby lost all purpose. Instead of telling us what we are with godlike finality and what to do as an expression of that essence, philosophy's task is to allow us to "stray afield" of ourselves: "There are times in life when the question of knowing if one can think differently than one thinks . . . is absolutely necessary if one is to go on thinking and reflecting at all." [67] Note that this "straying afield" is valued not so much because it creates something new but because only through this invitation to deviation is reflection itself kept alive. We can encounter ourselves as we are only when we become something at least a little different from what we are. The quotation above continues as follows: "People will say, perhaps, that these games with oneself would be better left backstage. . . . But then, what is philosophy today—philosophical activity, I mean—if it is not the critical work that thought brings to bear on itself? In what does it consist, if not in the endeavor to know how and to what extent it might be possible to think differently, instead of legitimating what is already known?" [68]

Does anything besides Foucault's personal whims stand behind the high value ascribed to thinking and being differently? In fact, as we have already seen, Foucault does provide us with a kind of "life philosophy" in his introduction to Georges Canguilhem's *The Normal and the Pathological*.[69] There Foucault spoke of error as something that was itself "hereditary" in humans. It "produces a living being who is never completely at home, a living being dedicated to 'error' and destined, in the end, to 'error.' " [70] It appears, then, that the positive value that Foucault ascribes to "straying afield of oneself," which is presented in a personal-philosophic mode in the introduction to *L'usage des plaisirs,* is given a similarly central treatment in the introduction to Canguilhem's book, but this time in a less specialized manner. In the latter essay, error is presented as something biologically fundamental to the process of (human) life itself. Of course, the kind of error Foucault is thinking of is not the genetic kind that accompanies Darwin's theory of evolution but is social in character.

We can note one more time, without insisting too much on its importance, the political value of this notion of error. Power structures create and maintain themselves by concocting and reproducing individuals who will function efficiently for the power relation in question. The production of these individuals, as we have noted before, is intimately bound up with the invention of experiences that individuals go through, which in turn become modes of thought. From the perspective of broader organizations of power, individuals are genes helping to make up the strand of DNA that produces and reproduces power relations. A mutation of one of these genes can, as it were, change the balance of factors making up the broader unit, thus producing a mutation. For Foucault, such mutations are as close to a general description of human existence as he is likely to endorse. The whole purpose of philosophy is redescribed in a way that will promote such mutations. Today, there is no "sovereign philosophy" but rather a "philosophy-in-activity," which can be understood as "the move-ment by which—not without effort and uncertainty, dreams and illusions—one detaches oneself from what is accepted as true and seeks other rules. . . . The displacement and transformation of frameworks of thinking, the chang-ing of received values and all the work that has been done to think otherwise, to do something else, to become other than what one is—that, too, is philoso-phy. From this point of view, the last thirty years or so have been a period of intense philosophical activity."[71] This kind of philosophy joins forces with a description of life as "the play of coding and decoding," which "leaves room for chance" and "acts as a mistake."

Both James Bernauer (in *Michel Foucault's Force of Flight*) and William Con-nolly (in *The Augustinian Imperative*) have argued for the existence of a kind of Foucauldian spirituality that draws on a relationship to the life sciences dif-ferent from the one for which I have argued here.[72] This reading is part of the effort to find a moral position of some kind that will provide Foucault's criti-cal efforts with an anchor in a structure of values. Gilles Deleuze was perhaps the first to raise this possibility in his *Foucault:* "When power becomes bio-power, resistance becomes the power of life, a vital power that cannot be con-fined within species, environment or the paths of a particular diagram. Is not the force that comes from outside a certain idea of Life, a certain vitalism, in which Foucault's thought culminates? Is not life this capacity to resist force?"[73] Bernauer's version has to do with what he identifies as a "negative theology" in Foucault that targets the tendency to essentialize and thus mythologize the particular form our being has taken in any one epoch; Connolly refers to "an abundance with respect to any actual organization of actuality."[74] The idea, then, would be that Foucault and Foucauldians can (or should) appeal to the infinite yet unexplored possibilities of existence that today's particular forms of life hide from us.

Such readings are not wrong in a straightforward textual sense, but I do think they take Foucault in directions he would resist. We might remind our-selves that Foucault insisted on seeing himself as a "specific intellectual" with no overall theory of the world.[75] The appeal to an unformed but somehow cre-ative principle of life would be much too vague to be of use to Foucault. Fou-cault's own "life philosophy," discussed above, focuses on the truth-mutating properties of error. In the introduction to *The Normal and the Pathological,* he argues that concepts — of truth, of the nature of reality, of morality — are a means for living life and not killing it, as life philosophers before him had argued.[76] As a result, he carefully avoids endorsing the kind of vitalism mentioned by the authors above, with its attention to the repression of abundance and difference. One might prefer that some expressions of "life," including some that have been repressed or silenced, should remain repressed and unrealized. In addition, there can be other kinds of "life" that have been institutionalized and made concrete — at the expense of other possibilities — that we would want to affirm. The "principle" of life itself would not provide us with a sufficiently fine-tuned critical apparatus to make such distinctions.[77]

With this interpenetrating union of biology and philosophy that can be found in Foucault's work, we have, I think, entered into the very heart of his thought. It is the foundation for the view, expressed most directly in "The Subject and Power," but found in dozens of other places as well, that "the target nowadays is not to discover what we are, but to refuse what we are."[78] If we refuse what we are, we will further the mutational capacities inherent in life. The justification for encouraging such variation is twofold: The deviation itself will open up a path to those new secrets, possible freedoms, and inventions that take us in unexpected directions and breathe life back into the human project. Second, the resulting cracks in our "being" will act as markers, allowing us to reflect comparatively on what we are as a whole. Self-knowledge and self-transformation come together in a way that requires and deserves an artistic and creative treatment.

CONCLUSION

Nietzsche's *Genealogy of Morals,* Weber's *Protestant Ethic and the Spirit of Capitalism,* Foucault's *Discipline and Punish*—three works that tell the story of the hard labor that goes into the manufacture of subjectivities. In each book the author describes concrete personalities, each specifically designed to both create and pursue the diverse paths on which meaning and being are discovered. Nietzsche's slave morality, Weber's Protestant ethic, Foucault's disciplines: these are descriptions of the response and creativity of particular historical actors in the face of necessity and opportunity. On Nietzsche's own account, the set of moral valuations grouped under the heading *ressentiment* was produced under conditions of profound stress, when some of the slaves of the Roman nobles were no longer able to read their existence through the lens of a promise concerning their life on this earth. The slaves faced a choice: in despair, collapse into the void of nihilism, where no values are possible and life has no meaning; or, create a new set of values that—with huge quantities of rich human passion thrown in—could once again make life livable. From here,

Nietzsche makes two observations. First, it appears to be very difficult to create new structures of value. These require a very long period of gestation and youth. Of course, changing values does not refer to this or that list of prudential or ethical considerations. Changing values means changing humans, and for that to happen an eruption of suffering and unwilling transformation must take place. The conditions that would make such a mutation necessary must be rare. Second, as a result, humanity is saddled with a mode of being that is the product of a condition that existed at some point in the past and is no longer appropriate to it. And this mode of being cannot be simply dismissed or artfully rearranged because the conditions needed for achieving a temperature capable of sustaining a period of value formation are positively pathological. One cannot merely will to change values. One must first be really sick.

Weber's Calvinist hero was hardly less troubled than the Jewish heroes of Nietzsche's account. Shut off from the company and grace of the confessional, confronting a wrathful God and pushed back uncompromisingly onto themselves, the Calvinist faithful were, in addition, told that only those predestined by God to join Him in heaven could hope for an afterlife — or a pleasant one, at any rate. It took the blind panic such a view would naturally produce to create the particular kind of personality that would positively value the pursuit of profit for its own sake and with no other end ultimately in view.[1] Just as in Nietzsche's account, however, we are not surprised to see that this unique and peculiar "protestant ethic" did not long survive the immediate conditions of its emergence. Weber's well-known concern is that while the objective circumstances of capitalist development will push us to work more and more frantically, the motivational fire that provided the passion needed for such a project — namely, Am I one of the elect? — has gone cold. The result is a race of humans that has — for the moment, at least — lost its capacity to give meaning to its existence.[2]

Both Nietzsche and Weber go on to make dire predictions about humanity's capacity for exiting from a world devoid of value. Like others before and after him, Nietzsche worried that the democratic slogans concerning equality and liberty contained a dangerous tendency to reduce humanity to a superficial, bland mediocrity, with no distinguishing traits, and certainly no values.[3] Weber's themes are similar. There is, he says, an inexorable process of bureaucratization that accompanies the increasing complexity of administration on the level of the nation-state. Expert officials tend to hijack one area of state policy after another by opposing their full understanding of a particular problem or range of issues to the manifest superficiality of a dilettantish political leader. On the one hand, a bureaucracy is an incredibly efficient tool for handling the massive amounts of input and output that a modern government must expect. On the other, it stifles creative policymaking in the name of the very rules that make it such a useful instrument. Government agencies, large private companies, political parties of every persuasion—all succumb to the organizational imperative of bureaucratization. In turn, the imperatives of bureaucratic organizational forms require that human passions and value commitments be excluded from decision making.[4]

In addition to providing a description of the forces that produce subjectivity, Nietzsche and Weber supply a comparative grid with which to assess the product. Master and slave morality are contrasted in Nietzsche, and charismatic politicians and soulless bureaucrats, in Weber. Unfortunately, the slaves and bureaucrats far outnumber their value-creating counterparts. Is there perhaps something about the study of subjectivity—the academic discipline begun by these two thinkers—that lends itself to the kinds of dark conclusions typical of its original practitioners? It could be that here, more than anywhere else, philosophy is blind to the forces currently at work, so that what appears to it as an exhausted and final collapse of meaning is better understood as the moment when new kinds of meaning—and new forms of subjectivity to act as their vehicle—are assembling. Or could there be a simpler, more "political" explanation? Does a new discipline, a new orientation for study, need the apocalyptic gesture to defend itself, attract adherents, and in general to make itself an object of interest? Or, finally, is there something about the times, something in the air of the late nineteenth and early twentieth centuries, that both bred and demanded such conclusions?

I cannot pursue these possibilities here, though an examination of the historical and comparative analysis of subjectivity would undoubtedly be worthwhile. What is relevant in this context is Foucault's own effort—which included hesitations and false steps—to free himself and the tradition he worked in from what has become a tired cliché, which runs as follows: the particular form of subjectivity with which we are cursed today dehumanizes us; makes us incapable of creation or meaningful choice; condemns us to experience false desires and unsuitable values; turns us into mediocre last men and women, rule-worshiping bureaucrats, unthinking agents of external powers—in other words, the whole weary refrain of the totality and our powerlessness in the face of it. As recruiting lures such stories have, or had, their value, but now they act as more of a bar to the valuations whose loss they mourn than as spurs to their invention.

Curiously, both Nietzsche and Weber had similarly contradictory attitudes to the phenomena they described. As a dominant value structure, Nietzsche certainly was the enemy of slave morality. He was not, on that account, opposed to the existence of slaves. He wanted, we could say, the physiological condition of slavery to exist without its associated peculiar valuations playing the leading role.[5] Weber also combined warnings concerning the mass production of barren souls—which could be traced both to the withering of the calling as a locus of meaning and the increasing sway of instrumental rationality—with an insistence that most humans *remain* in a state that Foucault would later call (borrowing from Kant) immature. Bureaucrats should not stop being bureaucrats but should stop trying to be politicians. Taking a stand, he makes clear, is the politician's element.[6] The people should not revolt against the intellectual and political leveling that accompanies democracy and modernity; on the contrary, the masses as both platform and instrument are an important condition for the rise of value-creating charismatics.[7] For both Nietzsche and Weber, then, the subordination of vast quantities of human material to the values, rankings, and projects of a small elite is a necessary precondition for the development of humanity as a whole. The problem arises, however, when people who should be instruments—slaves, bureaucrats—appropriate the creative role that they are simply unfit to perform. It is the perversely irreversible tendency of the modern world to allow the instruments to call the tune that prompts the dark predictions for which both authors are known.

While Foucault is rooted firmly in the tradition of inquiry pioneered by Weber and Nietzsche, his purposes for employing it differ considerably. Though not everything Foucault is after is captured in this way, one could say that what Nietzsche presents as a *complaint*—namely, that a bland, mediocre, last man has come to dominate Western society—Foucault presents as a *criticism*. As we have seen, disciplines produce individuals with a heightened productive and an inhibited political capacity. Such individuals will not intervene in the process of their own manufacture, nor will they question the ends for which they are employed. In other words, Foucault is not so much concerned to lament the rise of a slave morality and demand that its progenitors return to the salt mines where they belong as he is to reveal and criticize the process through which we become disciplined slaves. The same difference separates Foucault from Weber. Where Weber worries that the spread of instrumentally rational forms of organization will inhibit the rise of leaders proficient at creating value structures, Foucault focuses on the tendency of the same structures to produce a quiescent population. In other words, Foucault takes the criticism of modern forms of subjectivity in Nietzsche and the concern over the inherently expansive drift of bureaucratic organizational forms in Weber and radicalizes them in a democratic direction. Neither Nietzsche nor Weber thinks "the crowd" is capable of value creation, a claim that is immediately contradicted, however, by these two authors' own complaints over the kinds of values produced by the crowd. For both, the masses are capable of little more than ill-informed support for this or that value which was created elsewhere. If this is not how the masses in fact act, it is how they should act.[8]

When not prophesying the end of meaning, Nietzsche and Weber tell us about the conditions necessary for reintroducing it into our lives. If the slave revolts and the bureaucratic ethos of the modern era leads us into an ice age with the potential to wipe civilization clean from the face of the earth, it follows that only similarly dramatic developments can generate a thaw. For Nietzsche, a mythical *Übermensch* will provide humanity with new goals and thus transcend the *Letztemensch*, or "last man."

Weber is a bit less poetic, but the conditions he identifies for the reinfusion of meaning into our world are similarly daunting. The true politician creates or works on behalf of specific value structures. What makes this activity heroic for Weber is that the modern era naturally tends to undermine the traditional and religious sources of meaning. The politician works, then, in a demanding field against increasingly difficult odds. To succeed, passionate devotion to a cause, combined with a cool and analytical perspective on political realities, is needed.[9] It is no accident, of course, that the individuals needed to create new kinds of meaning are not that different from the Calvinists in Weber's *Protestant Ethic*.

Weber puts the question in a way that, with suitable modifications, would not be foreign to Nietzsche's conception of the problem: "What kind of a man must one be if he is to be allowed to put his hand on the wheel of history?"[10] Nietzsche's response was the mythical, quasi-Olympian figure of Zarathustra, and Weber's, the hard saintliness of the Calvinist faithful.

Foucault wishes, once again, to democratize the insights and conclusions of his mentors. The pursuit of meaning—reserved for near deities and an exemplary pious few in Nietzsche and Weber—must be more broadly and "locally" available. Foucault's "specific intellectual" is none other than the bureaucrat that Weber told to get out of politics. Similarly, what is his discussion of the "plebeian aspect," reviewed in detail earlier, but a partial response to and distancing from Nietzsche's own rejection of the "plebs."[11] And, finally, what could Foucault's intent be when discussing "technologies of the self" other than to argue that the art linking the cultivation of subjectivity with the capacity to give one's actions value be fostered by broader circles of political agents than usually allowed for (or desired) by the founders of the tradition in which he worked.

On what does Foucault base his relatively more optimistic assessment of our ability to play a role in our own self-formation? Foucault's answer, as reviewed here, refers to his specific account of the dynamics of modern power. That power proceeds neither in a top-down direction nor according to the dictates of a totality. The creative sites of modern power are not located at the center of some all-encompassing web but in the restricted confines of the hospital, clinic, school, factory, and other conceivable loci of experimentation in the manufacture of subjectivity. If it is possible for subjects of these disciplines to reverse and revalue the psychic states pursued by them, it is also possible to generate new styles of existence. True, oppositional activity in the West has not, up to this point, been primarily concerned with this kind of activity.[12] But then it was precisely Foucault's intention to make possible new reflections on the way forward for political thought and action, as well as to thematize in a new way the more local struggles over subjectivity that have, in fact, developed over the past several decades.

NOTES

Abbreviations

All works given below are by Michel Foucault.

FR   *The Foucault Reader,* ed. Paul Rabinow (New York: Pantheon, 1984).

"GE"   "On the Genealogy of Ethics: An Overview of Work in Progress," in Hubert L. Dreyfus and Paul Rabinow, *Michel Foucault: Beyond Structuralism and Hermeneutics,* 2d ed. (Chicago: University of Chicago Press, 1983), 229–252.

LMC; OT   *Les mots et les choses* (Paris: Gallimard, 1966); trans. under the title *The Order of Things* (New York: Pantheon, 1971).

"NGH"   "Nietzsche, Genealogy, History," in *Language, Counter-Memory, Practice,* ed. Donald F. Bouchard (Ithaca: Cornell University Press, 1977).

P/K   *Power/Knowledge: Selected Interviews and Other Writings, 1972–1977,* ed. Colin Gordon (New York: Pantheon, 1980).

PPC   *Politics, Philosophy, Culture: Interviews and Other Writings, 1977–1984,* ed. Lawrence D. Kritzman (New York: Routledge, 1988).

Le souci de   *Le souci de soi* (Paris: Gallimard, 1984); trans. Robert Hurley under the title *The*
soi; CS   *Care of the Self* (New York: Pantheon, 1986).

SP; DP   *Surveiller et punir: Naissance de la prison* (Paris: Gallimard, 1975); trans. Alan Sheridan under the title *Discipline and Punish* (New York: Pantheon, 1977).

"SuP"   "The Subject and Power," afterword to *Michel Foucault: Beyond Structuralism and Hermeneutics,* Hubert L. Dreyfus and Paul Rabinow, 2d ed. (Chicago: University of Chicago Press, 1983).

UDP; UP   *L'usage des plaisirs* (Paris: Gallimard, 1984); trans. Robert Hurley under the title *The Use of Pleasure* (New York: Random House, 1985).

VS; HSI   *La volonté de savoir* (Paris: Gallimard, 1976); trans. Robert Hurley under the title *The History of Sexuality,* vol. 1, *An Introduction* (New York: Random House, 1978).

"WIE"   "What Is Enlightenment?" in *The Foucault Reader,* ed. Paul Rabinow (New York: Pantheon, 1984), 32–50.

Preface

1 In the interview "Non au sex roi," Foucault acknowledges his status as a symbol, commenting that it is "personally embarrassing for me that all my work is seen as a sign for belonging to the 'good side.' But there is a good side, which must be reached however by dissolving the illusory 'nature' ('naturalness') of this other side with which we have taken sides" (*PPC,* 120).

2 This is, of course, a composite sketch drawn from a variety of secondary readings of Foucault.

3 Michel Foucault, "On Power," in *PPC,* 108.

Introduction: Rethinking "Critique"

1 The "realist" school is well represented by Machiavelli, who tells his readers in chapter 15 of *The Prince* that whereas others had dreamed of principalities that had never existed, he would restrict his discourse to practical matters. Plato returns the compliment in his *Republic,* arguing (for the "ought" school) that "practical" politicians have no understanding of the purposes for which they wield political power. Niccolò Machiavelli, *The Prince,* trans. George Bull (New York: Penguin, 1981), chap. 15; and Plato, *The Republic,* trans. Robin Waterfield (Oxford: Oxford University Press, 1994).

2 Plato, *Republic,* 487b–502c. See especially the analogy of the Navigator, 488a–489a.

3 Michel Foucault, "Qu'est-ce que la critique?" *Bulletin de la Société française de Philosophie* 84 (1990): 35–63; trans. Kevin Paul Geiman under the title "What Is Critique?" in *"What Is Enlightenment?" Eighteenth-Century Answers and Twentieth-Century Questions,* ed. James Schmidt (Berkeley: University of California Press, 1996).

4 Martin Heidegger, *Being and Time,* trans. John Macquarrie and Edward Robinson (New York: Harper and Row, 1962), 174, 219–224.

5 Ibid., 98.

6 Ibid., 95–107.

7 *HSI,* p. 86. See also the preface to *The History of Sexuality,* vol. 2, in *FR,* 334–336.

8 Michel Foucault, "Practicing Criticism," in *PPC,* 154.

9 Michel Foucault "Prison Talk," in *P/K,* 53, and "NGH," 139–64.

10 Friedrich Nietzsche, *On the Genealogy of Morals,* trans. Walter Kaufmann (New York: Random House, 1969), 15–20.

11 Ibid., 27–34.

12 Nietzsche's views are, of course, much more sophisticated than the simplified version presented here.

13 Nietzsche, *On the Genealogy of Morals*, 31; emphasis added.

14 Michel Foucault and Richard Sennett, "Sexuality and Solitude," in *Humanities in Review*, vol. 1, ed. David Rieff (Cambridge: Cambridge University Press, 1982), 3–21. Foucault's contribution to the discussion begins on page 8. On page 9 he says: "I have tried to get away from the philosophy of the subject, through a genealogy of the modern subject as a historical and cultural reality. That means as something that can eventually change, which is of course politically important."

15 See "WIE," 32–50, and Michel Foucault, "The Art of Telling the Truth," in *PPC*, 86–95.

16 "WIE," 33; Foucault, "The Art of Telling the Truth," 88.

17 Michel Foucault, "Power and Sex," in *PPC*, 121.

18 "WIE," 34.

19 Immanuel Kant, "An Answer to the Question: 'What Is Enlightenment?'" in *Kant: Political Writings*, ed. Hans Reiss (Cambridge: Cambridge University Press, 1991), 54.

20 Michel Foucault, "The History of Sexuality," in *P/K*, 190.

1. Confronting New Forms of Power

1 I want to use the word "individual" in a very general sense throughout this book to mean "center of force" or of activity. The empirical individual that we see walking around with (usually) two legs, a mouth, and so on, is just one kind of individual. There are supraindividual entities (states) and subindividual entities (psychic forces).

2 The literature on power is extensive. A useful introduction can be obtained by looking at Robert A. Dahl, "The Concept of Power," *Behavioral Science* 2 (1957): 201–215; David A. Baldwin, *Paradoxes of Power* (New York: Basil Blackwell, 1989); Peter Bacharach and Morton S. Baratz, "Two Faces of Power," *American Political Science Review* 56 (1967): 947–952; Steven Lukes, *Power: A Radical View* (London: Macmillan, 1974); Dennis Wrong, *Power: Its Forms, Bases, and Uses* (New York: Harper and Row, 1980); and James G. March, "The Power of Power," in *Varieties of Political Theory*, ed. David Easton (Englewood Cliffs, N.J.: Prentice Hall, 1966).

3 Of course, not everyone believes that hitting the child accomplishes this. But even those who do not believe corporal punishment of children "works" refrain from interfering in the physical punishment of children from other families because the supposed intent of the punishing parent is the "improvement" of the child. The exercise of power is "legitimate," as it were, on the *intentional* side.

4 Think of "government" as that set of institutions formally established through the consent of the governed to create formal rules (laws) for the interaction of citizens, and "civil society" as the informal mix of noncoordinated social forces—the economy, public opinion, and so forth—that produces informal rules for the interaction of individuals.

5 Thomas Hobbes, *Leviathan* (New York: Penguin, 1981); and John Locke, *The Second Treatise of Government*, in *Two Treatises of Government*, ed. Peter Laslett (Cambridge: Cambridge University Press, 1960).

6 Thus, not only does the procedure that produces the social contract respect the

equality of the participants, but the conditions agreed to—protection of persons and property—are essential to the well-being and independence of the persons involved.

7   A foreign power could conceivably invade a country and take over the legitimate functions of the previous government but nevertheless be considered illegitimate because it was not consented to. On the other hand, an elected or otherwise domestically invested power can act contrary to its intended purposes and in this way become objectionable.

8   John Stuart Mill, *On Liberty*, in *Utilitarianism, On Liberty, and Considerations on Representative Government*, ed. H. B. Acton (New York: J. M. Dent and Sons, 1972), 69–83.

9   Or, if they saw the need, they saw no effective way to challenge the system. Or, if individuals saw what they thought were effective ways to challenge the system, they were in fact channeled into avenues that did not actually threaten it.

10 See the introduction to this volume, above.

11 Michel Foucault, "Truth and Power," in *P/K*, 121.

12 Michel Foucault, "Two Lectures," in *P/K*, 91.

13 Jeremy Bentham, in his *Theory of Legislation* (London: Oxford University Press, 1914), 200, urges governments to encourage the invention and propagation of games of all kinds as a way of drawing citizens away from antisocial behavior. He particularly recommends card games. Such amusements "have brought the sexes in closer association, and have diminished ennui, the special ailment of the human race, and in particular of wealth and old age."

14 Here I use "governmental" not in the usual liberal sense of formal institutions of government but more loosely in the sense of being governed by a power structure of some kind. Foucault often uses the word "government" in the latter sense. See Michel Foucault, "Governmentality," *Ideology and Consciousness* 6 (1979): 5–21, and Foucault, "What Is Critique?" trans. Kevin Paul Geiman, in *"What Is Enlightenment?" Eighteenth-Century Answers and Twentieth-Century Questions*, ed. James Schmidt (Berkeley: University of California Press, 1996).

15 For Foucault on the relation between disciplines and the sovereignty model, the reader should consult "Two Lectures," 94–108, and "Truth and Power," 64.

16 *VS*, 113; *HSI*, 86.

17 Foucault, "Two Lectures," 97.

18 Ibid., 104.

19 *SP*, 185; *DP*, 183.

20 *SP*, 149; *DP*, 147.

21 *SP*, 185; *DP*, 182–183.

22 Locke, *Second Treatise*, sec. 171, 428.

23 Locke is explicit on this point: "By *Property* I must be understood . . . to mean that Property which Men have in their Persons as well as Goods." See ibid., sec. 173, 430.

24 *SP*, 172; *DP*, 170.

25 Locke, *Second Treatise*, sec. 202, 448. The quotation goes on to read: "And whosoever in Authority exceeds the Power given him by the Law, and makes use of the Force he has under his Command, to compass that upon the Subject, which the Law allows not, ceases in that to be a Magistrate, and acting without Authority, may be opposed, as any other Man, who by force invades the Right of another."

26   Michel Foucault, "Prison Talk," in *P/K*, 52.

27   Foucault, "Two Lectures," 88.

28   *SP,* 31; *DP,* 26.

29   Foucault, "Two Lectures," 106.

30   This is why scientists employed by the R. J. Reynolds Institute on Tobacco Research have a hard time being taken seriously.

31   Nietzsche argues that knowledge should be regarded "in a strict and narrow anthropocentric and biological sense. For a particular species to maintain itself and increase its power, its conception of reality must comprehend enough of the calculable and constant for it to base a scheme of behavior on it. The utility of preservation — not some abstract-theoretical need not to be deceived — stands as the motive behind the development of the organs of knowledge." See Nietzsche, *The Will to Power,* trans. Walter Kaufmann (New York: Vintage, 1968), sec. 480, 266–267.

32   Foucault, "Truth and Power," 112.

33   Take as an example the criticism of Donald Duck in Max Horkheimer and Theodor W. Adorno, *Dialectic of Enlightenment* (New York: Continuum, 1987), 138. This is part of Horkheimer and Adorno's general criticism of the "culture industry" and its capacity to produce shallow, hard-working, and uncomplaining cogs in the capitalist machine. In his cartoons, Donald Duck is constantly frustrated by little chipmunks. He screams in rage, but the more he rages, the more impotent he becomes and the more crushing the chipmunks' victories over him. We laugh at these scenes — a knowing laugh that empathizes with the cruelty of Donald's fate, a submissive laugh that says Donald gets only what he deserves for being so disagreeable, and a complicitous laugh that responds favorably to seeing him crushed. "Donald Duck in the cartoons and the unfortunate in real life get their thrashing so that the audience can learn to take their own punishment" (138). The culture industry, then, is a favorite example from the Frankfurt School of exercises of power where the "consent-coercion" dynamic plays little, if any, role.

34   For instance, Horkheimer and Adorno repeatedly refer to the "false" quality of post–World War II societies in *Dialectic of Enlightenment,* 120–121, 136, 141, 154. What is *falsch* — "artificial," "spurious," and "counterfeit" are some of the meanings of this German word — about these societies is the nature of the relationship between the individual and the social whole. Instead of acting as the condition for the development of diverse individual powers, society and the technological rationality that determine it provide nonhuman and diversionary satisfactions, thus producing a "false identification" of the individual with society (120–121). See also the articles titled "The Individual," "Prejudice," and "Ideology" in Frankfurt School of Social Research, *Aspects of Sociology,* trans. John Viertel (Boston: Beacon, 1972).

35   Michel Foucault, "Critical Theory/Intellectual History," 26, and Foucault, "The Art of Telling the Truth," 95, both in *PPC.*

36   In *Minima Moralia,* trans. E. F. N. Jephcott (New York: Schocken, 1978), pt. 1, sec. 5, Adorno criticizes those who partake of "little pleasures." There is, he says, "nothing innocuous left," not even nature. "Even the blossoming tree lies the moment its bloom is seen without the shadow of terror; even the innocent 'How lovely!' becomes an excuse for an existence outrageously unlovely, and there is no longer beauty or

consolation except in the gaze falling on horror, withstanding it, and in unalleviated consciousness of negativity holding fast to the possibility of what is better." Such as a blossoming tree?

37   *SP*, 218–219; *DP*, 217.

38   For an excellent discussion of Foucault's notion of power-knowledge and the oppositional possibilities linked to it, see Joseph Rouse, "Power/Knowledge," in *The Cambridge Companion to Foucault*, ed. Gary Gutting (Cambridge: Cambridge University Press, 1994), 92–114, esp. 104–112.

39   Karl Marx and Friedrich Engels, *The German Ideology* (1964), rpt. in *The Marx-Engels Reader*, ed. Robert C. Tucker (New York: W. W. Norton, 1972), 149 and 164–165, contains representative statements of this view.

40   Jürgen Habermas, *Knowledge and Human Interests* (Boston: Beacon, 1971), 301–317; Friedrich Engels, *Socialism: Utopian and Scientific*, rpt. in *The Marx-Engels Reader*, ed. Robert C. Tucker (New York: Norton, 1972), 683–717, esp. 714–717.

41   *SP*, 197–229; *DP*, 195–228.

42   Jürgen Habermas, *The Philosophical Discourse of Modernity: Twelve Lectures*, trans. Frederick Lawrence (Cambridge: MIT Press, 1987), 127. It is important to note that Habermas has missed a stage of the discussion. It is not Foucault who "replaces the model of domination based on repression . . . by a plurality of power strategies." That, according to Foucault, was done by the bourgeoisie and cannot be blamed on him. Of course, Habermas is free to disagree with Foucault's account of some of the forces making up Western societies, but until he does it makes no sense to complain that the usual critical tools fail to apply to the power formations described by Foucault. To say that disciplines "cannot be *judged* under the aspect of their validity" simply means we need to think about ways of opposing power constructs that do not rely on "judging their validity" (read: assessing their fitness or unfitness for expressing our human nature).

43   Foucault, "Critical Theory/Intellectual History," 43.

44   "Resistances . . . are all the more real and effective because they are formed right at the point where relations of power are exercised; resistance does not have to come from elsewhere to be real, nor is it inexorably frustrated through being the compatriot of power." Michel Foucault, "Power and Strategies," in *P/K*, 142.

45   A hermeneutic interpretation proceeds from within the phenomenon to be studied (a text, a historical period, a kind of knowledge, etc.), rather than bringing external criteria to bear on it. From within a text we develop a certain interpretation of it and then turn to the text for confirmation and challenges. What we find there not only confirms or denies our initial reading but probably enriches it or even sends it in new directions: thus the hermeneutic circle, which encloses—but does not trap!—the interpreter and excludes the introduction of external perspectives. In addition, the items we study are not chosen randomly but for their interest. To an extent, we are ourselves constituted by the thing we study—the Bible, the French Revolution, Bentham's Panopticon—and so our reading does not stand outside the text but is accomplished in it. At the same time, however, this interpretation does not leave unaffected the thing interrogated. Thus, Luther's reading of the Bible was done within a certain tradition, but when he was done neither Luther nor the Bible were the same. What Luther did

was to free another possible reading of the Bible through reinterpretation, thus adjusting its horizons of meaning. Similarly, Foucault wants to locate critique within the horizon of particular power-knowledge dynamics. For a review of the possibilities of hermeneutic interpretation, see Hans-Georg Gadamer, *Truth and Method*, 2d ed. (New York: Continuum, 1994), 265–379.

46   Foucault, "What Is Critique?"

47   Foucault, "Two Lectures," 107–108.

2. Disciplines and the Individual

1   The first task is the province of political *science* (Hobbes, Hume, and behaviorism comes to mind), and the second, of political *philosophy* (Aristotle, Plato, Kant, Rawls, and many others).

2   Aristotle, *The Politics*, trans. Trevor J. Saunders (New York: Penguin, 1981), bk. 1; Thomas Hobbes, *Leviathan*, ed. C. B. Macpherson (New York: Penguin, 1981), 118–119, 129–130.

3   Ibid., 229–270.

4   Immanuel Kant, *Foundations of the Metaphysics of Morals*, 2d ed., trans. Lewis White Beck (New York: Macmillan, 1985), 51–58.

5   Hobbes, *Leviathan*, 161.

6   Foucault is far from the first theorist to make claims about the historical constitution of the human subject. And yet others who make similar claims often seem to give in to the temptation to describe one particular kind of human nature as the one to be preferred, as the most human, the one history is leading up to, the most authentic, and so forth.

7   Michel Foucault, "Two Lectures," in *P/K*, 94–95.

8   For such assessments, see, for example, Michel Foucault, "SuP," 208; and Foucault, "Technologies of the Self," in *TS*, 17–18. And just because Foucault says "this is how you should read my work," one is not compelled to do so. But in fact this suggestion is a productive one.

9   Michel Foucault, "Governmentality," *Ideology and Consciousness* 6 (1979): 5.

10   Jeremy Bentham, *Theory of Legislation*, vol. 2 (London: Oxford University Press, 1914), 175.

11   Ibid., 177.

12   Ibid.

13   Ibid., 182 and 193.

14   Ibid., 181.

15   Ibid., 196–201. Of course, what might have worked in Bentham's time may not apply to ours. Today it is clear that something besides tea would be needed to replace alcohol.

16   "There is," Bentham confides to his reader, "a way of guiding and controlling public opinion in secret—that is to say, without anyone suspecting that it is being done. . . . Matters are so arranged that the occurrence we wish to prevent cannot come to pass without the happening of some previous event, which the popular voice has already condemned as undesirable" (ibid., 282). The example Bentham gives is the requirement of an oath concerning the payment of a tax. Many might be willing to avoid

paying the tax but are unwilling to perjure themselves or use an oath falsely. Result: the tax gets paid. Again, Bentham's specific expedients may seem unconvincing, but the direction of his comments is, hopefully, clear.

17 Ibid., 175.
18 *SP,* 9–11; *DP,* 3–6.
19 *SP,* 93; *DP,* 90.
20 But it does seem perverse and gratuitous for Foucault to insist that reformers felt none of the horror they so loudly expressed. Foucault appears to be confusing the intentions of a group of individuals with a retrospective assessment of the results of their actions.
21 *SP,* 105; *DP,* 102. See also the discussion of the Ideologues in *LMC,* 249–256; *OT,* 236–243.
22 *SP,* 105; *DP,* 103.
23 *SP,* 108; *DP,* 106.
24 *SP,* 109 and 113; *DP,* 107 and 111.
25 *SP,* 118; *DP,* 116.
26 *PPC,* 104–105; Graham Burchell, Colin Gordon, and Susan James, eds., *The Foucault Effect: Studies in Governmentality* (Chicago: University of Chicago Press, 1991), 75.
27 *SP,* 132; *DP,* 129.
28 *SP,* 105; *DP,* 103.
29 *SP,* 134; *DP,* 131.
30 *SP,* 83; *DP,* 80.
31 See chap. 4, below.
32 *SP,* 132; *DP,* 128–129.
33 *SP,* 132; *DP,* 129; emphases added. The first sentence in the French is, "L'agent de punition doit exercer un pouvoir total, qu'aucun tiers ne peut venir perturber; l'individu à corriger doit être entièrement enveloppé dans le pouvoir qui s'exerce sur lui."
34 *SP,* 139 and 141; *DP,* 137 and 139.
35 *SP,* 217–218; *DP,* 216.
36 *SP,* 218–219; *DP,* 217.
37 Foucault, "Two Lectures," 98.
38 Steven Best and Douglas Kellner, *Postmodern Theory* (New York: Guilford, 1991), 54.
39 Ibid., 55.
40 For "fragility," see *PPC,* 36, 37, 156; Foucault, "Two Lectures," 80; and Michel Foucault, "Questions of Method," in Burchell, Gordon, and James, *Foucault Effect,* 76–78. For "contingency," see "WIE," 45, and Michel Foucault, introduction to *The Normal and the Pathological,* by Georges Canguilhem (New York: Bone, 1989), 11–12.
41 Thomas McCarthy, "The Critique of Impure Reason: Foucault and the Frankfurt School," *Political Theory* 18, no. 3 (August 1990): 443.
42 See Karl Marx, *Capital,* vol. 1, trans. Ben Fowkes (New York: Vintage, 1977), 899.
43 For comments linking Foucault and his problematic to other twentieth-century thinkers, see Fred Dallmayr, "Pluralism Old and New: Foucault on Power," in *Polis and Practice: Exercises in Contemporary Political Theory* (Cambridge: MIT Press, 1984), 77–100, esp. 96–97.
44 Peter Dews, in "Power and Subjectivity in Foucault," *New Left Review* 144 (1984): 72–95, argues that "a theory of power with radical intent requires an account of that which

power represses, since without such an account relations of power cease to appear objectionable" (73). But doesn't a theory of power with radical intent — really, with any kind of intent — also need to reflect the ways in which power actually functions? Foucault's whole point is that power can be and often is *productive*. Productive forms of power do not repress; they create. If Foucault is right — and for some reason Dews skips this stage of the discussion — then a theory of power with radical intent cannot remain satisfied with a description of what it is power represses. Such an approach will inevitably miss all sorts of ways in which we are constituted as subjects and will cease — intentions not withstanding — to be radical.

45   The key criticisms of Foucault can be found in the following essays: Jürgen Habermas, "The Entwinement of Myth and Enlightenment: Max Horkheimer and Theodor Adorno," and "Some Questions Concerning the Theory of Power: Foucault Again," both in *The Philosophical Discourse of Modernity: Twelve Lectures,* trans. Frederick Lawrence (Cambridge: MIT Press, 1987); Nancy Fraser, "Foucault on Modern Power: Empirical Insights and Normative Confusions," in *Unruly Practices: Power, Discourse, and Gender in Contemporary Social Theory* (Minneapolis: University of Minnesota Press, 1989), 17–34 and also chaps. 2 and 3; and Charles Taylor, "Foucault on Freedom and Truth," and Michael Walzer, "The Politics of Michel Foucault," both in *Foucault: A Critical Reader,* ed. David Couzens Hoy (Oxford: Basil Blackwell, 1986), 51–102.

46   Leslie Paul Thiele makes interesting suggestions along these lines in "The Agony of Politics: The Nietzschean Roots of Foucault's Thought," *American Political Science Review* 84, no. 3 (September 1990): 907–925. She argues that it is quite possible to desire and defend civil and other rights not because such rights express an essential human nature but because many of them are useful tools for the struggle against whatever happens to be the "main danger" at a particular moment. See 916–919, esp. 919. I disagree, however, with Thiele's attempt, as I see it, to provide a philosophic grounding for Foucault's "pessimistic hyper-activism" (916). For Foucault, Thiele claims, "one acts not because goals are attainable but because it is one's fate to struggle valiantly. One struggles because the uncontested life is not worth living" (916). This quasi-romantic reading is unconvincing. Mental patients, prisoners, homosexuals, and so on, struggle for much more pragmatic reasons than this — and definitely with particular goals in mind.

47   *SP,* 220; *DP,* 218.

48   This dual program — combining political docility with a heightened economic usefulness — is discussed throughout *SP.* See, for instance, *SP,* 222–223; *DP,* 220–221.

49   Foucault also asserts that technologies often take three forms in the course of their history: first, as a dream of utopia; then, as a practice for actual institutions; and then, as an academic discipline. Perhaps *DP* could be thought of as a combination of the first two, with an emphasis on the "dream" stage. See Michel Foucault, "The Political Technology of Individuals," in *TS,* 154.

50   *SP,* 35; *DP,* 31.

51   Michel Perrot, ed., *L'impossible prison: Debat avec Michel Foucault* (Paris: Editions du seuil, 1980), 33. My translation.

52   Ibid., 42; Burchell, Gordon, and James, *Foucault Effect,* 75.

53   *SP,* 220; *DP,* 218.

54   See the discussion of the various programs of the penal reformers in *SP,* 75–134; *DP,* 73–131.

55   *SP,* 145; *DP,* 144.

56   *SP,* 146; *DP,* 144.

57   "SuP," 217.

58   *SP,* 199; *DP,* 198.

59   *SP,* 197 and 197 n. 1; *DP,* 195, and see also 316 n. 1.

60   *SP,* 200; *DP,* 198–199.

61   See the discussion in Perrot, *L'impossible prison,* 29–39.

62   Foucault specifically distances himself from a Frankfurt School–style attempt to criticize Western societies in terms of a rationality that produces an unassailable "totality." See "Political Technology of Individuals," 161.

63   Perrot, *L'impossible prison,* 34–35.

64   In French the first clause reads: "La discipline 'fabrique' les individus." *SP,* 172; *DP,* 170.

65   Ibid.

66   *SP,* 228; *DP,* 221.

67   *SP,* 186; *DP,* 184.

68   *SP,* 137–138; *DP,* 135.

69   *SP,* 220; *DP,* 218.

70   *SP,* 182; *DP,* 179.

71   *SP,* 182; *DP,* 180. Foucault is quoting from a manual on regulations for schools.

72   *SP,* 182–183; *DP,* 180.

73   *SP,* 183; *DP,* 181.

74   Friedrich Nietzsche, *The Will to Power,* trans. Walter Kaufmann (New York: Vintage, 1968), aphorism 481, 267.

75   *SP,* 181; *DP,* 179.

76   One is reminded in this context of Foucault's discussion of man in *Les mots et les choses* as an "empirico-transcendental doublet."

77   *SP,* 183; *DP,* 181.

78   *SP,* 200; *DP,* 198.

79   Ibid.

80   The first clause is more graphic in French: "D'un côté, on 'pestifère' les lépreux." *SP,* 201; *DP,* 199–200.

81   *SP,* 201; *DP,* 200.

82   *SP,* 163; *DP,* 161.

83   See, for instance, Friedrich Nietzsche, *On the Genealogy of Morals,* trans. Walter Kaufmann and R. J. Hollingdale (New York: Random House, 1967), "Second Essay," secs. 1, 12, and esp. 18, where Nietzsche maintains that the same creative force that builds up nation-states out of dispersed principalities also shapes the modern individual.

84   Duccio Trombadori, *Colloqui con Foucault* (Salerno: 10/17 Cooperative editrice, 1981), 20; Michel Foucault, *Remarks on Marx,* trans. R. James Goldstein and James Cascaito (New York: Semiotext(e), 1991), 31–32.

85   *SP,* 137–138; *DP,* 135–136.

86   *UDP,* 10–11; *UP,* 4–5.

87   *UDP,* 11; *UP,* 5.

88   When he writes of "first studying the games of truth," Foucault appears to refer to *Madness and Civilization* and *The Birth of the Clinic*—though he could have *Les mots et les choses* in mind as well. *UDP,* 12; *UP,* 6.

89   *UDP,* 12–13; *UP,* 6–7.

90   An excellent discussion of Foucault's attempt to provide his readers with "experiences" rather than with fully worked out theories can be found in the essay by Ladelle McWhorter, "Foucault's Analytics of Power," in *Crises in Continental Philosophy,* ed. Arleen B. Dallery and Charles E. Scott (Albany: State University of New York Press, 1990), 119–126.

91   *UDP,* 15; *UP,* 9.

92   Trombadori, *Colloqui con Foucault,* 22; Foucault, *Remarks on Marx,* 35–36.

93   Trombadori, *Colloqui con Foucault,* 25; Foucault, *Remarks on Marx,* 42.

94   *PPC,* 155.

3. Governmentality and Population

1   Critical readers of Foucault often attack his oppositional stances outside the context of his claims about what characterizes our political situation. Thomas McCarthy, for instance, insists on seeing Foucault's discussion of technologies of the self late in his career as nonsensical given his earlier discussion of disciplines and their effect on the individual. Foucault's focus has shifted, McCarthy claims, from an earlier "social ontology of power . . . from which there is no escape" to a discussion of self-fashioning that has "scant regard for social, political, and economic context." See McCarthy, "The Critique of Impure Reason: Foucault and the Frankfurt School," *Political Theory* 18, no. 3 (August 1990): 463. Both readings—that Foucault describes a society-wide prison in the 1970s followed by a timely focus on self-absorption in the 1980s—are wrong and can be corrected only if Foucault's overall picture of power in the West is considered.

   McCarthy, however, explicitly decides against taking seriously Foucault's own assessments of the themes that unify his work (in places such as "SuP," 208–209). These recastings of earlier periods, McCarthy suggests, "are . . . better read as *retrospectives* from newly achieved points of view" than as accurate "redescriptions" of them ("Critique of Impure Reason," 465). Perhaps. But what, in any event, is McCarthy's objection to this retrospective reading? McCarthy says he finds the "straightforward acknowledgment of a 'theoretical shift' [in Foucault's work] hermeneutically more satisfying than any of the attempts to read his earlier work as if it had been written from the perspective of the 1980s." But no one suggests we should read Foucault's earlier works as if they had been written from the perspective of the 1980s. That is an unhelpful distortion of what is at issue. What Foucault and others have suggested is that despite the different paths they take, there is a comprehensible sense in which the works from the different periods hang together. Certainly no one is required to agree with Foucault's reading of his own intellectual history. The question for scholars is, Which perspective yields greater insight? We can also wonder why McCarthy finds it hermeneutically more satisfactory to ascribe a fundamental incoherence to Foucault's efforts. Indeed, it is not difficult to describe someone as self-contradictory, inconsistent, and thus useless, when the *préjugés* that is brought to the issues is that the individual in question is flighty. The hermeneutic circle strikes again, with the result that Foucault is thrown into the Habermasian wastebasket of irrational postmodernists. But then, that conclusion was always already there in McCarthy's *Vor-urteil.*

2   See the first section in chap. 5, below.

3   Michel Foucault, "Governmentality," *Ideology and Consciousness* 6 (1979): 20.

4   Ibid.

5   There are, it is true, moments when Foucault has described the interaction between "power" and "knowledge" as a universal condition of power's functioning (see his "Two Lectures," in *P/K,* 93). I believe, however, that the Foucault that is the most helpful in understanding modern power formations is the one that presents "power-knowledge" as part of—and as product of—a historically situated confluence of factors rather than as an unchanging condition for the functioning of power.

6   An excellent overview of the industrial revolution is provided in John R. Gillis, *The Development of European Society, 1770–1870* (Boston: Houghton Mifflin, 1977).

7   *VS,* 187; *HSI,* 142.

8   *VS,* 188; *HSI,* 143. Translation slightly modified.

9   Karl Marx, *Grundrisse* (New York: Random House, 1973), 471–514.

10   *VS,* 187–188; *HSI,* 142–143.

11   *VS,* 35; *HSI,* 25.

12   *VS,* 180; *HSI,* 137.

13   An insightful overview of Foucault's notion of governmentality can be found in Peter Miller and Nikolas Rose, "Governing Economic Life," in *Foucault's New Domains,* ed. Mike Gane and Terry Johnson (New York: Routledge, 1993). The authors focus especially on the psychological aspects of governmentality.

14   *PPC,* 57–85.

15   Ibid., 79.

16   Ibid., 74. See also *TS,* 148.

17   *TS,* 147.

18   Ibid., 152.

19   *P/K,* 167.

20   Ibid.

21   *VS* gives a beginning account of the origins of the "pastoral" practice in the Christian confession and its mutation into elements of modern psychiatry and "sexology." See *VS,* 27–28 and 153–154; *HSI,* 18–19 and 118–119. Foucault provides a more developed treatment of the role of "pastoral power" in the modern context in "SuP," 213–215, and "Politics and Reason," in *PPC,* 67–73.

22   *PPC,* 125–151.

23   Ibid., 137.

24   Ibid., 134.

25   Ibid.

26   Ibid., 138.

27   Ibid., 135.

28   *VS,* 34–35; *HSI,* 24.

29   "Sexologists" is not Foucault's term. I use it to refer to the wide variety of practitioners, not all of whom were psychiatrists.

30   *VS*, 131–132; *HSI*, 99–100.
31   *PPC*, 128.
32   Foucault's emphasis. *VS*, 140; *HSI*, 106.
33   *VS*, 141; *HSI*, 107.
34   *P/K*, 142.
35   *VS*, 125; *HSI*, 94–95.
36   *VS*, 146; *HSI*, 110.
37   *VS*, 145–146; *HSI*, 110–111.
38   *VS*, 146–147; *HSI*, 111.
39   *VS*, 143; *HSI*, 109.
40   Ibid.
41   *VS*, 144–145; *HSI*, 109.
42   *PPC*, 28–29.
43   "SuP," 209.
44   This same point is pursued in the context of an overall treatment of genealogy in chapter 5 below.
45   *PPC*, 37.
46   Places where Foucault talks about the fragility of power explicitly or implicitly are *PPC*, 37, 156; *P/K*, 80; *TS*, 11; and James Bernauer and David Rasmussen, eds., *The Final Foucault* (Cambridge: MIT Press, 1988), 12.
47   *PPC*, 118. They are "best hidden" not in the sense that power is not visible but in the sense that it is not understood. We are not "enlightened" concerning its operations.
48   Ibid., 156.
49   *P/K*, 191. See also *VS*, 51–52 and 142; *HSI*, 37 and 107–108.
50   *PPC*, 114.
51   "SuP," 214.
52   *PPC*, 71.
53   "GE," 237.
54   Ibid., 244.
55   *P/K*, 108.
56   See chap. 1, above.
57   *VS*, 133–134; *HSI*, 101–102.
58   Ibid.
59   *P/K*, 108.
60   *VS*, 134; *HSI*, 102.
61   "SuP," 216.

4. Genealogy in the Disciplinary Age

1   See chap. 1 in this volume, and Michel Foucault, "Two Lectures," in *P/K*, 107–108.
2   Friedrich Nietzsche, *On the Genealogy of Morals*, trans. Walter Kaufmann and R. J. Hollingdale (New York: Vintage, 1989).
3   Nietzsche did dispute the tenets of Christian morality, but when in that mode he was not practicing genealogy.
4   Nietzsche, *On the Genealogy of Morals*, First Essay.

5 It is possible that we will then go on to affirm Christian principles despite the revelations of genealogy. But even in this case our cognitive relationship to Christian beliefs will have undergone a significant critical and reflective shift.

6 See, for instance, aphorisms 642 and 643 in Friedrich Nietzsche, *The Will to Power*, trans. Walter Kaufmann (New York: Vintage, 1968), 342; and Nietzsche, *On the Genealogy of Morals*, Second Essay, sec. 12, 79, and sec. 18, 87.

7 Arnold I. Davidson, "Archaeology, Genealogy, Ethics," in *Foucault: A Critical Reader*, ed. David Couzens Hoy (Oxford: Basil Blackwell, 1986), 225.

8 One of the best critical essays on Foucault is Charles Taylor's "Foucault on Freedom and Truth," in Hoy, *Foucault: A Critical Reader*, 69–102. There Taylor makes just the kind of mistake concerning Foucault's genealogies that I am concerned with here, namely, that their purpose is to expose the workings of "power." He does this by claiming that "as is well known," Foucault "wants to take a stance of neutrality" (73) regarding the discrete systems of power he describes, in this case the sovereign and disciplinary modes of punishment discussed in *DP*. "Here are just two systems of power," Taylor has Foucault say, "classical and modern" (73–74), with no way to distinguish them along ethical lines. I would argue, however, that Taylor's sense of bewilderment in the face of this "Nietzschean stance of neutrality" (80) comes from placing too much weight on the unveiling of power as the purpose of genealogy. That Taylor is mistaken in placing the emphasis where he does would explain why no one reading Nietzsche or Foucault ever comes away from their genealogies with a feeling that either author is neutral with regard to the discrete valuations embodied in the institutions and practices their histories describe. It is true: both the moral valuations of the Roman lords and their Jewish victims, along with the sovereign-centered and disciplinary modes of punishment, arise from the exercise of "power" of some kind. The point, then, is not that Nietzsche and Foucault are neutral with regard to these various expressions of power but that their evaluations pivot on some factor other than the presence or absence of power.

9 Thomas McCarthy, "The Critique of Impure Reason: Foucault and the Frankfurt School," *Political Theory* 18, no. 3 (August 1990): 445.

10 Judith Butler, *Gender Trouble: Feminism and the Subversion of Identity* (New York: Routledge, 1990), x.

11 *VS*, 133; *HSI*, 100–101.

12 *VS*, 134–135; *HSI*, 101–102.

13 *VS*, 134; *HSI*, 101.

14 See *VS*, chaps. 1 and 2, and chap. 1, above.

15 *VS*, 18; *HSI*, 10.

16 Michel Foucault, "Power and Sex," in *PPC*, 114.

17 *VS*, 133; *HSI*, 101.

18 This centrally important question is discussed at length in the next two chapters.

19 Foucault, "Power and Sex," 120.

20 Foucault, "Two Lectures," 107.

21 Ibid., 103.

22 "NGH," 151.

23 Michel Foucault, "Critical Theory/Intellectual History," in *PPC*, 37.

24   Michel Foucault, "Politics and Reason," in *PPC*, 83.
25   Michel Foucault, "Body/Power," in *P/K*, 62.
26   "NGH," 148.
27   Ibid., 149.
28   Ibid., 150.
29   Ibid., 152.
30   Foucault, "Body/Power," 61.
31   Michel Foucault, *Madness and Civilization* (New York: Random House, 1965), 38–64.
32   Ibid., 241–278.
33   Ibid., 241–242.
34   "NGH," 142.
35   Michel Foucault, "The Discourse on Language," in *The Archaeology of Knowledge*, trans. A. M. Sheridan Smith (New York: Pantheon, 1972), 231.
36   "NGH," 155, 154.
37   Foucault, "Two Lectures," 99.
38   See the first two sections of chap. 3, above.
39   Foucault, "Politics and Reason," 69.
40   See "Plurality of Power in the West" in chap. 3, above.
41   Max Horkheimer and Theodor W. Adorno, *Dialectic of Enlightenment* (New York: Continuum, 1987); see the essays "The Concept of Enlightenment," "Excursus 1: Odysseus or Myth and Enlightenment," and "The Culture Industry: Enlightenment and Mass Deception." An excellent review and critique of this text is contained in Paul Connerton, *The Tragedy of Enlightenment* (Cambridge: Cambridge University Press, 1980), chap. 4.
42   Foucault, "Politics and Reason," 73.
43   Ibid., 59.
44   Foucault, "Critical Theory/Intellectual History," 37.
45   Foucault, "Politics and Reason," 84.
46   Ibid.
47   Ibid., 85. The individualization that Foucault criticizes here is of a certain kind.
48   "NGH," 147.
49   See "Plurality of Power in the West" in chap. 3, above.
50   *VS*, 125; *HSI*, 95.
51   Michel Foucault, "The Confession of the Flesh," in *P/K*, 209.
52   *UDP*, 88; *UP*, 75.
53   "GE," 238.
54   *UDP*, 33; *UP*, 26. See also ibid., 238–243.
55   "GE," 231; see also "Varieties of Morality" in chap. 5, below.
56   "GE," 231.
57   Ibid., 234; emphasis added.
58   Ibid., 236.
59   Foucault, "Power and Sex," 118. See also *VS*, 113; *HSI*, 86.
60   Michel Foucault, "Prison Talk," in *P/K*, 51.
61   Michel Foucault, "Confinement, Psychiatry, Prison," in *PPC*, 197.
62   "NGH," 156–157.

63   Michel Foucault, "The History of Sexuality," in *P/K*, 193. In *Foucault and the Political*, Jon Simons draws on Milan Kundera's *Unbearable Lightness of Being* as a way to schematize the diversity of Foucault's efforts. Existence can be "too light" when marked by a lack of purpose and "too heavy" when overburdened with the goals of an exhausted will to power. See Simons, *Foucault and the Political* (New York: Routledge, 1995), 3. By sorting Foucault's efforts with reference to the "heavy" and "light" poles, Simons hopes to avoid the error of reading him solely in terms of one or the other of the two poles. Although this is a very helpful way of thinking about Foucault, Simons seems to misapply it at times. Foucault's comment that he has written "nothing but fictions" is, according to Simons, a claim that veers too sharply in the direction of "lightness" (5). This criticism can be sustained, however, only by a more careful analysis of Foucault's use of the term "fiction" than the one Simons provides. Fictions can have effects of truth, and much of the material Foucault discusses has to do with just such creations, with Bentham's Panopticon being the most familiar. Indeed, if a key element of Foucault's argument is that power is "productive," as Simons himself explains to us (33), then we should be very careful about dismissing fictions as "too light."

64   Michel Foucault, "Polemics, Politics, and Problemizations: An Interview," in *The Foucault Reader*, ed. Paul Rabinow (New York: Pantheon, 1984), 385.

65   "GE," 232.

66   Foucault, "Two Lectures," 81.

67   Ibid., 82.

68   Ibid.

69   Ibid.

70   Foucault, "The History of Sexuality," 186.

71   Foucault, "Two Lectures," 82.

72   Ibid., 83.

73   Ibid.

74   Ibid., 81, 85.

75   Ibid., 82.

76   Ibid., 86.

77   Ibid.

78   Ibid., 83.

79   *VS*, 131–132; *HSI*, 99.

80   "GE," 231–232.

81   Foucault, "Two Lectures," 80.

82   Ibid., 81.

83   "WIE," 46.

5. The "Plebeian Aspect"

1   A contemporary example is as follows: During the Persian Gulf War, it was reported that psychiatrists hired by the army had developed a new understanding of and thus a new approach to battle fatigue. In the Second World War and the Korean War, soldiers experiencing battle fatigue as the result of exposure to the sudden and horrific death of comrades were relieved of combat duty and returned home to recuperate in hospi-

tals. They were not returned to the battlefield. Psychiatrists concluded, however, that this solution was no longer the appropriate one. Instead, individuals suffering from this kind of shock could be successfully treated by spending several days in the rear and engaging in a number of group discussions of their experiences under the leadership of psychiatric personnel. Thus, a different knowledge leads to a new set of rules and a new disposition of human material. See Daniel Goleman, "In Gulf War, Many Wounds Will Be Mental," *New York Times*, 22 January 1991: C1.

2   Michel Foucault, "The History of Sexuality," in *FR*, 333–334.

3   See Michel Foucault, "Two Lectures," in *P/K*, 98: "The individual is an effect of power, and at the same time, or precisely to the extent to which it is that effect, it is the element of its articulation. The individual which power has constituted is at the same time its vehicle."

4   For this point, see the excellent discussion by R. N. Berki, *The Genesis of Marxism* (London: J. M. Dent and Sons, 1988), 1–89.

5   Very helpful in this context are James Bernauer's reflections on Foucault's reading of the French Revolution and the theme of revolution generally, in *Michel Foucault's Force of Flight* (London: Humanities Press International, 1990), 148–153.

6   Michel Foucault, "The Concern for the Truth," in *PPC*, 267. In 1977 Foucault was asked about an alternative to political forms in the West, given the seemingly poor record of accomplishments in the socialist world. His answer:

> La réponse à votre question est triste, étant donné les jours sombres que nous vivons et que la succession du président Mao Tsé-toung a été réglé par les armes. Des hommes ont été fusillés ou emprisonnés, des mitrailleuses ont été mises en action. Aujourd'hui, 14 octobre, jour dont on peut dire, peut-être, depuis la révolution russe d'octobre 1917, peut-être même depuis les grands mouvements révolutionnaires européens de 1848, c'est-à-dire depuis soixante ans ou, si vous voulez, depuis cent vingt ans, que c'est la première fois qu'il n'y a plus sur la terre un seul point d'où pourrait jaillir la lumière d'une espérance. Il n'existe plus d'orientation. Même pas en Union soviétique, cela va de soi. Ni non plus dans les pays satellites. Cela aussi, c'est clair. Ni à Cuba. Ni dans la révolution palestinienne, et pas non plus en Chine, évidemment. Ni au Viêt-nam ni au Cambodge. Pour la première fois, la gauche, face à ce qui vient de se passer en Chine, toute cette pensée de la gauche européenne, cette pensée européenne révolutionnaire qui avait ses points de référence dans le monde entier et les élaborait d'une manière déterminée, donc une pensée qui s'orientait sur des choses qui se situaient en dehors d'elles-mêmes, cette pensée a perdu les repères historiques qu'elle trouvait auparavant dans d'autres parties du monde. Elle a perdu ses points d'appui concrets. Il n'existe plus un seul mouvement révolutionnaire et à plus forte raison pas un seul pays socialiste, entre guillemets, dont nous pourrions nous réclamer pour dire: c'est comme cela qu'il faut faire! C'est cela le modèle! C'est là la ligne! C'est un état de choses remarquable! Je dirais que nous sommes renvoyés à l'année 1830, c'est-à-dire qu'il nous faut tout recommencer. Toutefois, l'année 1830 avait encore derrière elle la Révolution française et toute la tradition européenne des Lumières; il nous faut tout recommencer depuis la début et nous demander à partir de quoi on peut faire la critique de notre société dans

une situation où ce sur quoi nous nous étions implicitement ou explicitement appuyés jusqu'ici pour faire cette critique; en un mot, l'importante tradition du socialisme est à remettre fondamentalement en question, car tout ce que cette tradition socialiste a produit dans l'histoire est à condamner.

Roughly translated, the passage reads as follows:

The response to your question is sad, given the somber days in which we live and that the succession of President Mao Tse-tung has been settled by arms. People have been shot or imprisoned, machine guns have been put into action. Today, October 14, is a day of which it can be said: Not since the Russian Revolution of October 1917, maybe not even since the great European revolutionary movements of 1848—that is to say, for the first time in sixty years or, if you like, 120 years— there is no longer anywhere a single point from which the light of hope shines. There is no longer an orientation. Certainly not the Soviet Union, or any of the satellite countries. That too is clear. Neither Cuba, nor the Palestinian revolution, nor, it now appears, China. The same is true of Vietnam and Cambodia. For the first time, the left confronting what has just happened in China, all this "way of thinking" of the European left, this European revolutionary thought which had its points of reference throughout the world and elaborated on them in a deter- mined manner—and thus a thought that oriented itself on things which were situated outside of itself—this thought has lost its historical reference points that it had found previously in other parts of the world. It has lost its points of concrete support. There no longer exists a single revolutionary movement and certainly not a socialist country, in quotation marks, that we can point to and say: This is how it must be done! That's the model! There's the line! That's a re- markable state of things! I would say that we have returned to the year 1830, that is, we must start over again. Anyway, 1830 had the French Revolution and the whole European tradition of the Enlightenment behind it. We must begin from the beginning and ask ourselves, Starting from what is it possible to engage in a critique of our society in a situation where the thing we have implicitly or explic- itly relied on for support to make this critique, namely, the important tradition of socialism, has been placed fundamentally in question—because all that this socialist tradition has produced in history is to be condemned.

Michel Foucault, "La torture, c'est la raison," in *Michel Foucault: Dits et écrits*, vol. 3 (Paris: Gallimard, 1994), 397–398; translation mine.

7   See Michel Foucault, "The Art of Telling the Truth," in *PPC*, 86–95, and Immanuel Kant, *The Contest of the Faculties*, in *Kant: Political Writings*, ed. Hans Reiss (Cam- bridge: Cambridge University Press, 1991), 177–190.

8   Kant, *Contest of the Faculties*, 183.

9   Ibid., 182.

10 Foucault, "Art of Telling the Truth," 92.

11 Emphasis in original. Karl Marx, *Contribution to the Critique of Hegel's Philosophy of Right: Introduction* (1844), in *The Marx-Engels Reader*, ed. Robert C. Tucker (New York: W. W. Norton, 1972), 54–55.

12 Marx, *Critique of Hegel's Philosophy of Right*, 55. The original reads, "Der Geist jener Zustande ist widerlegt." See *MEGA*, vol. 2, 172.

13 Jürgen Habermas, *Legitimation Crisis* (Boston: Beacon, 1975); and Habermas, *Towards a Rational Society* (Boston: Beacon, 1971), esp. chap. 6. Ceauşescu headed the Romanian state until his dramatic overthrow and execution in 1989. Hoxha, the leader of Albania, died in office, but the regime he left behind was quickly pressed into the ranks of reform.

14 "GE," 343.

15 William Connolly, *Political Theory and Modernity* (Ithaca: Cornell University Press, 1993), 177–178.

16 Judith Butler, "Gender Trouble, Feminist Theory, and Psychoanalytic Discourse," in *Feminism/Postmodernism*, ed. Linda J. Nicholson (New York: Routledge, 1990), 339.

17 Ibid., 325.

18 Judith Butler, *Gender Trouble: Feminism and the Subversion of Identity* (New York: Routledge, 1990), 15.

19 William Connolly, "Beyond Good and Evil: The Ethical Sensibility of Michel Foucault," *Political Theory* 21, no. 3 (August 1993): 366.

20 Butler, *Gender Trouble*, 2.

21 Ibid., 5.

22 Ibid., 142–149.

23 For further positive treatments of the "politics of difference" approach, see Stephen K. White, *Political Theory and Postmodernism* (Cambridge: Cambridge University Press, 1991); Anna Yeatman, *Postmodern Revisionings of the Political* (New York: Routledge, 1994); Iris Young, *Justice and the Politics of Difference* (Princeton: Princeton University Press, 1990); and Young, "The Ideal Community and the Politics of Difference," in Nicholson, *Feminism/Postmodernism*. For Foucault's own objection to the use of abstract normative terms, see his comment concerning "humanism," in "WIE," 44, and in "Truth, Power, Self," in *TS*, 15.

24 "SuP," 215–216.

25 Kant, *Kant: Political Writings*, 54.

26 Ibid., 55.

27 Ibid.

28 Optimistic, because there is another version of liberalism coming out of the Enlightenment that points to the depravity of human nature as the key argument for liberal protections. For an especially extravagant and overblown version of the pessimistic-liberal argument, see Alexander Hamilton, James Madison, and John Jay, *The Federalist Papers* (New York: New American Library, 1961), esp. no. 10 and no. 51, but throughout as well.

29 Karl Marx and Friedrich Engels, *The German Ideology* (1964), rpt. in Tucker, *Marx-Engels Reader*, 197–199; Karl Marx, *Grundrisse*, trans. Martin Nicolaus (New York: Random House, 1973), 162–165.

30 I will have more to say about liberal theory proper in chapter 6, below.

31 See Karl Marx, "Sixth Thesis on Feuerbach," in Tucker, *Marx-Engels Reader*, 145.

32 Marx and Engels, *German Ideology*, 150.

33 Ibid., 165.

34 Karl Kautsky, *The Class Struggle* (New York: W. W. Norton, 1971), esp. chaps. 3 and 4; and Georg Lukács, *History and Class Consciousness: Studies in Marxist Dialectic*, trans.

Rodney Livingstone (Cambridge: MIT Press, 1968), esp. the essays "What Is Orthodox Marxism?" and "Class Consciousness."

35   Max Weber, "Parliament and Government in a Reconstructed Germany," in *Economy and Society*, ed. Guenther Roth and Claus Wittich (Berkeley: University of California Press, 1978), 2: 1381–1469. Many of Weber's most pointed comments on the threat represented by bureaucratization are in his political writings, which are scattered in his letters and talks. These comments are usefully pulled together in Wolfgang J. Mommsen, *Max Weber and German Politics* (Chicago: University of Chicago Press, 1984), esp. chap. 6. See also David Beetham, *Max Weber and the Theory of Modern Politics* (Oxford: Basil Blackwell, 1985), chap. 3.

36   Max Weber, "Socialism" (1919), rpt. in *Occasional Paper no. 11* (Durban, Natal: Institute for Social Research, University of Natal, 1967).

37   Compare, for instance, Max Horkheimer, "Traditional and Critical Theory," in *Critical Theory* (New York: Continuum, 1972), 188–252, which was written in the 1930s, with Horkheimer and Theodor W. Adorno, *Dialectic of Enlightenment* (New York: Continuum, 1987).

38   Karl Mannheim, *Ideology and Utopia* (New York: Harcourt, Brace and Company, 1936), 211–263, esp. 211–219 and 239–247.

39   Theodor W. Adorno, "Resignation," *Telos*, no. 35 (Spring 1978): 165–168. Adorno argues, "The administered world has a tendency to strangle all spontaneity or at least to channel it into pseudo-activity" (167). It is "the uncompromisingly critical thinker . . . who . . . in truth . . . does not give up," as only "thinking is not the spiritual reproduction of that which exists" (168).

40   Michel Foucault, "Critical Theory/Intellectual History," in *PPC*, 35–36.

41   Kant, "What Is Enlightenment?" in *Kant: Political Writings*, 54.

42   Michel Foucault, "What Calls for Punishment?" in *Foucault Live: Interviews, 1966–84* (New York: Semiotext(e), 1989), 281–282.

43   Michel Foucault, "Power and Sex," in *PPC*, 122, 123.

44   Michel Foucault, "On Revolution," *Philosophy and Social Criticism*, no. 1 (1981): 5–9.

45   Ibid., 6.

46   From a liberal perspective, this point is developed in classic fashion by T. H. Marshall in *Class, Citizenship, and Social Development: Essays by T. H. Marshall* (Garden City, N.Y.: Doubleday, 1964), chap. 4, "Citizenship and Social Class."

47   Berki, *Genesis of Marxism*, 11–12.

48   Foucault, "On Revolution," 6.

49   Ibid., 8.

50   Ibid.

51   According to Nancy Fraser: "Foucault calls in no uncertain terms for resistance to domination. But why? Why is struggle preferable to submission? Why ought domination to be resisted? *Only with the introduction of normative notions of some kind* could Foucault begin to answer such questions." See Fraser, "Foucault on Modern Power: Empirical Insights and Normative Confusions," in *Unruly Practices: Power, Discourse, and Gender in Contemporary Social Theory* (Minneapolis: University of Minnesota Press, 1989), 29; emphasis added. See also "The Demand for Criteria" in chap. 6, below.

52   Foucault, "On Revolution," 5.

53   "WIE," 44.

54   Michel Foucault, "Politics and Ethics," in *FR*, 374.
55   Marx, *Critique of Hegel's Philosophy of Right*, 62–63; Marx and Engels, *German Ideology*, 160–161.
56   "SuP," 226.
57   Michel Foucault, "Power and Strategies," in *P/K*, 136.
58   Ibid., 137–138.
59   Friedrich Nietzsche, *On the Genealogy of Morals*, trans. Walter Kaufmann (New York: Random House, 1969), Second Essay, sec. 1.
60   "In order for a particular species to maintain itself and increase its power, its conception of reality must comprehend enough of the calculable and constant for it to base a scheme of behavior on it. The utility of preservation—not some abstract-theoretical need not to be deceived—stands as the motive behind the development of the organs of knowledge—they develop in such a way that their observations suffice for our preservation. . . . A species grasps a certain amount of reality in order to become master of it, in order to process it into service." Friedrich Nietzsche, *The Will to Power*, trans. Walter Kaufmann (New York: Vintage, 1968), sec. 480, 266–267.
61   *VS*, 18–19, 139; *HSI*, 10–11, 105; *SP*, 29, 169–170, 172, 195–196, 218–219; *DP*, 24, 167, 170, 194, 217; Michel Foucault, "Body/Power," in *P/K*, 59; Foucault, "Two Lectures," 89–90, 98; Foucault, "Truth and Power," in *P/K*, 118–121; Foucault, "Power and Sex," 114; James Bernauer and David Rasmussen, eds., *The Final Foucault* (Cambridge: MIT Press, 1988), 2–3.
62   Again, a good short summary of Adorno's views is contained in his brief essay "Resignation."
63   Honi Fern Haber, *Beyond Postmodern Politics* (New York: Routledge, 1994), 89.
64   Ibid., 101.
65   See, for instance, Peter Dews, "Power and Subjectivity in Foucault," *New Left Review* 144 (1984): 72–95, esp. 77 and 82; Lois McNay, *Foucault: A Critical Introduction* (New York: Continuum, 1994), 5; and Thomas McCarthy, "The Critique of Impure Reason: Foucault and the Frankfurt School," *Political Theory* 18, no. 3 (August 1990): 437–469, esp. 437–441.
66   Up to this point Nietzsche and Marx would agree.
67   That subjective constructs such as the ego are incomplete and selective operations is one of the primary arguments in a very interesting piece by Eugene T. Gendlin, "A Philosophical Critique of the Concept of Narcissism," in *Pathologies of the Modern Self: Studies on Narcissism, Schizophrenia, and Depression*, ed. David Michael Levin (New York: New York University Press, 1987), 251–304, esp. 254–256.
68   Michel Foucault, "The Return of Morality," in *PPC*, 253.
69   Jane Flax, "Beyond Equality: Gender, Justice, and difference," in *Beyond Equality and Difference*, ed. Gisela Bock and Susan James (New York: Routledge, 1992).
70   Ibid., 198.
71   Ibid., 205–206.
72   Quoted in Nat Hentoff, "The Enemy within Gay Pride Day," *Village Voice*, August 8, 1995, 22. In *The Augustinian Imperative* (Newbury Park, Calif.: Sage, 1993), 154–158, William Connolly briefly discusses how proponents of a politics of difference might respond to deep societal divisions over issues like abortion.
73   See "Genealogy and the Uses of History," chap. 4, above.

74 *VS*, 132–135; *HSI*, 100–102.

75 Foucault, "Power and Sex," 115.

76 Michel Foucault, "The Ethic of the Care of the Self as a Practice of Freedom," in Bernauer and Rasmussen, *The Final Foucault*, 10; emphasis added.

77 See Marx and Engels, *German Ideology*, 150: "As individuals express their life, so they are. What they are, then, coincides with their production—both with what they produce and how they produce it. The nature of individuals depends on material conditions determining their production."

78 "SuP," 220.

79 Ibid., 221.

80 Immanuel Kant, *Foundations of the Metaphysics of Morals*, trans. Lewis White Beck (New York: Macmillan, 1990). See also Charles Taylor, "Kant's Theory of Freedom," in *Conceptions of Liberty in Political Philosophy*, ed. Zbigniew Pelcynski and John Gray (London: Athlone, 1984), 100–122; and Patrick Riley, *Kant's Political Philosophy* (Totowa, N.J.: Rowman and Littlefield, 1983), esp. chap. 1–3.

81 "SuP," 222.

82 A number of Foucault's readers have understood him to be arguing for a particular kind of polity that would promote rather than hinder agonistic activity. According to Jon Simons in his *Foucault and the Political* (New York: Routledge, 1995), "Foucault's politics aims not for a world without power but to prevent the solidification of strategic relations into patterns of domination by maintaining the openness of agonistic relations" (4). Later Simon adds: "Foucault's conceptualization of power relations as agonistic implicitly includes a regulative principle for the assessment of political regimes. If there is legitimation for resistance in Foucault's work, it is that it is the condition of possibility for further resistance and the constitution of agonal subjectivity" (86). But isn't it circular—and thus logically unhelpful—to say that resistance is legitimated as the condition of possibility for further resistance? On a practical level, the claim that people resist to be able to resist seems implausible. For Foucault, resistance occurs as the necessary concomitant of exercises of power. Leslie Paul Thiele makes an argument similar to that of Simons. In her article "The Agony of Politics: The Nietzschean Roots of Foucault's Thought," *American Political Science Review* 84, no. 3 (September 1990), she states that "Foucault's political project is founded on the valorization of struggle." It follows that "the ethicopolitical choice to be made every day consists in a judgment as to what form of power most threatens the possibility of its continued resistance" (918).

   Notice the persistent effort commentators engage in to "normalize" Foucault. He can be swallowed, it appears, only with a heaped spoonful of sugary commitments to some legitimatory device or another. In Thiele's case, this requires a serious misreading of Foucault's comment concerning the "main danger." Foucault introduces this term in "On the Genealogy of Ethics" (232). It has a vaguely (and probably misleading) Maoist flavor to it; see in this regard Mao Tse-tung, "On Contradiction," in *Selected Readings from the Works of Mao Tse-tung* (Peking: Foreign Languages Press, 1971), 111–112. See too Foucault's own discussion of the left's attempt to think about opposition through use of the idea of "contradiction" and its associated notions of "main danger" and "weak link" in "Power and Strategies," 143–144. That Foucault is not making either strategic or legitimating noises in the "Genealogy" interview is made clear by the example he immediately discusses there following the "main danger" phrase. The struggle against the treatment of those with mental illness in large state institutions led to the disestablishment of many of those centers and a concomitant rise in homelessness among the mentally ill. But this consequence, Foucault argues, does not disqualify the efforts of the original antipsychiatry movement that addressed the abuses of psychiatric hospitals and homes. It does, however, mean that the target of attack (the treatment of the mentally ill by society as a whole, the availability of housing, and so forth) has changed for activists in that particular domain (see "Genealogy," 232). No broader point is being made concerning the need to discover and concentrate one's fire on those forms of power that most effectively frustrate resistance.

83   Michel Foucault, "Politics and Reason," in *PPC*, 79; "WIE," 47–48.

84   "SuP," 223.

85   Foucault, "On Revolution," 5.

86   Michel Foucault, "Power and Norm: Notes," in *Michel Foucault: Power, Truth, Strategy*, ed. Meaghan Morris and Paul Patton (Sydney, Australia: Feral, 1979), 60. It should be pointed out that these notes were taken at a lecture given by Foucault in 1973.

87   "SuP," 235.

88   Ibid., 216.

89   Michel Foucault, "The History of Sexuality," in *P/K*, 190.

90   "WIE," 41.

91   Foucault, "Truth, Power, Self," 15.

92   Michel Foucault, introduction to *The Normal and the Pathological*, by Georges Canguilhem (New York: Zone, 1989); hereinafter referred to as "Introduction."

93   Henri Bergson is the most prominent spokesperson for this school. See his *La Pensée et le Mouvant* (Paris, 1946), trans. Mabelle L. Andison under the title *The Creative Mind* (New York: Philosophical Library, 1946); and Bergson, *L'évolution créatrice* (Paris, 1914), trans. Arthur Mitchell under the title *Creative Evolution* (New York: Henry Holt, 1944). See also Georg Simmel, *Der Konflikt der modernen Kultur* (Munich, 1918), trans. K. Peter Etzkorn under the title *The Conflict in Modern Culture and Other Essays* (New York: Teachers College Press, 1968); and Lukács, *History and Class Consciousness*, esp. "Reification and the Consciousness of the Proletariat."

94   Foucault, "Introduction," 21. See also Bernauer, *Foucault's Force of Flight*, 178–180; and Connolly, *Augustinian Imperative*, 143–151.

95   Foucault, "Introduction," 21.

96   Ibid., 22.

97   Ibid.

98   Ibid. For Nietzsche's comment see *On the Genealogy of Morals*, Third Essay, sec. 24, 152; and Nietzsche, *The Gay Science*, trans. Walter Kaufmann (New York: Random House, 1974), bk. 5, sec. 344, 280–283.

99   Foucault, "Truth and Power," 131–133.

100 Foucault, "Politics and Polemics," 388; emphasis added.

101 It does not refer to philosophical reflection in the sense, for instance, that Adorno uses the term in "Resignation."

102 "WIE," 46. See also Foucault, "On Power," in *PPC*, 107: "When I say 'critical,' I don't

mean a demolition job, one of rejection or refusal, but a work of examination that consists of suspending as far as possible the system of values to which one refers when testing and assessing it. In other words: what am I doing at the moment I'm doing it?"

103   Michel Foucault, preface to *The History of Sexuality*, vol. 2, in *FR*, 335. This preface is not, for some reason, included in either the original or the English translation of *L'usage des plaisirs*.

104   Ibid.; emphasis added.

105   Foucault, "Prison Talk," in *P/K*, 51.

106   Foucault, "Power and Strategies," 138.

107   Foucault, "Two Lectures," 98.

108   "SuP," 220.

109   Ibid., 221.

110   Foucault, preface to *The History of Sexuality*, 335.

111   Ibid.

112   Michel Foucault, "Practicing Criticism," in *PPC*, 155.

113   Ibid.

114   Wilhelm Reich is cited a number of times as a spokesperson for the repressive hypothesis. See Foucault, "Power and Sex," 113, and "Two Lectures," 91; *VS*, 173; *HSI*, 131.

115   *UDP*, 10; *UP*, 4.

116   Ibid.

117   *UDP*, 12; *UP*, 6.

118   *UDP*, 16; *UP*, 10.

119   *UDP*, 32; *UP*, 25.

120   Ibid.

121   *UDP*, 33; *UP*, 26.

122   Ibid.

123   *UDP*, 35; *UP*, 28.

124   *UDP*, 34, 35; *UP*, 26, 27, 28.

125   *UDP*, 34; *UP*, 27.

126   Peter Dews, "The Return of the Subject in the Late Foucault," *Radical Philosophy* 51 (Spring 1989).

127   Michel Foucault, "The Confession of the Flesh," in *P/K*, 208.

128   Nietzsche argues along similar lines: "The assumption of one single subject is perhaps unnecessary; perhaps it is just as permissible to assume a multiplicity of subjects, whose interaction and struggle is the basis of our thought and our consciousness in general." See *Will to Power*, sec. 488. At section 492 he speaks of the subject as a succession of "living unities" that "continually arise and die."

129   *UDP*, 35; *UP*, 28.

130   Ibid. I have modified the translation a bit at the beginning. The relevant text is: "Toute action morale, c'est vrai, comporte un rapport au réel où elle s'effectue et un rapport au code auquel elle se réfère; mais elle implique aussi un certain rapport à soi."

131   Foucault, "Return of Morality," 253.

132   *Le souci de soi*, 55; *CS*, 41.

133   "I believe in the freedom of people. To the same situation, people react in very different ways." See Foucault, "Truth, Power, Self," 14. These differing reactions to similar

situations are the stuff Foucault's "genealogical" method is made of: they force the received and familiar to appear contingent and perhaps unacceptable. See also Foucault, "Concern for the Truth," 264–265.

134 *Le souci de soi*, 56; *CS*, 42.
135 *Le souci de soi*, 57; *CS*, 43.
136 *Le souci de soi*, 56; *CS*, 42.
137 *Le souci de soi*, 81; *CS*, 64.
138 *Le souci de soi*, 77; *CS*, 61.
139 *Le souci de soi*, 61; *CS*, 47.
140 *Le souci de soi*, 81; *CS*, 64.
141 Howison Lecture, transcript, October 20, 1980, 8. For a similar comment, see "About the Beginning of the Hermeneutics of the Self," *Political Theory* 21, no. 2 (May 1993): 204.
142 Foucault, "About the Beginning," 204.
143 For comments along the lines of such warnings, see Foucault, "Body/Power," 59, and "Two Lectures," 89–91; *SP*, 32–33; *DP*, 27–28.
144 *Le souci de soi*, 82; *CS*, 65.
145 "GE," 236.
146 *Le souci de soi*, 83; *CS*, 66.
147 *Le souci de soi*, 55; *CS*, 41.
148 This is precisely Thomas McCarthy's argument in "The Critique of Impure Reason, 437–469, esp. 463. For an insightful discussion of Foucault's notion of self-care and the critical reaction to it, see Bernauer, *Foucault's Force of Flight*, 158–183, esp. 160.
149 "SuP," 213.
150 *SP*, 195; *DP*, 193.
151 Foucault, "Politics and Reason," 71.
152 For a refutation of the claim that Foucault's ethic of the care of the self promotes individualistic withdrawal, see Connolly, "Beyond Good and Evil," 365–389, esp. 373.
153 *Le souci de soi*, 102; *CS*, 82.
154 *Le souci de soi*, 102–103; *CS*, 82–83.
155 *Le souci de soi*, 103; *CS*, 83.
156 *Le souci de soi*, 107; *CS*, 86.
157 Michel Foucault, "Technologies of the Self," in *TS*, 22.
158 Ibid.
159 Ibid.
160 Ibid.
161 "GE," 234.
162 *Le souci de soi*, 67: "Elle constitue, non pas un exercice de la solitude, mais une véritable pratique sociale"; *CS*, 51.
163 *Le souci de soi*, 69; *CS*, 53.
164 *Le souci de soi*, 68–69; *CS*, 52–53.
165 *Le souci de soi*, 116–117; *CS*, 95.
166 "WIE," 49.
167 "GE," 231.
168 *Le souci de soi*, 69; *CS*, 54.

169   *Le souci de soi*, 175; *CS*, 149.
170   *Le souci de soi*, 191; *CS*, 163.
171   "GE," 238.
172   Ibid., 239; *Le souci de soi*, 112; *CS*, 91.
173   *Le souci de soi*, 61; *CS*, 47.
174   Foucault, "Politics and Reason," 71; and "SuP," 216.
175   "GE," 236.
176   Ibid., 231.
177   Dews, "Return of the Subject in the Late Foucault," 37–41. He characterizes technolo-
      gies of the self as "the advocacy of an arbitrary stylization of life" that can act only
      as a "reinforcement of social tendencies towards atomization" (40). See also Thomas
      McCarthy, "Critique of Impure Reason," 437–469, esp. 459–464.
178   This does not mean it is impossible to conceive of a link between the ethical and
      political aspects of a focus on the individual. This possibility will be discussed below.
179   Foucault, "Truth and Power," 126–133.
180   Ibid., 128.
181   Ibid., 126.
182   Ibid.
183   Foucault, "Two Lectures," 107.
184   Foucault, "On Power," 107. Foucault goes on to characterize himself as a specific intel-
      lectual: "I work in a specific field and do not produce a theory of the world" (108).
185   Foucault, "Truth and Power," 128.
186   Friedrich Nietzsche, *Human, All Too Human*, trans. R. J. Hollingdale (Cambridge:
      Cambridge University Press, 1986), 41 (sec. 55).
187   Foucault, "Power and Strategies," 143.
188   Foucault, "Critical Theory/Intellectual History," 38.
189   Foucault, "Power and Strategies," 144.
190   Foucault, "Truth and Power," 130.
191   Ibid., 132.
192   "WIE," 49.
193   *VS*, 122; *HSI*, 93.
194   Emphasis in original. Foucault, "Two Lectures," 99.
195   *VS*, 122; *HSI*, 93.
196   "WIE," 46–47.
197   Vladimir Ilyich Lenin, "The Immediate Tasks of the Soviet Government," in *The Lenin
      Anthology*, ed. Robert C. Tucker (New York: W. W. Norton, 1975), 448–449.
198   "WIE," 46–47.
199   Ibid., 47.
200   Ibid., 41.
201   Ibid., 41–42.
202   Ibid., 49.
203   Kant, *Kant: Political Writings*, 55.

6. Politics, Norms, and the Self

1   Michel Foucault, "Practicing Criticism," in *PPC*, 155.
2   Michel Foucault, "Qu'est-ce que la critique?" *Bulletin de la Société française de Philosophie* 84 (1990): 53.
3   Ibid., 39.
4   See "Varieties of Morality" in chap. 5, above.
5   Foucault, "Qu'est-ce que la critique?" 48.
6   This desire to promote reflective indocility is reminiscent of Schürmann's argument that, for Foucault, oppositional possibilities can be pursued more successfully not by creating new forms of subjectivity but by resisting the continuous efforts by a wide variety of forces to turn us into subjects of this or that kind. It seems, however, that although the refusal of certain kinds of subjectivity can be analytically distinguished from the conscious shaping of psychic structures, the same separation is much more difficult to achieve in practice. One way to read Foucault's later writings is as an attempt to bring together the "arts of refusal" discussed in the late 1970s with arts of self-fashioning characteristic of Greek and Roman antiquity. See Reiner Schürmann, "On Constituting Oneself as an Anarchistic Subject," *Praxis International* 6 (1986): 294–310, esp. 304–305.
7   Michel Foucault, "The Return of Morality," in *PPC*, 252–253.
8   "Who fights against whom? We all fight each other. And there is always within each of us something that fights against something else." See "The Confession of the Flesh," in *P/K*, 208, where Foucault also explicitly refers to the "subindividuals" that take up residence in "empirical" individuals. For similar views in Nietzsche, see his *Beyond Good and Evil*, trans. Walter Kaufmann (New York: Random House, 1966), pt. 1, sec. 12, 20–21, and sec. 19, 26–27; and Nietzsche, *The Will to Power*, trans. Walter Kaufmann (New York: Vintage, 1968), sec. 660, 348–349.
9   Foucault, "Return of Morality," 253.
10 Ibid.
11 These rights can be "inalienable"—inherent in the human personality—or the products of bargaining and even the outcome of conflict. Even with the second, more "pragmatic" version of the argument, however, there is an underlying belief in the individual as that which society must in one way or another respect and defend.
12 The reader can find view 2 in Michel Foucault, "Two Lectures," in *P/K*, 95–96, 107–108; view 3 in Foucault, "The Social Triumph of the Sexual Will," *Christopher Street* 6, no. 4 (1982): 36–41, and Foucault, "Truth, Power, Self," in *TS*, 15; and view 4 in *VS*, 107–120, and *HSI*, 81–91. Tom Keenan provides an excellent discussion of Foucault on rights in his "Reading Foucault on a Bias," *Political Theory* 15, no. 1 (February 1987): 5–37.
13 See "Foucault's Enlightenment" in chap. 5, above.
14 For instance, the United States Supreme Court had no trouble at all denying Eugene V. Dennis a right to free speech in *Dennis v United States* (1951). Indeed, what is the status of "fundamental protections," whose meaning shifts with each new Supreme Court majority?
15 Didier Eribon, *Michel Foucault*, trans. Betsy Wing (Cambridge: Harvard University Press, 1991), 259–260.
16 Foucault, "Two Lectures," 108.

17 See U.S. Constitution, art. 3, sec. 3.

18 But only at a *certain point*. A friend of mine who lived the housewife role in those days tells me how she would always vote for the same candidates as her husband, not because she always liked the same ones but because she did not want to "cancel out" her husband's vote. For a long time she had the right to vote and was free — in her own mind as well.

19 *VS*, 191; *HSI*, 145.

20 *VS*, 133; *HSI*, 101.

21 Michel Foucault, *Das Wahrsprechen des Anderen* (Verlag, 1988); and Foucault, "Discourse and Truth: The Problemization of 'Parrhesia,'" transcript, University of California, Berkeley, 1983. The second piece consists of verbatim transcripts from a seminar given by Foucault at the University of California at Berkeley. Both works deal with the same topic.

22 Foucault, *Wahrsprechen*, 30; "Discourse and Truth," 4.

23 Foucault, *Wahrsprechen*, 31-32.

24 Ibid., 23-32. Dionysius the Younger succeeded his father, Dionysius the Elder, in 367 B.C.

25 Ibid., 23.

26 Plato, *The Republic*, trans. Robin Waterfield (Oxford: Oxford University Press, 1994), bk. 9, 571-577.

27 Foucault, *Wahrsprechen*, 30.

28 Ibid., 32.

29 Foucault, "Discourse and Truth," 3; ibid., 34-35.

30 Foucault, "Discourse and Truth," 3.

31 "WIE," 42.

32 Michel Foucault, "Politics and Ethics," in *FR*, 379.

33 Foucault, "Truth, Power, Self," 15.

34 My goal in this section is not to review feminist responses to Foucault but to describe the dynamic that runs from "resistance" to "essentialism" using the early women's movement as an example. Without a doubt, however, some of the best, most engaged studies of Foucault have been written by feminists. In addition, these studies often confront — not always in ways I agree with — precisely the issue being discussed here: What should be the relationship between resistance to power and the creation or valorization of forms of subjectivity? See, in particular, Jana Sawicki, "Foucault, Feminism, and Questions of Identity," in *The Cambridge Companion to Foucault*, ed. Gary Gutting (New York: Cambridge University Press, 1994), 286-313; Sawicki, *Disciplining Foucault: Feminism, Power, and the Body* (New York: Routledge, 1991), 17-48 and 95-109; Judith Butler, *Gender Trouble: Feminism and the Subversion of Identity* (New York: Routledge, 1990); Nancy Hartsock, "Foucault on Power: A Theory for Women?" in *Feminism/Postmodernism*, ed. Linda J. Nicholson (New York: Routledge, 1990); and Diana Fuss, *Essentially Speaking* (New York: Routledge, 1989).

35 Niccolò Machiavelli, *The Discourses*, trans. Christian E. Detmold (New York: Random House, 1950), bk. 3, chap. 9, 442-443.

36 Michel Foucault, "Conversation with Michel Foucault," *Threepenny Review* 1, no. 1 (Winter/Spring 1980): 4.

37   Michel Foucault and Richard Sennett, "Sexuality and Solitude," in *Humanities in Review*, vol. 1, ed. David Rieff (Cambridge: Cambridge University Press, 1982), 9.
38   Betty Friedan, *The Feminine Mystique* (New York: W. W. Norton, 1963), chaps. 5 and 8.
39   Foucault and Sennett, "Sexuality and Solitude," 9.
40   "A Guide to Consciousness Raising," *Ms.*, July 1972, reprinted in *Women's Liberation in the Twentieth Century*, ed. Mary Lynn (New York: John Wiley and Sons, 1975), 111–118.
41   Part of the difference separating Foucault and Habermas can be located here. Habermas hinges his critical theory on the capacity of rational individuals to communicate their claims, interests, and needs to others. These and contrary claims are then discussed to produce an intersubjectively valid consensus on norms. If participants are unable to express their needs or the like, Habermas ascribes this to repressive "communicative distortions" that must be eliminated if the work of developing valid norms is to continue. But for Foucault a communicative distortion may very well be the salutary effect of a liberatory act. See Jürgen Habermas, *Moralbewusstsein und kommunikatives Handeln* (Frankfurt: Suhrkamp, 1983), 97–99; and Habermas, "Wahrheitstheorien," in *Wirklichkeit und Reflexion: Walter Schulz zum 60 Geburtstag*, ed. Helmut Fahrenbach (Pfullingen: Neske, 1973), 211–263, esp. 257. See also Stephen K. White, *The Recent Work of Jürgen Habermas: Reason, Justice, and Modernity* (Cambridge: Cambridge University Press, 1988), chaps. 3 and 4.
42   Foucault, *Wahrsprechen*, 33.
43   See chapter 5. See also Michel Foucault, *Remarks on Marx: Conversations with Duccio Trombadori*, trans. R. James Goldstein and James Cascaito (New York: Semiotext(e), 1991), 25–42.
44   Friedan, *Feminine Mystique*, 293.
45   Friedan, *Feminine Mystique*, 330.
46   Ibid., chap. 14.
47   Betty Friedan, *Second Stage* (New York: Summit, 1981), 31–32, 203.
48   For a review, see Susan Faludi, *Backlash: The Undeclared War against American Women* (New York: Crown, 1991), 318–332.
49   Carol Gilligan, *In a Different Voice* (Cambridge: Harvard University Press, 1982).
50   Clearly, however, Foucault is working against some deeply ingrained oppositional habits of thought. He does not want to refer to an essential human nature, either when describing the operations of power in various contexts or to justify oppositional activity. If an essential human nature is assumed at the start of concrete historical investigations, they will be compromised from the start. "The aim of [the refusal of the subject] is to bring to light the processes proper to an experience in which subject and object 'form and transform themselves' in relation to and as functions of one another." See Maurice Florence, "Foucault, Michel, 1926–," in Gutting, *Cambridge Companion to Foucault*, 317. (The editor of the *Companion* maintains that this brief article was authored by Foucault; see *Companion*, viii.) But as "Florence" argues, "one has to be careful: to deny the philosophic recourse to a constitutive subject does not amount to behaving as if the subject did not exist nor to setting it aside in favor of a pure objectivity" (317). It appears, then, that Foucault would be willing to say something similar to the following: "While I do not think of the subject as an anthropological constant and while I think that this view of the subject is an obstacle to historical research con-

cerning the constitution of subjects, actual subjects do exist! It follows that it is not wrong, meaningless, or self-defeating to say, 'I am a subject of such and such a kind, and in the name of this (constructed) subjectivity I demand equal treatment before the law, and so on.' "

51 "GE," 232. This same problem can be reflected on with reference to the Iranian revolution. See above, chap. 5.

52 Nancy Fraser, "Foucault on Modern Power," *Praxis International* 1, no. 3 (October 1981): 286.

53 See "Disciplinary Projects" and "Disciplines, Individuals, and Norms," in chap. 2, above.

54 By "personality structure" I mean whatever disposition of psychic forces exists at a particular time.

55 Foucault, "Truth, Power, Self," 15.

56 Foucault, "Social Triumph of the Sexual Will," 38.

57 Foucault, "Truth, Power, Self," 15.

58 Michel Foucault, introduction to *The Normal and the Pathological,* by Georges Canguilhem (New York: Zone, 1989), 21.

59 Foucault, *Remarks on Marx,* 122.

60 Foucault, "Truth, Power, Self," 15.

61 Foucault, "Politics and Ethics," 374.

62 Ibid.

63 Foucault, "Truth, Power, Self," 14.

64 Foucault, "The Concern for the Truth," in *PPC,* 255.

65 See "Criticism and Experience" in chap. 2, above.

66 Michel Foucault, "Foucault Responds to Sartre," in *Foucault Live: Interviews, 1966–84* (New York: Semiotext(e), 1989), 35.

67 *UDP,* 14; *UP,* 8.

68 *UDP,* 14–15; *UP,* 8–9.

69 See "The 'Plebeian Aspect' " in chap. 5, above, and n. 72, this chapter.

70 Foucault, introduction to Canguilhem, *The Normal and the Pathological,* 22.

71 Michel Foucault, "The Masked Philosopher," in *PPC,* 330.

72 James Bernauer, *Michel Foucault's Force of Flight* (London: Humanities Press International, 1990), 178–180; and William Connolly, *The Augustinian Imperative* (Newbury Park, Calif.: Sage, 1993), 143–151.

73 Gilles Deleuze, *Foucault,* trans. Sean Hand (Minneapolis: University of Minnesota Press, 1988), 92–93.

74 Connolly, *Augustinian Imperative,* 147.

75 Michel Foucault, "On Power," in *PPC,* 108.

76 Foucault, introduction to Canguilhem, *The Normal and the Pathological,* 21.

77 In addition, to the extent that the reference to life as some more innocently non-shaped and thus liberatory force is pursued, Foucault is opened up to the charge that he ultimately falls back on the very repressive hypothesis he dismissed in *HSI.* For an example of just such a criticism, see Hinrich Fink-Eitel, *Foucault,* trans. Edward Dixon (Philadelphia: Pennbridge, 1992), 64–65.

78 "SuP," 216.

Conclusion

1   According to Weber, the Calvinist looked around him to find signs of his election. The answer discussed by Weber is that signs of heavenly favor can be detected in the progress of one's calling. First, one must respond to the calling—that is, obey God's will and apply oneself to the assigned task. Second, it is wrong to waste the fruits of one's labor in a calling on frivolous or ungodly pursuits. The calling is, or should be, a labor of love for the faithful. In the case of business, profits from one cycle of production and sale were not to be spent in ways that did not promote the calling. They were, in other words, reinvested, thus promoting the process of capital accumulation. See Max Weber, *The Protestant Ethic and the Spirit of Capitalism*, trans. Talcott Parsons (New York: Charles Scribner's Sons, 1958), 98–122, 155–182. As is well known, for Weber one of the key problems for the development of capitalism was the need to construct forms of subjectivity that fit the new regimen of factory work. Certain subjective constraints concerning the accumulation of wealth had to be overcome for the process of capital accumulation to take off.

2   The bleakness of Weber's vision is best summarized by the well-known conclusion to *The Protestant Ethic and the Spirit of Capitalism:* "No one knows who will live in this cage in the future, or whether at the end of this tremendous development entirely new prophets will arise, or there will be a great rebirth of old ideas and ideals, or, if neither, mechanized petrification, embellished with a sort of convulsive self-importance. For of the last stage of this cultural development, it might well be truly said: 'Specialists without spirit, sensualists without heart; this nullity imagines that it has attained a level of civilization never before achieved' " (182).

3   See John Stuart Mill, *On Liberty*, in *Utilitarianism, On Liberty, and Considerations on Representative Government*, ed. H. B. Acton (New York: J. M. Dent and Sons, 1972), 134.

4   Max Weber, *Economy and Society*, ed. Geunther Roth and Claus Wittich (Berkeley: University of California Press, 1978), 975.

5   Friedrich Nietzsche, *Beyond Good and Evil*, trans. Walter Kaufmann (New York: Random House, 1966), sec. 258. A healthy aristocracy, Nietzsche says there, should be willing to accept with a good conscience the reduction of the vast majority of society's members to the status of incomplete human beings who will act as instruments for higher types of humans. See also section 257 of *Beyond Good and Evil* and Nietzsche, section 660 of *The Will to Power*, trans. Walter Kaufmann (New York: Vintage, 1968).

6   Max Weber, "Politics as a Vocation," in *From Max Weber: Essays in Sociology*, trans. H. H. Gerth and C. Wright Mills (New York: Oxford University Press, 1946), 95.

7   Weber, *Economy and Society*, 984–985.

8   See Weber, "Politics as a Vocation," 113: "The plebiscitarian leadership of parties entails the 'soullessness' of the following, their intellectual proletarianization, one might say."

9   Ibid., 115.

10 Ibid.

11 Friedrich Nietzsche, *On the Genealogy of Morals*, trans. Walter Kaufmann (New York: Random House, 1969), First Essay, sec. 2, 26.

12 The focus of oppositional thought in the West—of course I am speaking very generally here—has been on the reconstruction of the setting in which subjectivities are

fashioned. In other words, opposition has focused on the totality. But there are important exceptions to this rule. Antonio Gramsci was certainly concerned with the production of oppositional psychic states as an important prerequisite to revolutionary activity. But this insight, and others like it, was still trapped in the confines of a politics of the totality.

BIBLIOGRAPHY

Adorno, Theodor W. *Minima Moralia*. Trans. E. F. N. Jephcott. New York: Schocken, 1978.
———. "Resignation." *Telos*, no. 35 (Spring 1978): 165–168.
Aristotle. *The Politics*. Trans. Trevor J. Saunders. New York: Penguin, 1981.
Bacharach, Peter, and Morton S. Baratz. "Two Faces of Power." *American Political Science Review* 56 (1967): 947–952.
Baldwin, David A. *Paradoxes of Power*. New York: Basil Blackwell, 1989.
Beetham, David. *Max Weber and the Theory of Modern Politics*. Oxford: Basil Blackwell, 1985.
Bentham, Jeremy. *Theory of Legislation*. London: Oxford University Press, 1914.
Bergson, Henri. *Creative Evolution*. Trans. Arthur Mitchell. New York: Henry Holt, 1944.
———. *The Creative Mind*. Trans. Mabelle L. Andison. New York: Philosophical Library, 1946.
Berki, R. N. *The Genesis of Marxism*. London: J. M. Dent and Sons, 1988.
Bernauer, James. *Michel Foucault's Force of Flight*. London: Humanities Press International, 1990.
Bernauer, James, and David Rasmussen, eds. *The Final Foucault*. Cambridge: MIT Press, 1988.
Best, Steven, and Douglas Kellner. *Postmodern Theory*. New York: Guilford, 1991.
Bock, Gisela, and Susan James, eds. *Beyond Equality and Difference*. New York: Routledge, 1992.

Burchell, Graham, Colin Gordon, and Peter Miller, eds. *The Foucault Effect: Studies in Governmentality.* Chicago: University of Chicago Press, 1991.

Butler, Judith. *Gender Trouble: Feminism and the Subversion of Identity.* New York: Routledge, 1990.

Canguilhem, Georges. *The Normal and the Pathological.* New York: Zone, 1989.

Connerton, Paul. *The Tragedy of Enlightenment.* Cambridge: Cambridge University Press, 1980.

Connolly, William. *The Augustinian Imperative.* Newbury Park, Calif.: Sage, 1993.

————. "Beyond Good and Evil: The Ethical Sensibility of Michel Foucault." *Political Theory* 21, no. 3 (August 1993): 365–389.

————. *Political Theory and Modernity.* Ithaca: Cornell University Press, 1993.

Dahl, Robert A. "The Concept of Power." *Behavioral Science* 2 (1957): 201–215.

Dallmayr, Fred. "Pluralism Old and New: Foucault on Power." In *Polis and Practice: Exercises in Contemporary Political Theory.* Cambridge: MIT Press, 1984, 77–100.

Deleuze, Gilles. *Foucault.* Trans. Sean Hand. Minneapolis: University of Minnesota Press, 1988.

Dews, Peter. "Power and Subjectivity in Foucault." *New Left Review* 144 (1984): 72–95.

————. "The Return of the Subject in the Late Foucault." *Radical Philosophy* 51 (Spring 1989).

Engels, Friedrich. *Socialism: Utopian and Scientific* (1880). Rpt. in *The Marx-Engels Reader,* ed. Robert C. Tucker. New York: Norton, 1972.

Eribon, Didier. *Michel Foucault.* Trans. Betsy Wing. Cambridge: Harvard University Press, 1991.

Fahrenbach, Helmut, ed. *Wirklichkeit und Reflexion: Walter Schulz zum 60 Geburtstag.* Pfullingen: Neske, 1973.

Faludi, Susan. *Backlash: The Undeclared War against American Women.* New York: Crown, 1991.

Fink-Eitel, Hinrich. *Foucault.* Trans. Edward Dixon. Philadelphia: Pennbridge, 1992.

Foucault, Michel. *The Archaeology of Knowledge.* Trans. A. M. Sheridan Smith. New York: Pantheon, 1972.

————. "Conversation with Michel Foucault." *Threepenny Review* 1, no. 1 (Winter–Spring 1980).

————. "Discourse and Truth: The Problemization of 'Parrhesia.'" Transcript. University of California, Berkeley, 1983.

————. *Foucault Live: Interviews, 1966–84.* New York: Semiotext(e), 1989.

————. *The Foucault Reader.* Ed. Paul Rabinow. New York: Pantheon, 1984.

————. "Governmentality." *Ideology and Consciousness* 6 (1979): 5–21.

————. *Les mots et les choses.* Paris: Gallimard, 1966. Trans. under the title *The Order of Things* (New York: Pantheon, 1971).

————. *Madness and Civilization.* New York: Random House, 1965.

————. *Michel Foucault: Dits et écrits,* vol. 3. Paris: Gallimard, 1994.

————. "Nietzsche, Genealogy, History." In *Language, Counter-Memory, Practice,* ed. Donald F. Bouchard. Ithaca: Cornell University Press, 1977.

————. "On Revolution." *Philosophy and Social Criticism,* no. 1 (1981): 5–9.

————. "On the Genealogy of Ethics: An Overview of Work in Progress," in Hubert L.

Dreyfus and Paul Rabinow, *Michel Foucault: Beyond Structuralism and Hermeneutics,* 2d ed., 229–252. Chicago: University of Chicago Press, 1983.

———. *Politics, Philosophy, Culture: Interviews and Other Writings, 1977–1984.* Ed. Lawrence D. Kritzman. New York: Routledge, 1988.

———. *Power/Knowledge: Selected Interviews and Other Writings, 1972–1977.* Ed. Colin Gordon. New York: Pantheon, 1980.

———. "Qu'est-ce que la critique?" *Bulletin de la Société française de Philosophie* 84 (1990). Trans. Kevin Paul Geiman under the title "What Is Critique?" In *"What Is Enlightenment?" Eighteenth-Century Answers and Twentieth-Century Questions,* ed. James Schmidt (Berkeley: University of California Press, 1996).

———. *Remarks on Marx: Conversations with Duccio Trombadori.* Trans. R. James Goldstein and James Cascaito. New York: Semiotext(e), 1991.

———. "The Social Triumph of the Sexual Will." *Christopher Street* 6, no. 4 (1982): 36–41.

———. *Le souci de soi.* Paris: Gallimard, 1984. Trans. Robert Hurley under the title *The Care of the Self* (New York: Pantheon, 1986).

———. "The Subject and Power." Afterword to *Michel Foucault: Beyond Structuralism and Hermeneutics,* by Hubert L. Dreyfus and Paul Rabinow, 2d ed., 208–226. Chicago: University of Chicago Press, 1983.

———. *Surveiller et punir: Naissance de la prison.* Paris: Gallimard, 1975. Trans. Alan Sheridan under the title *Discipline and Punish* (New York: Pantheon, 1977).

———. *L'usage des plaisirs.* Paris: Gallimard, 1984. Trans. Robert Hurley under the title *The Use of Pleasure* (New York: Random House, 1985).

———. *La volonté de savoir.* Paris: Gallimard, 1976. Trans. Robert Hurley under the title *The History of Sexuality,* vol. 1, *An Introduction* (New York: Random House, 1978).

———. *Das Wahrsprechen des Anderen.* Verlag, 1988.

Foucault, Michel, and Richard Sennett. "Sexuality and Solitude." In *Humanities in Review,* vol. 1, ed. David Reiff. Cambridge: Cambridge University Press, 1982.

Frankfurt School of Social Research. *Aspects of Sociology.* Trans. John Viertel. Boston: Beacon, 1972.

Fraser, Nancy. *Unruly Practices: Power, Discourse, and Gender in Contemporary Social Theory.* Minneapolis: University of Minnesota Press, 1989.

Friedan, Betty. *The Feminine Mystique.* New York: W. W. Norton, 1963.

———. *Second Stage.* New York: Summit, 1981.

Fuss, Diana. *Essentially Speaking.* New York: Routledge, 1989.

Gadamer, Hans-Georg. *Truth and Method.* 2d ed. New York: Continuum, 1994.

Gendlin, Eugene T. "A Philosophical Critique of the Concept of Narcissism." In *Pathologies of the Modern Self: Studies on Narcissism, Schizophrenia, and Depression,* ed. David Michael Levin. New York: New York University Press, 1987.

Gilligan, Carol. *In a Different Voice.* Cambridge: Harvard University Press, 1982.

Gillis, John R. *The Development of European Society, 1770–1870.* Boston: Houghton Mifflin, 1977.

Gutting, Gary, ed. *The Cambridge Companion to Foucault.* New York: Cambridge University Press, 1994.

Haber, Honi Fern. *Beyond Postmodern Politics.* New York: Routledge, 1994.

Habermas, Jürgen. *Knowledge and Human Interests.* Boston: Beacon, 1971.

————. *Legitimation Crisis.* Boston: Beacon, 1975.

————. *Moralbewusstsein und kommunikatives Handeln.* Frankfurt: Suhrkamp, 1983.

————. *The Philosophical Discourse of Modernity: Twelve Lectures.* Trans. Frederick Lawrence. Cambridge: MIT Press, 1987.

————. *Towards a Rational Society.* Boston: Beacon, 1971.

Hamilton, Alexander, James Madison, and John Jay. *The Federalist Papers.* New York: New American Library, 1961.

Heidegger, Martin. *Being and Time.* Trans. John Macquarrie and Edward Robinson. New York: Harper and Row, 1962.

Hentoff, Nat. "The Enemy within Gay Pride Day." *Village Voice,* August 8, 1995, 22.

Hobbes, Thomas. *Leviathan.* Ed. C. B. Macpherson. New York: Penguin, 1981.

Horkheimer, Max. "Traditional and Critical Theory." In *Critical Theory.* New York: Continuum, 1972.

Horkheimer, Max, and Theodor W. Adorno. *Dialectic of Enlightenment.* New York: Continuum, 1987.

Hoy, David Couzens, ed. *Foucault: A Critical Reader.* Oxford: Basil Blackwell, 1986.

Kant, Immanuel. *Foundations of the Metaphysics of Morals.* 2d ed. Trans. Lewis White Beck. New York: Macmillan, 1990.

————. *Kant: Political Writings.* Ed. Hans Reiss. Cambridge: Cambridge University Press, 1991.

Kautsky, Karl. *The Class Struggle.* New York: W. W. Norton, 1971.

Keenan, Tom. "Reading Foucault on a Bias." *Political Theory* 15, no. 1 (February 1987): 5–37.

Lenin, Vladimir Ilyich. *The Lenin Anthology.* Ed. Robert C. Tucker. New York: W. W. Norton, 1975.

Locke, John. *Two Treatises of Government.* Ed. Peter Laslett. Cambridge: Cambridge University Press, 1960.

Lukács, Georg. *History and Class Consciousness: Studies in Marxist Dialectic.* Trans. Rodney Livingstone. Cambridge: MIT Press, 1968.

Lukes, Steven. *Power: Its Forms, Bases, and Uses.* New York: Harper and Row, 1980.

Lynn, Mary, ed. *Women's Liberation in the Twentieth Century.* New York: John Wiley and Sons, 1975.

Machiavelli, Niccolò. *The Prince.* Trans. George Bull. New York: Penguin, 1981.

Mannheim, Karl. *Ideology and Utopia.* New York: Harcourt, Brace, and Company, 1936.

Mao Tse-tung. *Selected Readings from the Works of Mao Tse-tung.* Peking: Foreign Languages Press, 1971.

March, James G. "The Power of Power." In *Varieties of Political Theory,* ed. David Easton. Englewood Cliffs, N.J.: Prentice Hall, 1966.

Marshall, T. H. *Class, Citizenship, and Social Development: Essays by T. H. Marshall.* Garden City, N.Y.: Doubleday, 1964.

Martin, H. Luther, Huck Gutman, and Patrick H. Hutton, eds. *Technologies of the Self: A Seminar with Michel Foucault.* Amherst: University of Massachusetts Press, 1988.

Marx, Karl. *Capital: A Critique of Political Economy.* Trans. Ben Fowkes. New York: Vintage, 1977.

————. *Contribution to the Critique of Hegel's Philosophy of Right: Introduction* (1970). In *The Marx-Engels Reader,* ed. Robert C. Tucker. New York: W. W. Norton, 1972.

―――. *Grundrisse.* Trans. Martin Nicolaus. New York: Random House, 1973.

Marx, Karl, and Friedrich Engels. *The German Ideology* (1964). Rpt. in *The Marx-Engels Reader,* ed. Robert C. Tucker. New York: W. W. Norton, 1972.

McCarthy, Thomas. "The Critique of Impure Reason: Foucault and the Frankfurt School." *Political Theory* 18, no. 3 (August 1990).

McNay, Lois. *Foucault: A Critical Introduction.* New York: Continuum, 1994.

McWhorter, Ladelle. "Foucault's Analytics of Power." In *Crises in Continental Philosophy,* ed. Arleen B. Dallery and Charles E. Scott, 119–126. Albany: State University of New York Press, 1990.

Mill, John Stuart. *Utilitarianism, On Liberty, and Considerations on Representative Government.* Ed. H. B. Acton. New York: J. M. Dent and Sons, 1972.

Miller, Peter, and Nikolas Rose. "Governing Economic Life." In *Foucault's New Domains,* ed. Mike Gane and Terry Johnson. New York: Routledge, 1993.

Mommsen, Wolfgang J. *Max Weber and German Politics.* Chicago: University of Chicago Press, 1984.

Morris, Meaghan, and Paul Patton, eds. *Michel Foucault: Power, Truth, Strategy.* Sydney, Australia: Feral, 1979.

Nicholson, Linda J., ed. *Feminism/Postmodernism.* New York: Routledge, 1990.

Nietzsche, Friedrich. *Beyond Good and Evil.* Trans. Walter Kaufmann. New York: Random House, 1966.

―――. *The Gay Science.* Trans. Walter Kaufmann. New York: Random House, 1974.

―――. *Human, All Too Human.* Trans. R. J. Hollingdale. Cambridge: Cambridge University Press, 1986.

―――. *On the Genealogy of Morals.* Trans. Walter Kaufmann and R. J. Hollingdale. New York: Random House, 1967.

―――. *The Will to Power.* Trans. Walter Kaufmann. New York: Vintage, 1968.

Pelcynski, Zbigniew, and John Gray, eds. *Conceptions of Liberty in Political Philosophy.* London: Athlone, 1984.

Perrot, Michel, ed. *L'impossible prison: Debat avec Michel Foucault.* Paris: Editions du seuil, 1980.

Plato. *The Republic.* Trans. Robin Waterfield. Oxford: Oxford University Press, 1994.

Riley, Patrick. *Kant's Political Philosophy.* Totowa, N.J.: Rowman and Littlefield, 1983.

Rouse, Joseph. "Power/Knowledge." In *The Cambridge Companion to Foucault,* ed. Gary Gutting, 92–114. Cambridge: Cambridge University Press, 1994.

Sawicki, Jana. *Disciplining Foucault: Feminism, Power, and the Body.* New York: Routledge, 1991.

―――. "Foucault, Feminism, and Questions of Identity." In *The Cambridge Companion to Foucault,* ed. Gary Gutting, 286–313. New York: Cambridge University Press, 1994.

Schürmann, Reiner. "On Constituting Oneself as an Anarchistic Subject." *Praxis International* 6 (1986): 294–310.

Simmel, Georg. *The Conflict in Modern Culture, and Other Essays.* Trans. K. Peter Etzkorn. New York: Teachers College Press, 1968.

Simons, Jon. *Foucault and the Political.* New York: Routledge, 1995.

Thiele, Leslie Paul. "The Agony of Politics: The Nietzschean Roots of Foucault's Thought." *American Political Science Review* 84, no. 3 (September 1990): 907–925.

Trombadori, Duccio. *Colloqui con Foucault.* Salerno: 10/17 Cooperative editrice, 1981.

Weber, Max. *Economy and Society.* Ed. Guenther Roth and Claus Wittich. Berkeley: University of California Press, 1978.

———. *The Protestant Ethic and the Spirit of Capitalism.* Trans. Talcott Parsons. New York: Charles Scribner's Sons, 1958.

———. "Socialism" (1919). Rpt. in *Occasional Paper no. 11.* Durban, Natal: Institute for Social Research, University of Natal, 1967.

White, Stephen K. *Political Theory and Postmodernism.* Cambridge: Cambridge University Press, 1991.

———. *The Recent Work of Jürgen Habermas: Reason, Justice, and Modernity.* Cambridge: Cambridge University Press, 1988.

Yeatman, Anna. *Postmodern Revisionings of the Political.* New York: Routledge, 1994.

Young, Iris. *Justice and the Politics of Difference.* Princeton: Princeton University Press, 1990.

INDEX

Emancipation, 83, 102, 104. *See also* Revolution
Enlightenment, 2, 143, 153; and Foucault, 144–153
Epictetus, 138–139
Experience, 55; and book-experience, 57, 175; and the subject, 156; and thought, 132

Flax, Jane, 120–121
Foucault: his critics, 23, 38–39, 120–121, 140–141, 145, 147, 171–172, 193 n.45, 195 n.1, 198 n.8; and prisons, 31; and solemnity as a flaw, 113
Frankfurt School, 13, 20–21, 24, 36, 45, 88–89; and Donald Duck, 189 n.33; and little pleasures, 189 n.36; and the totality, 112, 119
Fraser, Nancy, 37, 38, 171, 172, 173
Freedom, 124, 125, 126; an error, 128–129; and imagination, 127
French Revolution, 32
Friedan, Betty, 169–170

Genealogy, 78–100; and chance, 88, 89
Government, 28–29, 31, 123, 131, 155, 188 n.14; and the management of populations, 39–40, 53–54, 60–64. *See also* Biopower
Gulag, 117–118

Haber, Honi Fern, 119
Habermas, Jürgen, 22–23, 190 n.42
Heidegger, Martin, 3–4, 81
History of Sexuality, 66–72
Hobbes, Thomas, 12, 14, 27, 157
Humanism, 117, 167

Individual, 26–28, 168, 187 n.1; and disciplines, 34, 45–46, 52; and individualism, 137–138; and liberalism, 108–109; and Nietzsche, 119–122; norm, 52; as product of power, 21, 27–28; and prospects for resistance, 49, 56–57, 118, 120, 123; and subindividuals, 156, 157; and truth, 52; as vehicle of power, 36. *See also* Self

Intellectuals, 85, 95; and the Oppenheimer effect, 148; universal and specific, x, 145–148, 150, 151–152

Julius, N. H., 35

Kant, Immanuel, 7; and categorical imperative, 27; and *Contest of the Faculties*, 103, 142, 143; and Enlightenment, 7–8, 108, 152
Knowledge: and genealogy, 84; and human nature, 22, 24; and its link to power, 19–20, 22, 23; and opposition, 102; and science, 20

Lenin: and Leninism, 147; and the Taylor system, 150
Liberalism, 108–109, 158
Life philosophy, x, 128, 177–178; and error, 128–129, 132, 176
Localism, 150
Locke, John, 12; and opposition, 17

Madness and Civilization, 55, 57, 86–87, 170–171
Marx, Karl, 2, 37; as critic of German politics, 103–104; and human nature, 109–111
Marxism, 21
McCarthy, Thomas, 37, 81, 195 n.1
Morality, 134; and relationship with the self, 136

Nietzsche, Friedrich, 5, 179, 180; and genealogy, 5, 79; master and slave morality, 181–183; and plebeian aspect, 118–119; and will to power, 6
Normativity, 107, 120, 129; and norms, 171–172, 174

Oppenheimer, J. Robert, 146
Oppositional ethos, 112–113
Optimism, 89, 184

Parrhesia, 163, 174; and free speech, 162–163
Pastoral power, 64–67, 74, 75

John S. Ransom is Assistant Professor of Political Science at
Dickinson College.

Library of Congress Cataloging-in-Publication Data
Ransom, John S.
Foucault's discipline : the politics of subjectivity /
John S. Ransom.
Includes bibliographical references and index.
ISBN 0-8223-1878-4 (cloth : alk. paper). — ISBN 0-8223-1869-5 (pbk. : alk. paper)
1. Foucault, Michel—Political and social views.   2. Political science—Philosophy.
3. Intersubjectivity.   I. Title.
B2430.F724B36   1997
320'.092—dc20   96-34130 CIP